First and Second Corinthians

Westminster Bible Companion

Series Editors

Patrick D. Miller
David L. Bartlett

First and Second Corinthians

JOHN PROCTOR

WESTMINSTER
JOHN KNOX PRESS
LOUISVILLE • KENTUCKY

© 2015 John Proctor

First edition
Published by Westminster John Knox Press
Louisville, Kentucky

15 16 17 18 19 20 21 22 23 24—10 9 8 7 6 5 4 3 2

All rights reserved. No part of this book may be reproduced or transmitted in any form or by any means, electronic or mechanical, including photocopying, recording, or by any information storage or retrieval system, without permission in writing from the publisher. For information, address Westminster John Knox Press, 100 Witherspoon Street, Louisville, Kentucky 40202-1396. Or contact us online at www.wjkbooks.com.

Unless otherwise indicated, Scripture quotations are from the New Revised Standard Version of the Bible, copyright © 1989 by the Division of Christian Education of the National Council of the Churches of Christ in the U.S.A., and are used by permission.

Map © Ben Pease and used by permission.

Book design by Publishers' WorkGroup
Cover design by Drew Stevens

Library of Congress Cataloging-in-Publication Data

Proctor, John
 First and Second Corinthians / John Proctor.
  pages cm. -- (Westminster Bible companion)
 Includes Bibliographical references
 ISBN 978-0-664-25262-5 (alk. paper)
1. Bible. Corinthians--Commentaries. 2. Bible. Corinthians--Study and teaching. I. Title. II. Title: 1st and 2nd Corinthians.
 BS2675.53.P76 2015
 227'.2077--dc23

2014031555

∞ The paper used in this publication meets the minimum requirements of the American National Standard for Information Sciences—Permanence of Paper for Printed Library Materials, ANSI Z39.48-1992.

Most Westminster John Knox Press books are available at special quantity discounts when purchased in bulk by corporations, organizations, and special-interest groups. For more information, please e-mail SpecialSales@wjkbooks.com.

Contents

Series Foreword	xi

FIRST CORINTHIANS

Introduction	**3**
Gospel Meets Corinth	3
Getting to Know Corinth	5
Paul and Corinth	7
Writing to Corinth	8
Mapping First Corinthians	9
First Corinthians: Symptoms and Causes	10
Jews and Gentiles	10
Bodies and Souls	11
Women and God	12
Pride and Power	13
No Single Key	14
Joining the Conversation	14

Part 1: People of the Cross: The Challenge of the Gospel:
1 Corinthians 1–4

1. Greeting and Grace: 1 Corinthians 1:1–9	**19**
Formalities and Friendship (1:1–3)	19
Prayer for a Gifted People (1:4–9)	20
2. Divisions and Leadership: 1 Corinthians 1:10–4:21	**22**
A Church Divided (1:10–17)	22
The Word of the Cross (1:18–2:5)	25
The Cross and the Foolishness of God (1:18–25)	26
The Church and the Choice of God (1:26–31)	27
The Preacher and the Power of God (2:1–5)	28

The Wisdom of God (2:6–16)	29
The Work of Church Leaders (3:1–23)	32
Flesh and Spirit (3:1–4)	32
Images of Leadership (3:2 and 3:5–9)	33
Building and Judgment (3:10–15)	34
Temple and Presence (3:16–23)	35
Pastor and People (4:1–21)	37
Serving in Trust (4:1–7)	38
Honor and Hardship (4:8–13)	39
Care and Confrontation (4:14–21)	40

Part 2: People of Corinth: The Guidance of the Gospel:
1 Corinthians 5–14

3. Commitments and Conflicts: 1 Corinthians 5:1–7:40	**45**
Conduct and Community (5:1–13)	45
Home Affair (5:1–5)	45
Passover People (5:6–8)	47
Church and World (5:9–13)	48
Courts of the Lord? (6:1–8)	49
Bodies and Belonging (6:9–20)	52
Past and Present (6:9–11)	52
Reasons for Restraint (6:12–20)	53
Marriage, Singleness, and Christian Faith (7:1–40)	56
Sex and Marriage (7:1–7)	57
Singleness and Marriage (7:8–9)	58
Separation and Marriage (7:10–16)	59
Circumstance and Service (7:17–24)	60
Single-Minded (7:25–38)	62
Bound and Blessed (7:39–40)	64
4. Other Gods in Town: 1 Corinthian 8:1–11:1	**66**
The Problem: One Person's Meat (8:1–13)	67
Knowledge and Love (8:1–3)	69
Christ and Creation (8:4–6)	69
Custom and Conscience (8:7)	71
Freedom and Family (8:8–13)	71
The Pattern: Service and Sacrifice (9:1–27)	72
The Rights of an Apostle (9:1–14)	73
Freedom to Serve (9:15–23)	75
Running Hard (9:24–27)	77
A Precedent: The Exodus as Example (10:1–13)	78

The Practicalities: Temples and Tables (10:14–11:1)	80
Sacrifice and Sharing (10:14–22)	80
Of Meat, Markets, and Meals (10:23–11:1)	82

5. The Church and Its Worship: 1 Corinthians 11:2–14:40 — 85

Grace and Gender (11:2–16)	85
Sharing the Supper (11:17–34)	90
Not the Lord's Supper (11:17–22)	92
"The Lord's Death, until He Comes" (11:23–26)	93
"Discerning the Body" (11:27–34)	94
Gifts and the Body (1): One in the Spirit (12:1–31)	95
Many Gifts, One Spirit (12:1–11)	96
Many Parts, One Body (12:12–31)	98
Gifts and the Body (2): All You Need Is . . . (13:1–13)	101
Love Is Primary (13:1–3)	101
Love Is Practical (13:4–7)	102
Love Is Permanent (13:8–13)	103
Gifts and the Body (3): With Spirit and Understanding (14:1–40)	104
Balancing the Gifts (14:1–25)	107
When You Gather (14:26–33 and 14:36–40)	109
Women's Voices (14:34–35)	110

Part 3: People of the Resurrection: The Hope of the Gospel: 1 Corinthians 15–16

6. Easter Gospel: 1 Corinthians 15:1–58 — 115

Resurrection Faith: Where It Comes From (15:1–19)	116
"Of First Importance" (15:3–4)	117
"He Appeared" (15:5–7)	118
"Also to Me" (15:8–11)	118
"If Christ Has Not Been Raised" (15:12–19)	119
Resurrection Faith: Where It Leads (15:20–34)	120
"For He Must Reign" (15:20–28)	120
"If the Dead Are Not Raised" (15:29–34)	122
Resurrection Faith: What It Means (15:35–58)	123
"How Are the Dead Raised?" (15:35–41)	123
"So It Is with the Resurrection" (15:42–44)	124
"The Image of the Man of Heaven" (15:45–49)	125
"Thanks Be to God, Who Gives Us the Victory" (15:50–58)	126

7. Plans and Personalities: 1 Corinthians 16:1–24 — 129

Paul's Projects (16:1–9)	129

"Concerning the Collection" (16:1–4)	129
"I Will Visit You" (16:5–9)	131
God's People (16:10–24)	132
Friends and Journeys (16:10–12)	132
Strength and Love (16:13–14)	133
People to Respect (16:15–18)	133
Christian Greetings (16:19–20)	135
His Own Hand (16:21–24)	135

SECOND CORINTHIANS

Introduction	**139**
Stress and Service	139
A New Situation	139
Clash and Challenge	140
Gathering Gifts	141
Titus and the Team	141
"A Different Gospel"	142
Coming to Town	143
One Letter or Many?	144
Mapping Second Corinthians	147
Listening to Second Corinthians	148
Service	148
Suffering	149
Speech	149
Spirituality	149

Part 4: Paul's Ministry: A Call to Trust: 2 Corinthians 1–7

8. Comfortable Words: 2 Corinthians 1:1–11	**153**
Saluting the Saints (1:1–2)	153
God of Comfort (1:3–7)	154
Pressure and Prayers (1:8–11)	155
9. Difficult Days: 2 Corinthians 1:12–2:13	**157**
Changed Plans (1:12–22)	157
With Candor and Clarity (1:12–14)	158
Sealed and Certain (1:15–22)	158
"I Did Not Come" (1:23–2:4)	159
Moving On (2:5–13)	161
10. Confidence and Integrity: 2 Corinthians 2:14–5:10	**163**
"Sufficient for These Things" (2:14–3:6)	163

Images of the Gospel (2:14–17)	163
Living Letters (3:1–3)	165
Resources and Sufficiency (3:4–6)	166
Spirit of Glory: The Face of Jesus Christ (3:7–4:6)	167
Glory after Glory (3:7–11)	167
Veil and Vision (3:12–18)	168
Face of Christ (4:1–6)	170
Hope of Glory: Suffering and Renewal (4:7–5:10)	172
Treasure in Clay Jars (4:7–12)	172
Faith and Hope (4:13–18)	174
Dwelling Place (5:1–10)	175
11. Repair and Reconciliation: 2 Corinthians 5:11–7:16	**179**
God and Reconciliation: The Cross of Christ (5:11–21)	179
Love That Motivates (5:11–14)	179
Life That Transforms (5:15–17)	181
God Who Reconciles (5:18–21)	182
Paul and Reconciliation: "Open Your Hearts" (6:1–7:4)	184
Acceptable Time (6:1–2)	184
Marks of Ministry (6:3–10)	185
Open Mouth, Open Heart (6:11–13)	187
A People Apart (6:14–7:1)	187
Comfort and Joy (7:2–4)	190
Corinth and Reconciliation: Grief and Comfort (7:5–16)	190

Part 5: Collecting for the Saints: 2 Corinthians 8–9

12. A Call to Contribute: 2 Corinthians 8–9	**197**
Opportunity for Giving: As Others Have Given (8:1–15)	197
Friends in the North (8:1–6)	197
Completers in Christ (8:7–15)	198
Occasion for Giving: Titus's Visit and Paul's (8:16–9:5)	200
Titus and the Team (8:16–24)	200
A People Prepared (9:1–5)	202
Objects of Giving: Sharing and Praise (9:6–15)	203
Sowing and Reaping (9:6–9)	204
Harvest of Praise (9:10–15)	205

Part 6: Challenge to Corinth: 2 Corinthians 10–13

13. A Call to Discern and Decide: 2 Corinthians 10–13	**209**
Tension in the Air	209
Facing the Critics (10:1–18)	211

Weapons of Gentleness (10:1–6)	211
Building Up and Tearing Down (10:7–11)	212
New Territories (10:12–18)	213
"A Little Foolishness" (11:1–12:13)	214
Rough Résumé	214
Fearful for Friends (11:1–21)	215
Catalog of Weakness (11:22–33)	218
Vision and Thorn (12:1–10)	220
Back into Role (12:11–13)	223
Coming to Corinth (12:14–13:13)	224
Pastoral Care (12:14–21)	224
The Challenge of Christ (13:1–4)	225
Building Up (13:5–10)	226
The Grace of the Lord (13:11–13)	227

For Further Reading   229

Series Foreword

This series of study guides to the Bible is offered to the church and more specifically to the laity. In daily devotions, in church school classes, and in listening to the preached word, individual Christians turn to the Bible for a sustaining word, a challenging word, and a sense of direction. The word that Scripture brings may be highly personal as one deals with the demands and surprises, the joys and sorrows, of daily life. It also may have broader dimensions as people wrestle with moral and theological issues that involve us all. In every congregation and denomination, controversies arise that send ministry and laity alike back to the Word of God to find direction for dealing with difficult matters that confront us.

A significant number of lay women and men in the church also find themselves called to the service of teaching. Most of the time they will be teaching the Bible. In many churches, the primary sustained attention to the Bible and the discovery of its riches for our lives have come from the ongoing teaching of the Bible by persons who have not engaged in formal theological education. They have been willing, and often eager, to study the Bible in order to help others drink from its living water.

This volume is part of a series of books, the Westminster Bible Companion, intended to help the laity of the church read the Bible more clearly and intelligently. Whether such reading is for personal direction or for the teaching of others, the reader cannot avoid the difficulties of trying to understand these words from long ago. The Scriptures are clear and clearly available to everyone as they call us to faith in the God who is revealed in Jesus Christ and as they offer to every human being the word of salvation. No companion volumes are necessary in order to hear such words truly. Yet every reader of Scripture who pauses to ponder and think further about any text has questions that are not immediately answerable simply by reading the text of Scripture. Such questions may be about historical and geographical details or about words that are obscure or so loaded with meaning that one cannot tell at a glance what is at stake. They may be about the fundamental meaning of a passage or about what connection a particular text might have to our contemporary world. Or a teacher preparing for a church school class may simply want to know: What should I say about this biblical passage when I have to teach it next Sunday? It is our hope that these volumes, written by teachers and pastors with long experience studying and teaching Bible in the church, will help members of the church who want and need to study the Bible with their questions.

The New Revised Standard Version of the Bible is the basis for the interpretive comments that each author provides. The NRSV text is presented at the beginning of the discussion so that the reader may have at hand in a single volume both the Scripture passage and the exposition of its meaning. In some instances, where inclusion of the entire passage is not necessary for understanding either the text or the interpreter's discussion, the presentation of the NRSV text may be abbreviated. Usually, the whole of the biblical text is given. We hope this series will serve the community of faith, opening the Word of God to all the people so that they may be sustained and guided by it.

From almost the beginning of our work on the Westminster Bible Companion, Stephanie Egnotovich of Westminster John Knox Press was our editor, encourager, and friend. Her death was a great loss to us and to this project, and with gratitude we dedicate these volumes to her memory.

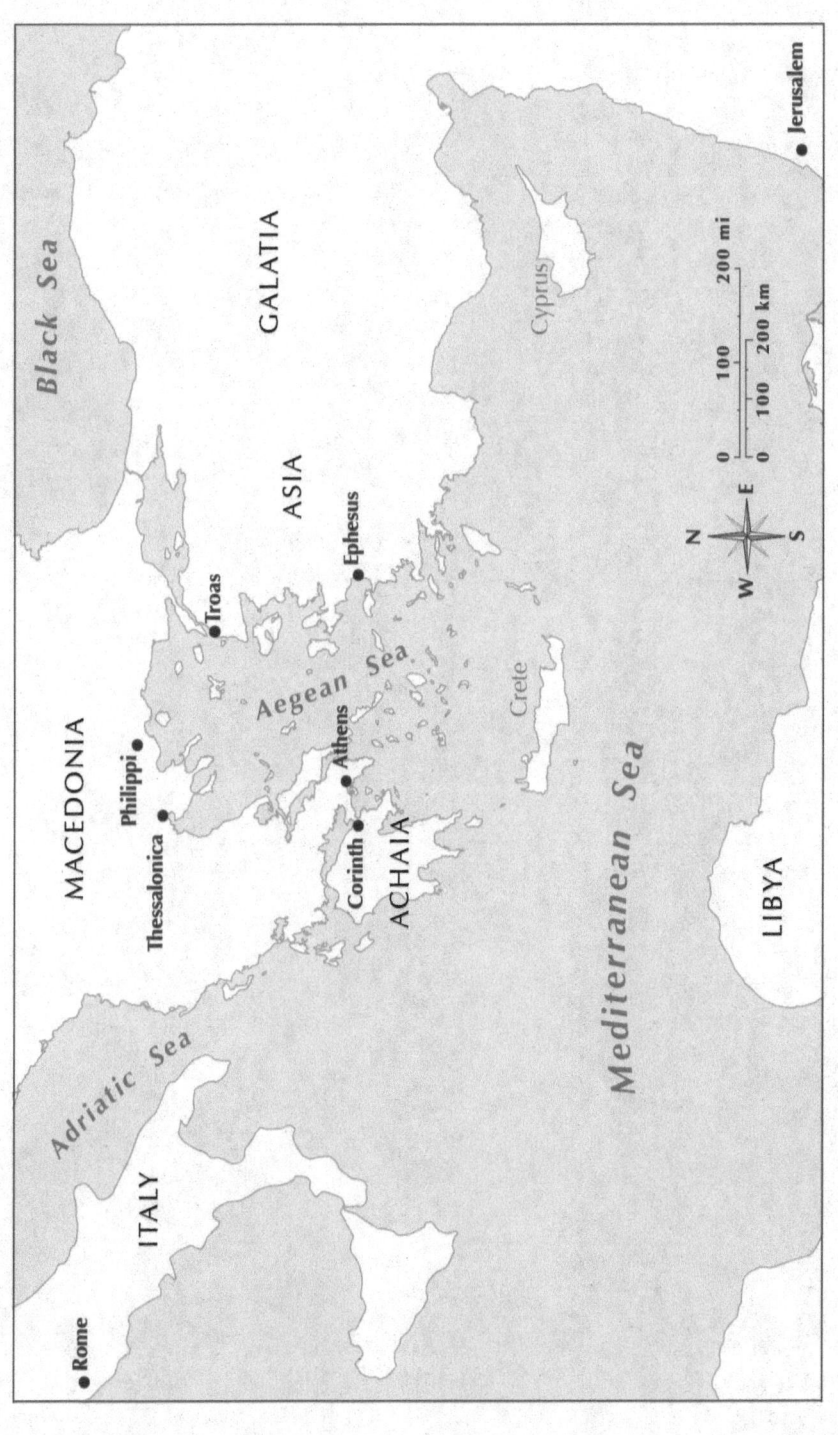

First Corinthians

Introduction

GOSPEL MEETS CORINTH

Places form people. The place where we live shapes our habits, our relationships, and the kind of people we become. Faith forms people too. It influences our character, behavior, and personality. So every local church is a meeting point of two powerful forces: place and faith. The culture and customs of the locality meet the values of the gospel in the lives of the members. Of course this is often a life-giving and happy encounter. But sometimes it is not so straightforward. There can be major tensions between culture—the kind of people our neighbors expect us to be—and the life of Christ.

In Corinth this encounter proved a fraught and complex business. The church there was new, and almost all its members had become Christian very recently. There was a lot to get used to, and quickly. Yet living in Corinth and loving the Lord Jesus did not go easily together. The values of the gospel clashed and contrasted in many ways with the culture of the city. Finding and following the Christian way was a tough task. Here are some of the questions these new Christians had to face:

- Corinth was a religious place. Worship was offered to the traditional gods of Greece, and to the Roman emperor. How far could a Christian get involved in all that without compromising loyalty to Christ?
- Corinth was divided economically. Many people were poor; some were rich. Rich people tended to take the lead in all sorts of spheres of life. Did that mean that rich people should also lead the church? Or did the gospel put everyone on the same level? If so, how might that play out in practice?
- Corinth was a status-conscious community. People liked to know where they stood on the social scale and to draw attention to their

rank and prestige. So how did that match up to a gospel about a man on a cross? Was the crucifixion rather an embarrassment to the Christians in Corinth?
- Men took a much more prominent role in Corinthian life than women did. Should the church copy that pattern, or should it try to balance the roles of women and men more equally?
- Sex outside marriage—on the part of men—was tolerated and even regarded as normal. Should the church accept this, or should it press its members to be faithful to their marriage commitments?
- Corinth was a competitive city. Rivalries in business, law, and local politics were sometimes very bitter affairs. How could people who were accustomed to behaving in this way contribute to church life? Might they have some serious new learning to do about unity, love, and service?
- In one important matter, Corinth was a painfully sad community. Few people in that era had much hope of life beyond death. How, then, would Christians deal with dying and bereavement? Would their faith help at all?
- Corinth was a proud city. So how would Christians there relate to churches elsewhere? Were they willing to learn from the wisdom of others? Or would they try to fix all their problems themselves?

All these issues were difficult for a newly founded church to handle. How do you lead, live, learn, and love when Christ and culture offer very different values? As these believers started to follow the Christian faith, they took time to find the right routes forward. They made some bad mistakes along the way. At times they disagreed over what to do. It was a slow learning process.

The two Corinthian letters take us to the inside of that process. As they do so, they also illuminate some of the demands and difficulties of our Christian lives. Of course the Corinthians' problems may not match ours in detail. Yet we too serve Christ in a complicated world. We are shaped by both faith and place. We seek to love the Lord Jesus, sometimes in settings that are not easy or straightforward. So as we open these letters and watch these Christians handling the encounter between their Lord and their city we may learn from the problems they meet, the pressures they bear, and from the pastoral wisdom that Paul shares with them.

Before we turn to the first letter, here is a bit more information about the kind of place Corinth was.

GETTING TO KNOW CORINTH

Corinth was a crossroads. The city sat on the west coast of Greece, at a place where a long arm of the sea, the Gulf of Corinth, comes in from the west and almost cuts Greece in two. The width of the land shrinks from over a hundred miles to just six. Today a canal has been cut through this neck of land, but in ancient times there was a paved diolkos (a "drag-way") and ships were pulled across to avoid a long voyage round the turbulent southern capes. So Corinth occupied an absolutely prime location. Sea routes stretched east and west, and the city had good harbors on each side. Land traffic from north to south had to pass this way; there was no other option. Corinth was a window on the world.

Corinth was a successful new town. A city had been there for centuries; it was a good site. But in 146 BCE its people went to war against the Roman Empire and lost badly. Everyone was either killed or deported, and the site sat almost empty for a hundred years. Then in 44 BCE Rome re-founded Corinth as a colony—an outpost and small-scale clone of the mother city. Rome hoped to develop its trade links with Greece and with lands farther east, and Corinth was a key point of contact and communication for this. So new settlers came. There was a small group of wealthy Roman families. Also a larger number of freedmen (former slaves), of low-to-middle social status; these people were mostly Greek in background. Corinth prospered. Before long it became the provincial capital of Achaia, and Rome's civic and political headquarters in southern Greece. By 50 CE when Paul visited, it was one of the empire's largest cities, with almost a hundred thousand people.

Corinth was a global city. As a port, it was bound to have international horizons. More than this, its nature and origin made it a city where two cultures met: it stood in Greece but belonged to Rome. So major buildings and the street plan were designed in Roman ways. Latin was the language of government and of public inscriptions. Top people would be keen to copy Roman habits, trends, and fashions. Yet many of the working people were Greek and spoke Greek in their daily lives. The city looked to Greece for some of its traditions, much of its trade, and many of its cultural contacts. In addition there were migrants from further east, including a Jewish community, which was strong enough to have its own synagogue. The world passed through Corinth, and a fair selection of the world's people lived there.

Corinth was both rich and poor. Trade was good, and there were those who made money from it. The imperial civil service offered a few prestigious and lucrative posts. There were stylish public buildings and a regular major sports meeting—the Isthmian games—brought visitors from far and wide and increased the city's kudos and prosperity. Yet wealth was not evenly shared. In many Western lands today society has quite a big middle layer, made up of people who may not be rich but are not hungry either. But in the ancient world, this middle layer was much thinner; many more people lived near the bottom of the economic scale than near the top. Most people were poor. Many were destitute. Few were really secure.

Corinth was a place of networks. Again there is a contrast with today's West, where most people have friends from their own income bracket. Friendships are "horizontal" we might say, linking people at a similar level. And there was some of this in Corinth: wealthy people mixed with others of their own kind; craft workers supported one another in trade guilds. However, other networks of friendship were pyramid shaped, involving dependence rather than equality. For those in the lower and middle layers of society, it was important to have "vertical" contacts. If you were connected with powerful people, they might offer you work, or help your family in hard times. In a world without decent pay-grades, this was the best source of security for many. Rich people also valued these friendships, to enhance their standing in the community. Corinth was a showy sort of town; it mattered to be seen as a person of influence and significance.

Corinth was religious. Across the Greco-Roman world generally, religion was a major presence. There were "many gods and many lords" (1 Cor. 8:5), with temples in towns, statues on quays and harbors, and shrines of various kinds almost anywhere. In Corinth several temples clustered around the forum (the main square), and other places of worship were scattered through the town and just outside. Imperial praise—honoring the Roman emperor, the empire, and the mother city—was evident. The traditional gods of Greece were remembered too, although the worship of these gods had become quite Roman in tone. Religion, under many names, was a major factor in the city's life. The new kid on the block was the Christian gospel.

Corinth has not vanished. As postscript to this section, if you want to introduce these letters to a church group, you might want first to look out some pictures of Corinth on the internet. Much of the city Paul knew is still there, in ruins admittedly, but extensive enough to set the scene for the letters. Corinth was a real place. Maps and photographs can help to introduce its realities and cast a new clarity onto much of the New Testament text.

PAUL AND CORINTH

Paul believed that God had called him as a missionary to the Gentiles. Under his leadership the church spread across the lands that we now call Turkey and Greece. He founded churches, and then he wrote letters to teach and encourage them. According to Acts (18:1–18) he got to Corinth toward the end of his second major missionary journey and stayed for eighteen months. Acts links this period to the tenure of the proconsul Gallio (the leading Roman official in the city), who served there briefly for a while around 51 CE.

After his months in Corinth Paul traveled east. He visited Jerusalem, then made his way gradually back to the west, visiting a number of churches on the way (Acts 18:22–23). So he may not have heard from Corinth for a long time. But when he got to Ephesus (Acts 19), which was just a few days' voyage away, friends from Corinth were able to visit him there. The news they brought troubled Paul: all was not well with this church, and he really wanted to go and help them. However, he was not free to visit immediately, so he wrote. First Corinthians is the result. It was drafted in Ephesus, about the year 54. Second Corinthians may have been sent a year or so later. (There is a fuller introduction to that letter midway through this book.)

We do not, however, have a complete record of Paul's correspondence with this church. Most obviously, no letters from Corinth to Paul have survived, although the church did write to him at least once (1 Cor. 7:1). More curiously, both of Paul's letters mention that he had written previously (1 Cor. 5:9; 2 Cor. 2:4). Therefore, he must have written at least three times altogether. Indeed some people reckon that Paul wrote even more than this—possibly up to seven times—and that the document we call "Second Corinthians" might be a composite of two or more of these letters. More is said about this in my introduction to Second Corinthians.

First Corinthians, however, is generally reckoned to be all-of-a-piece—one letter, written for one occasion. Problems and progress in the Corinthian church had been reported to Paul, both by personal contact and in writing, and 1 Corinthians is his response. What the problems were we have to reconstruct from the letter itself. But it also helps to use information about Corinth that has been gleaned in other ways. For example, archaeology tells us about the layout and atmosphere of an ancient city. Inscriptions—found on graves, monuments, buildings, and even coins—speak of people, events, and values. Literature of the period—poetry, political writing, and so on—teaches us about customs and attitudes. All of these sources help us to understand the culture and setting within which Paul writes and to make better sense of what he says.

Yet our sources are frustratingly elusive when it comes to personal information. We know the names of about fifteen church members in Corinth. But we do not know who did what—who hosted church meetings in their home, who was taking another Christian to court, who had been eating in a Greco-Roman temple, and so on. If you wanted to write a TV series about church life in Corinth, the letters would supply you with many issues to include, but you would have to guess which individuals were involved. Compared, for example, with the scenes we meet in the gospels, our knowledge of personalities in the Corinthian church is rather sketchy. We know more about the fellowship as a whole than about individuals within it.

WRITING TO CORINTH

One thing we know about the New Testament churches is that they often met in homes. Purpose-built church buildings came a few generations later. So we should imagine Christians in Corinth meeting in the home of one of the church families. It might well be a wealthier family, because they had larger houses than poor people. But we do not know whether all the church could get into one house at this stage or whether they were already splitting into several groups and meeting in different places. Opinions differ on this. My comments on 1 Cor. 11:17–34 give more detail. Either way, however, it is almost certain that homes were used.

This is the setting where Paul's letters were read. Only a small percentage of people could read and write. So documents—letters and books—often got read aloud by those who could read to the many who could not. Imagine, then, Paul's letters being read out for everyone to hear, in a setting with several dozen Christians present. It would take time. First Corinthians needs an hour of steady reading—more if you allow for pauses, questions, or time to reflect and discuss. Yet surely gaps of this kind would be necessary, for the writing is dense, and Paul's train of thought is often quite demanding and intricate.

So I wonder if the Corinthians read this letter in installments. Even then they might have found it quite a tough experience. This is not gentle writing. Paul's manner is candid and direct. At times he is quite combative and controversial. Some members might have felt he was attacking them personally. Yet this was much more than a personal letter. It was an explanation of the gospel, in a particular local context and culture.

MAPPING FIRST CORINTHIANS

This is one of the easiest of Paul's letters to divide into sections. It reminds me of a kind of writing that is quite common in Britain—a problem page in a newspaper or magazine. An expert on some aspect of living—perhaps on cooking or house repairs or relationships and marital problems—responds to readers' queries. So as you browse the page, you find yourself reading a question followed by an answer, then another question and an answer to it, and so on. The layout is clear; it is obvious where each new issue begins. That's how it is in 1 Corinthians, and it is pretty clear when Paul is moving on from one topic to another.

Here is an outline of the letter:

1 Corinthians 1–4	**People of the cross: the challenge of the gospel**	
1:1–9	Greeting and grace	
	1:1–3	Formalities and friendship
	1:4–9	Prayer for a gifted people
1:10–4:21	Divisions and leadership	
	1:10–17	A church divided
	1:18–2:5	The word of the cross
	2:6–16	The wisdom of God
	3:1–23	The work of church leaders
	4:1–21	Pastor and people
1 Corinthians 5–14	**People of Corinth: the guidance of the gospel**	
5:1–7:40	Commitments and conflicts	
	5:1–13	Conduct and community
	6:1–8	Courts of the Lord?
	6:9–20	Bodies and belonging
	7:1–40	Marriage, singleness, and Christian faith
8:1–11:1	Other gods in town	
	8:1–13	The problem: one person's meat
	9:1–27	The pattern: service and sacrifice
	10:1–13	A precedent: the exodus as example
	10:14–11:1	The practicalities: temples and tables
11:2–14:40	The church and its worship	
	11:2–16	Grace and gender
	11:17–34	Sharing the supper

	12:1–31	Gifts and the body (1): one in the Spirit
	13:1–13	Gifts and the body (2): all you need is …
	14:1–40	Gifts and the body (3): with Spirit and understanding
1 Corinthians 15–16	**People of the resurrection: the hope of the gospel**	
15:1–58	Easter gospel	
	15:1–19	Resurrection faith: where it comes from
	15:20–34	Resurrection faith: where it leads
	15:35–58	Resurrection faith: what it means
16:1–24	Plans and personalities	
	16:1–9	Paul's projects
	16:10–24	God's people

As we said above, this is rather like a newspaper problem page. But when all these problems crop up within the same group of people, we may ask if there is a common cause. Just as some diseases can produce symptoms in various parts of our body, is it possible that one difficult issue in the Corinthian church led to several problems and controversies all at once? Or did all these difficulties have different causes? Here are some theories that have been put forward.

FIRST CORINTHIANS: SYMPTOMS AND CAUSES
Jews and Gentiles

Several of the difficulties might be explained if some of the Corinthian Christians were Jewish by race and others were Gentile. Meat offered to idols (chaps. 8–10) is one obvious issue. Jews had learned to be wary about this; but Gentiles might be more casual. The name of Cephas (1:12; 3:22; 9:5)—the Aramaic name of Simon Peter—is interesting too. He seems to be known in Corinth. And elsewhere in the New Testament he clashes with Paul (Gal. 2:11–14). So might he have had a following in Corinth among Jewish believers in Jesus, and Paul among Gentile believers? Might this church be splitting along racial lines? Might some of the problems reflect the cultures and expectations of different ethnic groups?

A weakness with this theory is that so few of the issues Paul confronts in this letter seem to demand it. Almost everything can be explained, and often more naturally and plausibly, in different ways. A theory like this gains some momentum from the fact that there are tensions of this kind in Paul's other letters, notably in Galatians and Romans. But Corinth presents a different bag of issues than those two letters. The arguments that Paul uses most heavily in Galatians and Romans hardly appear at all in 1 Corinthians. In my view, we need to look for other explanations of what was happening in Corinth.

Bodies and Souls

A second suggestion is that the Corinthians distorted the Christian message by over-emphasizing one aspect of it. The theory goes like this: The worldview of many Greek people was dualist—they had a two-level understanding of reality and a split view of human nature to match. Philosophers had taught them to look on this world of sight and touch as a shadowy and insignificant realm; the true, eternal world counted for a lot more. But only the soul, not the body, could experience that higher reality. In matters spiritual the body was a mere shackle, confining the life of the soul.

So when Paul spoke about Christians being new people in Christ, some of his Greek hearers would think of rising above the ordinary, everyday world, of uplifting personal experiences, and of the inner life of the soul. The spiritual possibilities would excite them, but they might overlook the practical element of the gospel and its strong concern for neighbor. Above all they might ignore the Christian hope; they had such a keen sense of spiritual renewal that they would not care about future glories. They were more interested in their heady present experience.

All of this might explain the Corinthians' delight in being "spiritual" and in spiritual gifts (3:1; 12:1). It could be the reason that some of them thought "all things lawful" (6:12; 10:23): the body was not important, so they could eat anything they wanted and have sex with anyone they chose. Oddly this same notion, that the body did not matter, led others to ignore bodily desires entirely and even to abandon their marriages (7:1, 10). And if some "denied the resurrection of the dead" (15:12), that was because they thought they were already living an elevated life: what more resurrection need they hope for?

So this theory could make sense of many issues in this letter. It accounts for why this set of problems arose in this place, it explains the pride and enthusiasm of this church, and it shows why Paul was keen to correct them. His emphases on Christian behavior, on the church as body, on the importance of the cross, and on the hope of resurrection are all issues that the Corinthians had overlooked.

However, this theory may not tell the whole story. Indeed it may itself overlook some of the ways in which the local context of Corinth influenced this church. For there were many angles of contact and contrast between culture and gospel; it will not all reduce to a single factor. One particular aspect of this encounter concerned the role of women. Our next theory takes up that theme and links it to the issues in this letter.

Women and God

This third way of looking at the church in Corinth has some points in common with the theory outlined above. But it looks most directly at the issue of gender and at gender roles in church and society. In Corinth, men traditionally had a much better deal than women. Some boys received an education; girls generally did not. Men had fewer restrictions on their conduct than women did. Men could get more involved in life outside the home. So men generally took the lead in civic and community life—in politics, commerce, and religion.

However, this state of affairs had started to change, at least in the upper echelons of Roman society. Many women were keen to break free of the restrictions and conventions that limited their conduct and to claim a larger role in determining their own lives. So it is likely that this mood reached Corinth; the city was heavily influenced by Roman ways. And that may be the context in which a group of Christian women developed prophetic gifts and aspired to a kind of elevated spiritual life along the lines sketched out in the section above. Indeed the activity of such a group and the impact they made on the life of the church could explain most of the issues Paul addresses in this letter.

A number of the points mentioned above under "Bodies and Souls" could fit with this suggestion. More than this, the theory would make particularly good sense of a few sections of the letter. For example, some women in the church may have left their marriages, to devote themselves more fully to Christ (7:1, 10). If so, we are not surprised to find that they pray and prophesy in church without wearing the traditional headdress expected of a married woman (11:2–16). And the forceful influence of this group would account for Paul's attempt to silence them (14:34–35).

I think this theory is of some help. Several passages in the letter do concern matters of sex or gender. The writing on marriage suggests that some people were seeking a single life for spiritual reasons (7:1–16). We do need to look at the cultural background to understand the section on women and worship (11:2–16). And Chloe (1:11) may have been a powerful figure in the church, as might Prisca (16:19), before she left Corinth.

However, a problem with wholly accepting this theory is that Paul never talks directly about a high-profile or disruptive group of women. More of his concerns were caused, I think, by the behavior of Christian men. For example, litigation (6:1–8) and eating idol-meat (8:1–13) were likely to be male issues, and going to prostitutes certainly was (6:12–20). The leaders mentioned at the start (1:12) are men. So I suspect that further insights are needed before we understand the full background to the various Corinthian problems.

Pride and Power

A fourth theory, which has been popular in recent years, considers the competitive culture of Corinth and the assertive ways in which people—especially the wealthy—claimed and defended their position and privilege. You will find more about this in the comments on 1:12–17, because this approach makes a lot of sense of the initial chapters—of the Corinthian church's obsession with leadership and its tendency to value style over substance. But the theory would also help with most of the other issues that Paul discusses.

Litigation, and even the case of the incestuous man (5:1–13), may well be issues of wealth and status. The slogan "All things are lawful" (6:12; 10:23)—"I can do what I like"—was a typical upper-class attitude in the Greco-Roman world. The idol-meat issue may revolve around the conduct of rich Christians who insisted on their right to attend ceremonial dinners in the city. The divisions at the Lord's Supper seem to represent gulfs between people of different social class and income group (11:17–34). The quarrels about spiritual gifts may reflect the assertiveness that colored so much of Corinthian life rather than any deep theological error around the role of the Holy Spirit.

So this theory explains a host of particular issues. But it also accounts well for the general fact that Paul found this church a difficult group of people to deal with. In Corinth any difference of style could become a rivalry, and any divergence of opinion could turn into a quarrel. That had surely happened in the church. So Paul tackles first the divisiveness of this congregation, and their proud sense of their own wisdom (1:10–4:21). He insists on the cross as a pattern and standard, for Christian conduct, leadership, and service. The message of Jesus crucified subverts and rebuts all human arrogance and assertiveness. Affirming and emphasizing this gives Paul a basis to address a host of other problems in the church at Corinth.

So this fourth theory, about pride and power, strikes me as the most solid and far-reaching of the four. But I doubt if any of the four is so helpful as to override all the other three. The problems in Corinth were varied, and I think the causes were varied too. The fourth theory is particularly helpful; the second and third give us some useful insight; the first, however, might have less to offer.

No Single Key

You will gather, then, that this commentary will not use any one theory as a key to unlock all the doors in the letter. In general I think we can understand Corinth's problems better if we use background information about the city and its culture. But culture is not one-dimensional. It is a wrap-around reality; it meets us from all sorts of angles and influences many aspects of our living. The customs and context of Corinth affected the church in many different ways and raised a host of questions about how Christ's people should live.

Yet even when culture poses questions, it may not have all the answers. In this letter, Paul's great resource for responding to the questions of Corinth is the gospel of Christ. Paul takes Corinth seriously. But he wants the Christians there to take their faith seriously too and to let it guide and influence their living. So this letter is a conversation—a conversation between place and faith, between the life of this city and the good news of Jesus Christ.

JOINING THE CONVERSATION

If we think of this letter as a conversation, we might think of reading it as a kind of overhearing. We sit on the edge of the circle, not quite present but not quite absent either. Yet perhaps reading the letter is also a way of joining in. For the issues that the letter explores are not peculiar to Corinth.

Some of them are deep and vital concerns for every community and every generation. Here are tensions and frictions that people in our time also have to negotiate as we make our way through the years.

For the letter starts by talking of status, power, and leadership. In due course it turns to gender roles and relations and to sex, singleness, and marriage. Money matters come regularly into view. So do friendship and hospitality. And at the end we come to death, burial, and bereavement. None of this is narrow church stuff. These are the basic components of human living. Home, workplace, and neighborhood are here too. These are everyone's concerns. This letter does not show us the whole of human experience. But it does show us real people facing big but very normal human problems.

Within that whirlpool of experience, the letter brings a voice of faith—some of the central beliefs of the Christian good news. Again, you cannot quite say that the whole of our gospel is there. But many of the truths on which Paul draws in this letter will be celebrated and remembered next Sunday in your church and mine: the identity, cross, and resurrection of Jesus; the worship and unity of the Christian church; the work of the Holy Spirit; and the hope of eternal life.

First Corinthians brings these two collections of issues into conversation. It explores questions that life puts to faith and some of the ways that faith speaks to life. At times the encounter is untidy and even tense. But it is also honest, searching, and thoughtful. Here we meet life in its complexity, people with their dignity and difficulties, and the church's good news. We see how the gospel encounters Corinth and how Christianity can guide people amid the toils and temptations of living.

That's why I think this letter is worth reading. Faith ought to meet life, if it is to be worthwhile faith. In 1 Corinthians it does. This is not a book of easy answers or checklist theology. It is careful, practical writing about Christian beliefs, values, and behavior. And we are beckoned in: to follow Paul's thinking and writing; to try and understand events in the Corinthian church; to join this ancient conversation between gospel and life; and to reflect on the places where our faith connects with the tumults and tangles of living.

Yet as we try to do this, two potential pitfalls are waiting for us, and we need to navigate between them. The first of these is that we might never look past the words on the page. We try to receive from the text and to shape our belief or behavior by its words without ever really asking why it speaks as it does. We overlook the to-and-fro of this letter—for example, that sometimes Paul quotes views he disagrees with in order to argue against them. We do not notice the cultural background and the situations that made Paul write as he did. We fail to ask questions of the text or to probe beneath it. We want the text to speak to us, but we do not pause to see how it spoke to Corinth.

The second pitfall is the exact opposite of this: we are keen to understand how the text spoke to Corinth, but we do not trouble to let it speak to us. We treat it as an ancient curiosity, a piece of history, a distant object of study. So we investigate background issues, we discover the history and geography of Corinth, we discuss the subtleties of Paul's argument, and we conclude that it's all very interesting. But that is all. We stand over the text for a while, and then simply walk away. We have learned about it, but not learned from it.

This commentary aims to steer between these two extremes. I want to see how this letter spoke to Corinth, because that is the setting in which it was written. Respect for the author, for the writing itself, and for the historical nature of our faith means that we ought to take the original context seriously. So we shall often ask about the flow of a passage to highlight the main point Paul is making and to discover why. We shall use background information about Corinth to illuminate problems in the church. We shall aim to get beneath the surface of the text.

Yet I also want the letter to speak today, because this is the era in which it is being read. Although our setting is very different from theirs, we stand in the same heritage of faith as the Corinthians. There ought to be a word here that can help us. So as we read, we shall listen for the conviction and challenge of the gospel. We shall ask how Paul uses Christian beliefs to address Corinthian problems. We shall think about what is lasting and what is merely local. We shall look for values and insights that might travel from there to here.

Drawing out that wisdom cannot be an exact process. It will involve personal judgments and intuitions as well as careful study. Some of your opinions about what we can learn from the letter may differ from mine, and this commentary will not tell you what to think. But I hope it will help you, both to think clearly and to live faithfully. Reading 1 Corinthians ought to be more than mere study. This letter asks to come out with us, from study into life. It may lead us to audit our behavior and attitudes in the light of the gospel. It can help us to hold the faith with confidence and joy in the place where we serve God and follow Jesus.

Part 1: People of the Cross: The Challenge of the Gospel
1 Corinthians 1–4

1. Greeting and Grace
1 Corinthians 1:1–9

FORMALITIES AND FRIENDSHIP
1 Corinthians 1:1–3

> 1:1 **Paul, called to be an apostle of Christ Jesus by the will of God, and our brother Sosthenes,**
> ² **To the church of God that is in Corinth, to those who are sanctified in Christ Jesus, called to be saints, together with all those who in every place call on the name of our Lord Jesus Christ, both their Lord and ours:**
> ³ **Grace to you and peace from God our Father and the Lord Jesus Christ.**

Many a letter starts with some opening formalities before getting on to business. This is what Paul does here—greetings, good wishes, and a short thanksgiving prayer. This sort of beginning was typical of many letters in the ancient world. You would state your name, address the receiver, include a word of goodwill, and offer a brief prayer of thanks to the god (or gods) in whom you believed. So Paul follows the usual form. Yet he fills it with Christian content. Here we find words of gospel, and we start to be aware of a lively network of Christian friendships and pastoral concerns.

Most of Paul's letters include the name of a colleague, a fellow worker for the good news who was with him when he wrote. Sosthenes, mentioned in 1:1, also appears in Acts 18:17. When Paul preached in Corinth, this man was a leading member of the Jewish synagogue there. It seems that he came to faith in Jesus and joined Paul on his missionary travels. Indeed he may even have been scribe for this letter. For Paul mentions that he penned the last few lines himself (16:21); so probably he dictated the rest.

If Paul had simply addressed his letter, "To the church of God at Corinth" (1:2), his meaning would have been clear. They would have known it was for them. But by saying a little more than this, Paul reminds his readers that faith involves relationships and responsibilities. In calling them "sanctified" and "saints," he lets them know that Christians are a holy people, belonging to God and committed to a godly way of life. Loyalty and lifestyle—whom we serve and how we live—are meant to match.

So Christians have a direct responsibility to God—a "vertical" relationship, we might say. We also have "horizontal" loyalties, to the whole church on earth, to "all those who ... call on ... Jesus Christ" (1:2). There were some strong personalities in the church at Corinth, and at times these people acted as a law unto themselves. But Paul saw the matter differently. He realized that the Corinthians belonged to a much wider fellowship, and he wanted them to learn from the wisdom and experience of Christians elsewhere. The opening greeting hints at these concerns, and it foreshadows advice Paul will give as the letter proceeds.

Next come "grace" and "peace" (1:3). Every one of Paul's letters wishes his readers grace and peace. But these are more than simple good wishes. They are gospel words, speaking of the generous love of God and of the deep and secure well-being that Christians find in Jesus. This is a brief greeting with big substance, telling of a common fellowship, and grounded in God's goodness.

The Nicene Creed, which some Christian churches use in worship, speaks of the church as "holy," "catholic," and "apostolic". This is all here in the opening verses of this letter. "Holy" means belonging to God—"sanctified and saints,"—as Paul puts it. To be "catholic" is to be part of one worldwide fellowship with all other Christians. And "apostolic" means living by the church's ancient good news of grace and peace and passing this on in our own day.

PRAYER FOR A GIFTED PEOPLE
1 Corinthians 1:4–9

> 1:4 **I give thanks to my God always for you because of the grace of God that has been given you in Christ Jesus,** [5] **for in every way you have been enriched in him, in speech and knowledge of every kind—** [6] **just as the testimony of Christ has been strengthened among you—** [7] **so that you are not lacking in any spiritual gift as you wait for the revealing of our Lord Jesus Christ.** [8] **He will also strengthen you to the end, so that you may be blameless on the day of our Lord Jesus Christ.** [9] **God is faithful; by him you were called into the fellowship of his Son, Jesus Christ our Lord.**

There are thanksgiving prayers at the start of most of Paul's letters. Always the prayer seems to match the occasion and to reflect the situation and needs of the particular church to which Paul is writing. Often the prayer mentions briefly some of the important topics that will take up the main body of the letter.

There are probably two reasons that Paul does this. The first is spiritual: his prayers reflect genuine concerns. What he asked for when he prayed for his friends matched the hopes and fears that he carried on their behalf. So as he tells here of his prayers for Corinth, we expect to hear of the pastoral concerns and anxieties that shaped his care for this particular group of people.

The second reason has to do with Paul's method as a writer. He may have a deliberate purpose in mentioning issues at the start of the letter, to which he will return more fully later. He is alerting his readers, starting a train of thought in their minds so that they will not be surprised when these subjects come up again further on in the letter.

Paul's first theme for thanksgiving is that the Corinthians were a gifted people (1:7). God had been good to them: they were rich in Christ (1:5). Members of this church were well aware (possibly too aware) of their rich spiritual experience and inspired speech. But Paul wanted them to use these gifts more humbly and carefully. So in his prayer he stresses that these capacities are given; they are not earned or achieved but are gifts of heaven's grace. And these gifts are only temporary. God has greater purposes ahead.

So Paul speaks of waiting (1:7) for "the day of our Lord" (1:8). He is thinking of the return of Jesus Christ and of God's judgment of the whole world. This theme will return several times over in the letter. The Lord "will disclose the purposes of the heart" (4:5). Prophecies, tongues, and knowledge "will come to an end" (13:8). Paul wants to teach the Corinthians responsibility in the way they use their gifts and think about their blessings. He wants to remind them that they depend on God and must answer to God.

Yet as they wait, these Christians belong to the "fellowship of . . . Jesus Christ" (1:9). They share in a common life with a very wide community of believers, centered on Jesus. Their faith is not their own alone but is part of a much larger work of God. And as with relationships of any kind this brings demands and duties. A key sign of their bond to Christ should be their unity. That is the topic to which Paul is about to turn.

2. Divisions and Leadership
1 Corinthians 1:10–4:21

A CHURCH DIVIDED
1 Corinthians 1:10–17

1:10 Now I appeal to you, brothers and sisters, by the name of our Lord Jesus Christ, that all of you be in agreement and that there be no divisions among you, but that you be united in the same mind and the same purpose. ¹¹ For it has been reported to me by Chloe's people that there are quarrels among you, my brothers and sisters. ¹² What I mean is that each of you says, "I belong to Paul," or "I belong to Apollos," or "I belong to Cephas," or "I belong to Christ." ¹³ Has Christ been divided? Was Paul crucified for you? Or were you baptized in the name of Paul? ¹⁴ I thank God that I baptized none of you except Crispus and Gaius, ¹⁵ so that no one can say that you were baptized in my name. ¹⁶ (I did baptize also the household of Stephanas; beyond that, I do not know whether I baptized anyone else.) ¹⁷ For Christ did not send me to baptize but to proclaim the gospel, and not with eloquent wisdom, so that the cross of Christ might not be emptied of its power.

Names and News. This paragraph introduces a string of personal names. Crispus, Gaius, and Stephanas (1:14, 16) were members of the church in Corinth. Indeed Stephanas and his family were the first Christian converts there (16:15). Crispus, another early convert, had been a leading figure in the Jewish synagogue (Acts 18:8). And Gaius must have been among the wealthier church members, for his house was the congregation's meeting place (see Rom. 16:23, which was written in Corinth).

Cephas and Apollos (1:12) were not local men. They were Christian preachers, from elsewhere in the empire. Cephas is another name—an Aramaic name—for Simon Peter. He had been with Jesus, had led the church in Jerusalem, and traveled widely as a missionary. It is possible (see 9:5 as well as 1:12) that he spent time in Corinth. But even if he did not visit, he was known there by reputation. Perhaps those church members at Corinth who were Jewish by race and background would think of him with special appreciation.

Apollos too was Jewish, but a more cosmopolitan figure than Cephas. He had come from Egypt by way of Ephesus (Acts 18:24–28) and arrived in Corinth after Paul had left. He was a good debater, an able preacher, and quite an intellectual. He had probably been trained in Greek philosophy and in public speaking. Some of the wealthier and more educated Corinthians would have been impressed by Apollos. So although he had moved on by the time Paul wrote (16:12), his influence remained.

Lastly there is Chloe (1:11). Probably she was a church member at Corinth. Her "people"—her relatives, servants, or slaves—had been in Ephesus, perhaps on business, and had made contact with Paul there. Their news about the church made him anxious. The early chapters of this letter are a response.

The problem is that Corinth was a divided church. Several different preachers had acquired a personal fan base (1:12), and the fellowship had started to fragment. But Paul took no pleasure in this kind of support. He wanted followers of Jesus and not of himself. So he appealed for unity (1:10)—for "agreement" in common mind and common purpose.

Causes of Conflict. If we ask what was behind the splits, there may have been no great differences of belief among the parties. This letter does not deal with doctrinal controversy of the kind Paul faces in Galatians. There may be a simpler and more direct explanation for the splits, from within the local culture at Corinth. For there was a gene in the city's social DNA that tended to foster dispute and division. Christians in the city learned these habits almost instinctively and took up this pattern of behavior in their church life without really thinking.

Two factors had created this trend. First, ancient Greece had a strong tradition of local politics. In centuries past, towns had controlled their own affairs, and local politics was sometimes conducted in quite a heated way. Rivalry among leaders could be intense, and factions and parties would form around strong local figures. Competitiveness was part of the culture. So although the days of the Greek city-states had passed with the coming of the Roman Empire, these attitudes remained alive and found an outlet in groups such as trade guilds and religious movements. Second, the entire Roman world operated as a web of privilege and power. In a provincial city like Corinth, local dignitaries and business people worked hard to sustain their position. It mattered to have the right contacts. Patronage, as it was called, involved making powerful friends who could support you and help you to exercise control and leadership among people lower down the social grid. It was a manipulative little world where status mattered, and image and influence could gain you power and wealth.

With these habits ingrained in the culture, it is no surprise that they surfaced in the church. Groups, clusters, and factions would form easily. Comparison and preference of one leader against another would be quick to arise. Some of the Corinthian Christians were far too ready to rate their pastors, to revel in a preacher's gifts and talents, and to forget that every minister is called to represent Christ and the gospel. They were more impressed by style than by substance and by cleverness, eloquence, and skills of presentation than by the content of the good news. They were full of their own opinions and overlooked the fact that only God knows the real value of our Christian service. The local culture encouraged these attitudes, and the church provided an opportunity for expressing them.

Aims and Attitudes. Against this background, we hear Paul writing about Christian leadership. As his argument progresses in these four chapters, he appears to have two main aims. The first and more obvious aim concerns attitude. He urges the Corinthians to think in a new way. He tries to move their interest away from superficiality and style and to focus their faith more directly on the cross of Christ. This would take away some of their concern with personalities. It would help to knit them together as one church. It would enable them to discover again the unity and humility to which Christ had called them.

The second aim has a more personal aspect. Paul had many issues in mind on which he wanted to advise the Corinthians. We shall see these unfold in the rest of the letter. But first he had to claim a hearing. If some members of the church did not care for his ministry, they might not listen to the advice he intended to give. So he must establish the right to speak. By putting the cross front and center, by stressing the unity of the church, by portraying ministers as colleagues not competitors, he undercuts the Corinthian way of thinking and sets ministry in a truer light. These opening chapters on leadership lay a foundation for the rest of the letter. They refresh the pastoral relationship between Paul and this congregation. They take seriously the input of other leaders while resisting the Corinthian tendency to measure leaders against each other.

Christ at the Center. All of this may help us to make sense of the words "I belong to Christ," at the end of 1:12. I suspect this was not a particular group at all, not a "Christ-party" like the groups who favored Paul, Cephas, or Apollos. There is another way to hear these words. Suppose we were to read 1:12 and to pause for a second or so after the name of Cephas. Then we might discover Paul saying something like this: "Each of you allies yourself with a different leader—Paul, Apollos, or Cephas. But what I value most (and I wish you thought the same) is to belong to Christ." This would lead on well to the next sentence, "Has Christ been divided?" The point would be that belonging to Christ is the common possession of the whole church and is more important than all our separate factions, parties, denominations, and traditions. The Corinthians needed to hear this, and sometimes the church in our day does too.

So to help his readers take this challenge seriously, Paul makes three more points. First, he reminds them of the crucifixion. "Was Paul crucified for you?" (1:13). Of course not; the Corinthians knew this. But this was a step toward helping them to think about the cross, as a sign of their unity and a pattern for their Christian living. They would read much more about Christ's crucifixion in the verses ahead.

Then Paul reminds them of the name of Jesus in which they were baptized (1:13). Paul himself had baptized only a few of the Corinthians. Indeed he could scarcely remember who they were (1:14–16). But that did not matter. The power and promise in baptism come from Christ, not from the minister who happens to conduct the service.

Finally Paul speaks of the minister's prime duty, which is to tell the good news of Christ (1:17). In this task, substance matters much more than style. The wrong kind of style can even obscure the message. The preacher's cleverness is not the gospel. Power in preaching comes through letting the cross speak for itself. It speaks of values and standards very different to those that were current in Corinth.

THE WORD OF THE CROSS
1 Corinthians 1:18–2:5

Paul has said that if he preaches "with eloquent wisdom" (1:17), the message of the cross will lose its power. Now, in three separate but related ways, he explains why this would be. He talks about the cross (1:18–25), about the church (1:26–31), and about his own preaching (2:1–5). But first let us look at what he means by "wisdom."

Ways of Being Wise. "Wisdom" is an important biblical word with several different meanings in the various places where it appears. Occasionally in the Old Testament it refers to the creative love of God, the insight, care, and craft that shaped the world and made it good. In other Old Testament texts, wisdom is a human virtue—the capacity to handle life's varied challenges with integrity, sense, and skill. So wisdom can be a very positive quality. But as Paul thinks of the church in Corinth, the notion of wisdom has a much more negative feel.

The problem, again, is in the culture of the Greco-Roman world. Good public speaking was highly rated. Traveling orators were a familiar sight, and the best of them were among the top entertainers of the day. In the busy and contentious life of the city, skillful speech was an important way to win friends and influence people. One danger of all this, however, was that show could prevail over substance. Facility and fluency with words were valued for their own sake. There were many in Corinth who would judge a preacher by style. And evidently there were those in the church who thought themselves rather wise (3:18). They had some education, some ability to speak, status, and kudos in their city, and they had a high regard for their own opinion. All of this, in Corinth, could make a person feel very self-assured.

Yet this, for Paul, fell far short of true wisdom, and he was keen to distance himself from this way of thinking. He was concerned above all for the message he had to bring, and mere show and skill could not adequately tell the good news of a crucified savior. Paul was concerned, too, that the Corinthians were overconfident in their own wisdom. Indeed this was one of the factors that had strained and fragmented the church. He wanted to direct their thoughts into a different path. So he reminded them of the cross of Christ.

The Cross and the Foolishness of God
1 Corinthians 1:18–25

> 1:18 **For the message about the cross is foolishness to those who are perishing, but to us who are being saved it is the power of God.** [19] **For it is written,**
> **"I will destroy the wisdom of the wise,**
> **and the discernment of the discerning I will thwart."**
> [20] **Where is the one who is wise? Where is the scribe? Where is the debater of this age? Has not God made foolish the wisdom of the world?** [21] **For since, in the wisdom of God, the world did not know God through wisdom, God decided, through the foolishness of our proclamation, to save those who believe.** [22] **For Jews demand signs and Greeks desire wisdom,** [23] **but we proclaim Christ crucified, a stumbling block to Jews and foolishness to Gentiles,** [24] **but to those who are the called, both Jews and Greeks, Christ the power of God and the wisdom of God.** [25] **For God's foolishness is wiser than human wisdom, and God's weakness is stronger than human strength.**

In several letters Paul uses the cross like the needle of a compass to give orientation and direction to his thought and writing. From here he plots a course through the varied pastoral problems of his congregations. By this he brings the values of the gospel into contact with the questions of the people. With it he challenges attitudes and ambitions of the wider world. When we get to 2 Corinthians, we shall find Paul reflecting on the cross as a pattern for Christian ministry. Here in the first Epistle, he contrasts the crucifixion with "wisdom."

For the cross is "foolishness" (1:18). To preach about it is, by human standards, mad. People in the ancient world knew well about crucifixion. It was a public way to dispose of rebels and criminals with the fullest possible measure of suffering and shame. It would have seemed utterly crazy that the world should be saved in such a wretched and awful way.

There is, thank God, no very close equivalent to crucifixion in our time. But to speak of the cross in New Testament times might be rather like our discussing hanging or the electric chair. These are not subjects for polite company or dignified discourse. If you want to impress people with your wisdom, you do not take pride in execution or praise a man whom the state has killed. Do that, and you cause only scandal and offense. Nothing there will entice "the wise," "the scribe," and "the debater of this age" (v. 20). Neither Jews nor Greeks attributed much value to those who were crucified.

For Greek culture valued learning and sophistication (1:22). It was important to sound clever. Jews looked for a messiah to do deeds of power. They wanted a leader who would achieve something on his people's behalf. By both of these standards the crucifixion was mere madness and weakness.

Yet Paul knew, and he wanted to remind the Corinthians, that the cross has a paradoxical strength. In dying, God was weak as a way of showing power. God looked a fool, but there was meaning in the madness (1:25). Christians who had heard the call of the good news (1:24) and begun to discover Christ's saving love (1:18) would find the cross a place of wisdom and hope. Never again need they think that God judges by appearances. Never again need they confuse spiritual power with human pomp and pride. At the cross the church can gather as a united people, rich and poor, the wise and the weak, as one body in Christ.

The Church and the Choice of God
1 Corinthians 1:26–31

> 1:26 **Consider your own call, brothers and sisters: not many of you were wise by human standards, not many were powerful, not many were of noble birth.** [27] **But God chose what is foolish in the world to shame the wise; God chose what is weak in the world to shame the strong;** [28] **God chose what**

> is low and despised in the world, things that are not, to reduce to nothing things that are, ²⁹ so that no one might boast in the presence of God. ³⁰ He is the source of your life in Christ Jesus, who became for us wisdom from God, and righteousness and sanctification and redemption, ³¹ in order that, as it is written, "Let the one who boasts, boast in the Lord."

This understanding of the church as the people of the cross is Paul's theme from 1:26 onwards. The Christians at Corinth matched the gospel he had to tell. A few of them were rich—and these may be the ones who were most concerned for "wisdom" and status—but the majority were not. The God of the cross had called and gathered a fellowship made up mainly of lowly people. Most of these Corinthians had no great education, wealth or prestige. So Paul invites them to look at one another. They were not chosen because of their position, their learning or their achievements. No one should be proud before God. Salvation is a gift. Christian faith is a privilege we do not deserve. Our bond with Christ does not depend on our goodness but on God's sheer grace.

That is the point of the dense series of nouns in verse 30. The wisdom of God—a very different wisdom to that of Corinth and its world—is shown in the cross of Christ. By this strange good news, grace and hope reach out in unexpected ways to the lowly and needy of the earth. At the cross the church finds its pattern of life. Through Christ's death we are drawn into relationship with God (righteousness), released from old and destructive patterns of living (redemption), and given a new status as a holy people (sanctification). The idea of the church as a community of "saints" (1:2) gets its motive power from the death of Jesus.

The Preacher and the Power of God
1 Corinthians 2:1-5

> 2:1 When I came to you, brothers and sisters, I did not come proclaiming the mystery of God to you in lofty words or wisdom. ² For I decided to know nothing among you except Jesus Christ, and him crucified. ³ And I came to you in weakness and in fear and in much trembling. ⁴ My speech and my proclamation were not with plausible words of wisdom, but with a demonstration of the Spirit and of power, ⁵ so that your faith might rest not on human wisdom but on the power of God.

This theme of God's presence in the lowly and humble places of the world continues in chapter 2 as Paul contrasts the cross and "wisdom" in one further way. He reminds the Corinthians of his own preaching. As an orator might announce a subject before coming into town, so Paul committed himself to speak on the crucifixion (2:2). This, he decided, would be the hub and heart of his message in Corinth, from which he would not be distracted. This need not mean endless repetition of the same point. But it surely meant that Paul wanted to keep the crucifixion central, to relate all his preaching to this core truth. Indeed his manner as a speaker may have matched the message.

For Paul describes himself as an unimpressive preacher (2:3). Evidently others thought this about him too (2 Cor. 10:10). The "fear and trembling" of which he writes may have been caused by the turmoil he stirred up in Corinth (Acts 18:5–11). But he clearly felt he did not command the same fluency or technique as some other speakers of his day. An orator would "demonstrate" the point he had to make by a combination of logic and talent. Paul's "demonstration," by contrast, depended on God's Spirit rather than on the force of his own words (2:4).

So what did Paul mean by "demonstration of the Spirit and of power"? Had there been miracles or healings to reinforce his message and give it credibility? This could be. Paul mentions this kind of thing elsewhere (Rom. 15:19). But if he is referring to something like this in Corinth, it is odd that he contrasts the message of the cross with "signs" just a few verses earlier (1:22–23). So another meaning may make better sense. Paul may have simply meant that the converting power of his message was not based on his skills. That there was a church in Corinth at all was not the product of his ingenuity or rhetorical polish. It must be the work of God, of the convicting power of the Spirit.

In three different ways, then, Paul reminds his friends of their identity as Christians and of the contrast between "eloquent wisdom" (1:17) and the gospel. In the death of Christ (1:18–25), in the fellowship of the church (1:26–31), and in the message that was brought to them (2:1–5) lies the mysterious and life-giving wisdom of God, which is so different to the ostentatious wisdom of their Corinthian world. In the weakness of Christ are the power and purpose of heaven.

THE WISDOM OF GOD
1 Corinthians 2:6–16

2:6 **Yet among the mature we do speak wisdom, though it is not a wisdom of this age or of the rulers of this age, who are doomed to perish.** [7] **But we speak God's wisdom, secret and hidden, which God decreed before the ages** for our glory. ⁸ None of the rulers of this age understood this; for if they had, they would not have crucified the Lord of glory. ⁹ But, as it is written,

"What no eye has seen,
 nor ear heard, nor the human heart conceived,
what God has prepared for those who love him"—

¹⁰ these things God has revealed to us through the Spirit; for the Spirit searches everything, even the depths of God. ¹¹ For what human being knows what is truly human except the human spirit that is within? So also no one comprehends what is truly God's except the Spirit of God. ¹² Now we have received not the spirit of the world, but the Spirit that is from God, so that we may understand the gifts bestowed on us by God. ¹³ And we speak of these things in words not taught by human wisdom but taught by the Spirit, interpreting spiritual things to those who are spiritual.

¹⁴ Those who are unspiritual do not receive the gifts of God's Spirit, for they are foolishness to them, and they are unable to understand them because they are spiritually discerned. ¹⁵ Those who are spiritual discern all things, and they are themselves subject to no one else's scrutiny.

¹⁶ "For who has known the mind of the Lord
 so as to instruct him?"
But we have the mind of Christ.

Two Kinds of Wisdom. From the start of the letter proper, in 1:10, right through to 2:5, Paul has challenged the divisiveness of the church at Corinth. In tackling this issue, he has spoken of the cross as a lens into God, a leveler of human pride and a rebuke to the worst kind of "wisdom." Yet as he has explored this theme, he has touched on the fact that there are two kinds of wisdom (1:21). The readers may think themselves wise (3:18–20; 4:10), but there is a deeper and truer wisdom they have yet to discover. Their present wisdom, as they regard it, has too much of Corinth in it and not enough of Christ.

For God's wisdom has its center in Christ (1:24, 30) and in the seeming madness of the crucifixion. So it is a discerning wisdom. It conceals as well as reveals. The paradox and "folly" of the cross will always prevent people knowing God through human wisdom alone (1:21). Only through the work of the Holy Spirit can God be truly grasped. And that is the theme of 2:6–16.

Knowing God. These verses answer three questions: How can people know God? Who can know God? And what can we know about God? The first and third questions we shall discuss briefly. The second will take longer.

First, how can we know God? Paul's answer is direct and emphatic: by the Spirit. The Holy Spirit knows God from the inside. So only the Spirit can testify at firsthand about God and speak with proper understanding of the nature of God (2:10–13). It is the Spirit's task to witness with our Spirit that we are God's children and to pray for us when we do not know how to pray (Rom. 8:16, 26). This same theme of the Spirit as "go-between God," the great communicator between heaven and the human heart, is here in 1 Corinthians. The Spirit reveals and teaches to give intimate and inside knowledge of God's being and ways.

Second, who can know God? Paul's words suggest contrast and division. "Mature" (2:6) and "spiritual" (2:15) people know. Others cannot—the "unspiritual" (2:14) (although the word "natural" in the NRSV footnote would be a better translation) and the "rulers of this age" (2:6, 8).

Paul is not suggesting that Christians are cleverer than other people. Nor does he say that the understanding given to Christians is denied to everyone else. And he surely does not imply that a few "spiritual" Christians are given special knowledge, which is withheld from the rest of the church. Any of these claims would raise again the problem the Corinthians already had. It would invite, even incite, a sense of superiority and pride.

What Paul does mean is that there are two ways of knowing. Truly "mature" and "spiritual" knowing will use the cross as its lens into God. It will find in the crucifixion a sign of life and hope. It will not strive for glory or greatness of its own. It will "know nothing" of God that it cannot connect to "Jesus Christ, and him crucified" (2:2). This sort of knowing will be tuned to the wavelength of the Spirit. This approach to God will embody and express "the mind of Christ" (2:16).

In contrast to this cross-focused insight, Paul speaks of "the wisdom . . . of the rulers of this age" (2:6, 8). The political powers of the world operate, for good or ill, by the standards and lights of their culture, and culture can lead people into terrible mistakes. If "the rulers" had been better attuned to the ways of God, they would not have crucified Jesus (2:8). The wisdom of the world, which so impressed some in Corinth, can result in the sort of skewed and shallow judgment that put Christ on the cross.

So even though some in Corinth would gladly call themselves "mature" and "spiritual," Paul reckoned they were really no better than the "rulers" who crucified the Lord. They were judging by the same "wisdom" and applying the same standards. They were living in a way that was merely "natural" (2:14); there was too much Corinth in them and not enough Christ. Paul was not confident about speaking to them as "spiritual people" (3:1). The animating power of the Holy Spirit seemed to be dormant within them rather than active. They were Christians—Paul does not deny that—but they seemed to him to have forgotten their identity and mislaid their birthright.

So eventually we come to the third question. What can people know about God? Two answers stand out: "the depths of God" (2:10) and "the gifts bestowed on us by God" (2:12). These answers suggest that when our thinking starts at the cross, our journey will not end there. By the light from the cross, we shall discover a fuller and surer insight into God's own nature. And we shall know ourselves more realistically, as people gifted by God, committed to serving God, and accountable to God.

All this is "what God has prepared for those who love him" (2:9)—that people should know God by the wisdom of the cross, through the work of the Spirit, and with "the mind of Christ."

THE WORK OF CHURCH LEADERS
1 Corinthians 3:1–23

Flesh and Spirit
1 Corinthians 3:1–4

> 3:1 **And so, brothers and sisters, I could not speak to you as spiritual people, but rather as people of the flesh, as infants in Christ.** [2] **I fed you with milk, not solid food, for you were not ready for solid food. Even now you are still not ready,** [3] **for you are still of the flesh. For as long as there is jealousy and quarreling among you, are you not of the flesh, and behaving according to human inclinations?** [4] **For when one says, "I belong to Paul," and another, "I belong to Apollos," are you not merely human?**

This third chapter carries forward Paul's long argument about factions in the church. The opening paragraph leads on from chapter 2 and runs full circle back to where we came in. So the language of 3:4 resonates with 1:12. It is not "spiritual" (3:1), says Paul—indeed it is fleshly and "merely human" (3:3)—to divide into parties around particular leaders.

"Flesh" (3:3) is a complex term in Paul's writings. It refers most obviously to the physical dimension of human life, lived in the body, and handed on from one generation to another—"flesh and blood" (15:50): "my kindred according to the flesh" (Rom. 9:3). But on occasion the word "flesh" refers to the shadow side of human nature, the sort of life that does not rise above the natural and that lacks the renewing energy of God's Spirit. In this sense "flesh" is not merely physical human nature; it is also flawed human nature. Sin and selfishness are part of the package we inherit. This is the meaning Paul gives to the word "flesh" in 3:1–4. Flesh and Spirit stand in opposition to one another; to be "of the flesh" is not to be "spiritual"; it is to think and act in a manner at odds with the values of the cross. That is Paul's concern and criticism about the Christians in Corinth as they favor one leader over another.

Images of Leadership
1 Corinthians 3:2 and 3:5–9

> 3:2 **I fed you with milk, not solid food, for you were not ready for solid food. Even now you are still not ready, . . .** [3:5] **What then is Apollos? What is Paul? Servants through whom you came to believe, as the Lord assigned to each.** [6] **I planted, Apollos watered, but God gave the growth.** [7] **So neither the one who plants nor the one who waters is anything, but only God who gives the growth.** [8] **The one who plants and the one who waters have a common purpose, and each will receive wages according to the labor of each.** [9] **For we are God's servants, working together; you are God's field, God's building.**

So through most of chapter 3 Paul develops a more positive and creative account of church leadership. He works out fresh metaphors for the pastor's task and tries to lead the Corinthians into a more wholesome attitude. Leaders are servants, he says, working with one another and for God (3:5–9). They are called to be builders, and the fellowship they build is a temple for God to dwell in (3:16–17). And leaders are judged. Their work will be tested. They ought to work with care and awe (3:10–15). There is plenty of vivid illustration. We look at some themes and images that Paul uses.

The first of these pictures may surprise us: Paul as mother of the church. A little later he will speak of being the Corinthians' "father" (4:15). But in calling them "infants" who have to be "fed with milk" (3:1–2) he seems to see himself as a nursing mother, feeding a child. This was not a usual way to describe a religious teacher in ancient times, and this kind of language is not very common in Paul. But he does introduce a similar thought in a couple of other places. With the Thessalonians he was gentle, "like a nurse tenderly caring for her own children" (1 Thess. 2:7), and to the Galatians he writes of laboring like a birthing mother to bring the form of Christ to life in them (Gal. 4:19). In our time Paul has sometimes been thought of as a strict authoritarian, but he evidently tried to fill his ministry with compassion and care. The image of the mother speaks of tender love and patience, of self-giving and attentiveness, and of the willingness to let growth happen in its own time and in God's. These are still the marks of authentic pastoral ministry.

The next cluster of images comes from the world of the farmer and the gardener. In 3:5–9 Paul calls the work that he and Apollos have done "planting and watering." In several ways this image gently corrects some Corinthian attitudes:

- Planter and waterer depend on each other. Collaboration is their keyword, rather than competition and comparison. It would be foolish to regard them as rivals.
- Farm work was not a prestigious occupation. It is necessary: people need to eat. But it was not a high-status job. To status-conscious Corinth, Paul casts the pastor as a laborer and a servant (3:5), doing honest and needful work without great concern for kudos or honor.
- "God gives the growth" (3:6). Land work depends on nature, on weather, on creation, on God. Life and growth are not within our gift. It is the same in the work of the gospel. Pastors must work purposefully, but they cannot control the outcome; "neither the one who plants nor the one who waters is anything" (3:7). For that reason, if for no other, church members should look past their pastor and attach their faith firmly to God. For God's grace remains as pastors come and go.
- Farming requires patience. Crops take time. You have to wait for results. If some in Corinth valued instant and immediate spiritual experience, Paul reminds them that much of God's best work grows slowly.

Building and Judgment
1 Corinthians 3:10–15

> 3:10 **According to the grace of God given to me, like a skilled master builder I laid a foundation, and someone else is building on it. Each builder must choose with care how to build on it.** [11] **For no one can lay any foundation other than the one that has been laid; that foundation is Jesus Christ.** [12] **Now if anyone builds on the foundation with gold, silver, precious stones, wood, hay, straw—** [13] **the work of each builder will become visible, for the Day will disclose it, because it will be revealed with fire, and the fire will test what sort of work each has done.** [14] **If what has been built on the foundation survives, the builder will receive a reward.** [15] **If the work is burned up, the builder will suffer loss; the builder will be saved, but only as through fire.**

The idea of the church as "building" (3:9)—not meaning a literal church building, but as a metaphor for the fellowship of Christ's people—occurs in several places in the New Testament. This chapter develops the idea into the thought of the church as temple, where God's presence will be known in a special way (3:16–17). But first we look at the link between building and judgment, which appears in 3:10–15.

This connection is worked out at some length. Two main thoughts are involved. One is that some buildings get put up in stages. Again the theme of collaboration may be in view. Different contractors or successive owners extend and improve the original design. Sometimes you can see who has done what. Styles and materials tell the tale. Then the second thought, which develops this first theme, is that buildings ought to be, as far as possible, fireproof. The morning after a bad fire will show what sort of work the various builders have done. So builders, says Paul, are always liable to judgment. And "the Day" (3:13) of God's final and fiery judgment will show what Christ's ministers have accomplished. Until then we do not know for sure what God thinks of their life's work.

If all this seems to raise the issue of justification by works, we might reflect on a couple of issues. One is Paul's point in 3:15: our salvation is not gained or lost by the quality of our Christian service. The prospect of judgment ought to make us careful in doing God's work, but it need not scare us. A second point concerns the words "reward" (3:8, 14) and "loss" (3:15), which may be one aspect of Paul's building metaphor. For construction contracts in those days, as in ours, sometimes had penalty clauses if the job was not done properly. Only sound building work would be paid for in full. Yet if we reflect on this metaphor in relation to our own service, we may realize that God's good judgment would itself be a reward. If we discovered that our work for God had lasted, that it had weathered the tests of time and would count in eternity, this in itself would be deeply satisfying. We need not think of "reward" as some kind of heavenly bonus fund for the best church workers. That might be a very Corinthian way of thinking rather than a gospel insight.

Temple and Presence
1 Corinthians 3:16–23

> 3:16 **Do you not know that you are God's temple and that God's Spirit dwells in you?** [17] **If anyone destroys God's temple, God will destroy that person. For God's temple is holy, and you are that temple.**

¹⁸ Do not deceive yourselves. If you think that you are wise in this age, you should become fools so that you may become wise. ¹⁹ For the wisdom of this world is foolishness with God. For it is written,

> **"He catches the wise in their craftiness,"**

²⁰ and again,

> **"The Lord knows the thoughts of the wise,**
> **that they are futile."**

²¹ So let no one boast about human leaders. For all things are yours, ²² whether Paul or Apollos or Cephas or the world or life or death or the present or the future—all belong to you, ²³ and you belong to Christ, and Christ belongs to God.

Although there were many temples in Corinth to various gods and goddesses, when Paul says "God's temple" (3:16–17) he surely thinks of the temple in Jerusalem. This was Israel's pilgrim center and meeting place with God until it was destroyed in 70 CE. So at the time of this letter the temple was still standing. Yet Paul here takes the idea of the temple as God's dwelling and applies it to the church. He speaks of the fellowship of Christ's people as a home for the Holy Spirit. The common life that Christians share is a web woven by the Spirit, a place for God to dwell and to meet the world. So church life is sacred territory. It belongs in a peculiar way to God. It must be treated with respect and even with awe. Leaders and pastors should remember, when we deal with Christian lives, that we walk on holy ground. None of us may view the church as our own possession or project. Handle with care.

A thought that runs through all of these different illustrations is that God is in charge: God gives the growth (3:7); "God's servants . . . God's field . . . God's building" (3:9); God's grace (3:10); "God's temple," "God's Spirit" (3:16). The church does not belong to its members, its mentors, or its missionaries. The more surely we know this, the more truly we shall serve.

As so often in Scripture, this thought should give God's people both humility and confidence. Confidence comes from belonging to God, in Christ. Humility is needed, because nothing apart from God can give us true security or status. Before God, our own wisdom may seem both limited and misguided. Only the strange perspective of the gospel, which questions and turns upside-down so many worldly values, can make us truly wise (3:18–19). Nor shall we find refuge in groups and parties. Even the church leaders and preachers who have helped us most should not absorb our loyalty in a way that divides us from other Christians (3:21). For the deep truth is that we belong to God as part of the church (3:23).

We have no right to brag about anything or anyone other than Christ (1:31). There is nothing in the gospel that raises us above our sister or brother in Christ, just as nothing entitles us to split and strain the unity and love that bind Christ's church together. Corinth needed to hear this. The church today needs to hear it too.

PASTOR AND PEOPLE
1 Corinthians 4:1–21

Critical Love. As we approach the end of the initial portion of the letter, Paul's language becomes more direct, challenging, and personal. He talks at length about his own service and lifestyle and about his relationship to the church. Still the two aims that have guided these chapters remain in view. First, he wants his readers to alter their attitudes. He wants them to have the courage and commitment to live counterculturally. In proud and assertive Corinth, they need to be ready for a demanding and lowly kind of discipleship. Second, he has advice to give them on a range of issues, which will appear in the rest of the letter. So he needs to establish his credibility. It matters that the readers listen to him.

So as Paul describes his own ministry, he offers himself to the Corinthians as an example. He writes of his humility, to teach them; and of his integrity, so that they will trust him. There is love in his writing, a pastor's love for his people. But this is not a casual or careless affection. It is the kind of urgent and restless love that always wants the best for the beloved. We should keep this in mind as we follow the chapter through and encounter in places some quite confrontational language.

For when Paul writes of his work as an apostle, he does not hide his emotions. There is a sense of passion and of pressure. In defending himself he discloses himself. We feel his intense and committed personality within the text. Indeed we see quite deeply into Paul's character and nature, precisely because he feels that he is under challenge. But we shall only see him truly when we also notice how fully he has given himself to Christ. In this passage, self-defense and Christian commitment are deeply intertwined.

In parallel ways this same issue may apply to us. When we do Christ's work, we do it with the personality God has given us, and this is part of God's gift to the task and people that we serve. So when the work is tough and pressure is on, our personality will be on view. People will see deeply into us. But at that time we may also be closest to the cross, and we may show—even without knowing it—something vital of Christ to people around. In times of pressure, people see us as we are and Christ as he is. Paul knew this. It is the main theme of 2 Corinthians. It shapes our present chapter too.

Serving in Trust
1 Corinthians 4:1–7

> 4:1 **Think of us in this way, as servants of Christ and stewards of God's mysteries.** ² **Moreover, it is required of stewards that they be found trustworthy.** ³ **But with me it is a very small thing that I should be judged by you or by any human court. I do not even judge myself.** ⁴ **I am not aware of anything against myself, but I am not thereby acquitted. It is the Lord who judges me.** ⁵ **Therefore do not pronounce judgment before the time, before the Lord comes, who will bring to light the things now hidden in darkness and will disclose the purposes of the heart. Then each one will receive commendation from God.**
>
> ⁶ **I have applied all this to Apollos and myself for your benefit, brothers and sisters, so that you may learn through us the meaning of the saying, "Nothing beyond what is written," so that none of you will be puffed up in favor of one against another.** ⁷ **For who sees anything different in you? What do you have that you did not receive? And if you received it, why do you boast as if it were not a gift?**

Christian leaders are "servants and stewards" (4:1; the Greek words are *hypēretas* and *oikonomous*). A "steward" (*oikonomos*) was the principal employee, often in a large estate, who could be trusted to take initiatives and decisions on the owner's behalf. And the word *hypēretēs* for "servant" also suggests trust. Indeed this is one of three words that Paul uses that are translated "servant" in the NRSV, and each of them has its own shade of meaning. A *doulos* (Phil. 1:1) is a "slave," another person's property; *diakonos* (1 Cor. 3:5) has quite a wide spread of meaning. It can entail highly responsible duty. But it may also refer to lowly and humble domestic service. There is more about this word in our comment on 2 Cor. 4:1; thirdly *hypēretēs* (here in 4:1) is an "official," carrying out delegated business with some authority. So in this verse, both the words "servant" and "steward" imply that God mandates Paul and Apollos. They act responsibly, on God's behalf.

So how the Corinthians rate their leaders does not matter much. Servants are accountable to their employer. The only judgment that carries any real weight is God's, and this has not yet come into view (4:3–5). Only when "the Lord comes" will the true value of people's service be known. Until that time, even our own motivations are not fully known to us. It is important, then, to be humble, and not to jump to opinions about the merits of one leader over another (4:6).

There is a cryptic expression in the middle of verse 6: "Nothing beyond what is written." No one really knows what this means. But the general sense of the paragraph is plain enough. The Corinthians should be more measured in their opinions, more muted in their claims, more moderate in their pride. Their minds, says Paul, are inflated—filled with hollow self-confidence (4:6). They would be better to remember how completely they depend on God (4:7).

Honor and Hardship
1 Corinthians 4:8–13

4:8 Already you have all you want! Already you have become rich! Quite apart from us you have become kings! Indeed, I wish that you had become kings, so that we might be kings with you! ⁹ For I think that God has exhibited us apostles as last of all, as though sentenced to death, because we have become a spectacle to the world, to angels and to mortals. ¹⁰ We are fools for the sake of Christ, but you are wise in Christ. We are weak, but you are strong. You are held in honor, but we in disrepute. ¹¹ To the present hour we are hungry and thirsty, we are poorly clothed and beaten and homeless, ¹² and we grow weary from the work of our own hands. When reviled, we bless; when persecuted, we endure; ¹³ when slandered, we speak kindly. We have become like the rubbish of the world, the dregs of all things, to this very day.

We only understand 4:8–10 if we spot that Paul is writing ironically. He says things he does not truly believe to provoke thought and to make his meaning more pointed. He tells the Corinthains that they are full and rich and royal (4:8), as if it were really so. In truth he reckons that some of them are shallow and superficial. But he knows they think well of themselves, so for a moment he plays their own notions back to them. Then abruptly he turns the idea inside-out: "I wish that you had become kings." If they had, he might reign with them. But in truth the work of an apostle is far from kingly. It is a wretched, ragged task, despised by all (4:8, 9, 13).

Many of us who read this will be used to churches holding an honorable place in society and to pastors carrying respect in the local community. Yet through long eras of history, and still in many parts of the world, the status of the gospel has been very different. And to judge from Paul's writing, rank and respect are not the norm for a faith based on crucifixion. The wise, strong, and honored Christians of Corinth (4:10) miss the point if they judge by status. They should realize that humility and hardship are often the truest signs of God's involvement in the world. This is how it has been for Paul, as he now outlines in some detail.

Paul's account of his experiences, through 4:9–13, is intentionally eloquent. He tells of his work for God in nearly twenty different ways—"fools . . . weak . . . hungry and thirsty . . . beaten and homeless." There was no prestige or comfort in the life of an evangelist. Indeed he feels that he has often been treated like dirt, (4:13), the mere trash of the earth. Yet out of the dirt was growing the bloom of Christ's good news.

So the language is thick with contrast and paradox: weakness and strength, honor and contempt, persecution and endurance, slander and blessing. The gospel is gloriously incongruous. Things do not happen as you expect. Paul returns often to this theme in 2 Corinthians. There too, he lists all that he has borne and done for Christ (2 Cor. 6:4–7; 11:23–33). And there too he speaks of the great paradox and pattern of the gospel: that life emerges from places of death (2 Cor. 4:7–12; 6:8–10; 12:9–10). This principle and pattern—although Paul does not quite say so here—is the truth behind his words in 1 Corinthians 4.

Care and Confrontation
1 Corinthians 4:14–21

> 4:14 **I am not writing this to make you ashamed, but to admonish you as my beloved children.** [15] **For though you might have ten thousand guardians in Christ, you do not have many fathers. Indeed, in Christ Jesus I became your father through the gospel.** [16] **I appeal to you, then, be imitators of me.** [17] **For this reason I sent you Timothy, who is my beloved and faithful child in the Lord, to remind you of my ways in Christ Jesus, as I teach them everywhere in every church.** [18] **But some of you, thinking that I am not coming to you, have become arrogant.** [19] **But I will come to you soon, if the Lord wills, and I will find out not the talk of these arrogant people but their power.** [20] **For the kingdom of God depends not on talk but on power.** [21] **What would you prefer? Am I to come to you with a stick, or with love in a spirit of gentleness?**

These final verses of chapter 4 pave the way, both for the advice that Paul will give in the coming chapters and for the visit he hopes to make in due course. He will say more about visiting at the end of this letter (16:5–9). Yet the theme of presence and absence crops up in both letters (1 Cor. 5:3–4; 2 Cor. 10:1; 13:2, 10). Writing both testifies to Paul's absence from Corinth and carries something of his presence. He tries to speak as if present—to visit, as it were, through writing. He knows, however, that coming in person will be better when circumstances allow.

There are images in these verses of both care and authority. Paul writes as the church's "father through the gospel" (4:14–15). His preaching brought these people to life in Christ. His name was on their spiritual birth certificate. So there is feeling in his words. Paul had a deep sense of belonging to his churches, and here he wants the Corinthians to know how intimately and closely he cares. He calls them "my beloved children" (4:14). (Recall our comment at 3:2, on Paul as mother.)

As "father" Paul thinks of himself as a role model for the Corinthians to copy: "be imitators of me" (4:16). Indeed this theme of modeling and imitation appears in several of his letters. For Paul saw Jesus as the great template for all Christian people (Phil. 2:5–11), and he himself aimed to reflect and relay the way of life that Jesus had shown (1 Cor. 11:1). So he says not only "copy Jesus" but also "copy me" (to paraphrase Phil. 4:9; 1 Thess. 1:6; 2 Thess. 3:7–9). Those of us who lead in the church may want to ask how readily we could say this. What sort of Christians would we encounter if people copied us?

Meanwhile Timothy is on the way to Corinth (4:17), although he may not arrive before the letter does (16:10). Paul himself will come too, when he can (4:19–21). Although he will come to care, he will not shrink from conflict and criticism if he finds that these are needed. Any in Corinth who want to oppose him, to advance their own position against his leadership, should beware. If there are serious wrongs in the church, Paul will mount a vigorous challenge. A particular issue on which he has strong views is the theme of the next chapter.

Part 2: People of Corinth: The Guidance of the Gospel
1 Corinthians 5–14

3. Commitments and Conflicts
1 Corinthians 5:1–7:40

CONDUCT AND COMMUNITY
1 Corinthians 5:1–13

Home Affair
1 Corinthians 5:1–5

> 5:1 **It is actually reported that there is sexual immorality among you, and of a kind that is not found even among pagans; for a man is living with his father's wife.** ² **And you are arrogant! Should you not rather have mourned, so that he who has done this would have been removed from among you?**
> ³ **For though absent in body, I am present in spirit; and as if present I have already pronounced judgment** ⁴ **in the name of the Lord Jesus on the man who has done such a thing. When you are assembled, and my spirit is present with the power of our Lord Jesus,** ⁵ **you are to hand this man over to Satan for the destruction of the flesh, so that his spirit may be saved in the day of the Lord.**

We do not know how Paul learned about this odd relationship. The Corinthians had consulted him by letter (7:1), but this chapter does not read as a response to an inquiry. We know that a number of people from Corinth had visited him (1:12; 16:17), so probably they passed on the information. It disturbed him greatly.

Paul was anxious about the well-being of the Corinthian church. He wanted its members to mirror God's purity and goodness in their personal conduct and in their life as a Christian community. So a theme of this whole chapter is that Christians have a responsibility for one another. We belong together in our belonging to Christ. Part of being a church is that we help each other to live holy lives.

The words "his father's wife" (5:1) surely refer to a stepmother. If the man's mother were involved, Paul would say so directly. But there are other circumstances that we do not know—whether the father was still alive, for example. So we are to some extent guessing about the background. However, a likely scenario is that the father had died, and an adult son had then formed a relationship with the father's second wife. One reason for doing this could be to keep property within the family, which the widow would have taken with her if she had remarried elsewhere.

All this might imply that the man was among the church's wealthier members. His social rank might itself have deterred others in the fellowship from challenging him. But Paul's words—"you are arrogant" (literally "inflated") (5:2)—suggest that the church did not object to the man's incestuous relationship. Did some in Corinth even regard the couple's action as a welcome expression of Christian freedom? Paul would have preferred them to view it as a tragedy (5:2).

For Paul's beliefs about relationships and marriage owed much to the Hebrew Scriptures, and a union like this one—even after the father's death—broke a clear Old Testament command (Lev. 18:8). It was offensive to Greco-Roman custom too; both law and opinion spoke against it. "Not even pagans do this," says Paul (5:1).

We may wonder why so little is said about the woman. Maybe she was not a Christian, so not involved at all in church life. But even if she were Christian, the male head of household would be seen as the main player. He was—particularly if he now controlled the family fortune—the more powerful figure of the two, with the higher public profile. He was the one who had brought this situation about. Paul felt it necessary to confront the man.

In such a serious case, Paul tells the church members to expel this man from their company (5:3–5). They should proceed solemnly and deliberately, "in the name of the Lord Jesus" (5:4) and in the confidence that Paul too was acting with them. His "spirit" (5:3, 4) would give them courage and nerve to tackle a difficult confrontation. The power, however, would come neither from the pastor nor the church but from the Lord.

Yet although the language is severe, the long-term aim was evidently positive. Paul viewed the church as a little zone of holiness in an evil world. To "hand over to Satan" (5:5) would mean putting a person out of fellowship into territory unprotected by grace. There, as the man realized what he had lost, it was intended that he would come to his senses, find his way to repentance, and reform his life. The "destruction of the flesh" would be the withering and cleansing of sinful desire. (Recall our comment on the word "flesh" at 3:3.) Beyond that, the ultimate hope was for the man's salvation. Paul genuinely wanted to win this young man, not to lose him, and it seems quite likely that he eventually succeeded.

The reason for thinking this is that a couple of passages in 2 Corinthians (2:3–11; 7:6–12) recall a harsh letter Paul had written and the impact it had made on the church and on a particular wayward member. Those lines could well refer to this present chapter. If they do, then clearly Paul's advice not only challenged and alarmed his readers. It also led to repentance on the part of the man concerned and to some spiritual growth in the fellowship.

The details of this unhappy case in Corinth may seem far removed from our present church life. Yet there are features of Paul's response that can claim the church's attention in any age. Most obviously, Christian faith commits us to godly living. Second, church members ought to help each other to discover what holiness means in practice and to keep on track. Third, there are limits to the actions and lifestyles that we can ask God or our fellow Christians to bless. Last, even when things go badly wrong and fellowship has to break, we seek and pray for eventual restoration—of people, of faith, and of trust.

Passover People
1 Corinthians 5:6–8

> 5:6 **Your boasting is not a good thing. Do you not know that a little yeast leavens the whole batch of dough?** ⁷ **Clean out the old yeast so that you may be a new batch, as you really are unleavened. For our paschal lamb, Christ, has been sacrificed.** ⁸ **Therefore, let us celebrate the festival, not with the old yeast, the yeast of malice and evil, but with the unleavened bread of sincerity and truth.**

We have already seen the church described as God's temple (3:16–17). Now Paul draws another metaphor from Israel's worship. He invites the Corinthians to be Passover people. Passover was Israel's great festival of deliverance, an annual celebration of its ancient release from Egypt. The original Passover was the start of a journey to freedom. The power that held God's people captive had to let them go.

Every year at Passover-tide, Jewish people held a seven-day "Feast of Unleavened Bread" (Exod. 12:14–20). Families would scrub their kitchens clear of yeast and eat flat, unraised bread for the duration of the festival. Not a grain of yeast would be left. Even a little would taint the feast. So Paul refers to this custom and tells the Corinthians that they too are a tainted people. They have tolerated one very odd and unwholesome relationship within their company. They are like bread that is still alive with the yeast of an old way of living. With stuff as powerful and insidious as leaven, even a little reaches a long way.

"For our paschal lamb, Christ, has been sacrificed" (5:7). This is a rather unusual image for Paul. It is in John's writings, much more than Paul's, that we hear of Jesus as Lamb of God and see his ministry against the background of Israel's religious calendar. In John's eyes, Jesus was indeed God's great Passover sacrifice. Yet here in Paul the image is clear and potent too. The Corinthians have been released from an old way of living. Forces that once held them captive no longer do so. It is time, then, for them to be Passover people, to clean out the taint of old ways, and to grasp a new and godly lifestyle. This will mean church members pursuing holiness in their own living. It will also mean taking care for each other's growth in Christ and nurturing one another in faithful Christian service.

Church and World
1 Corinthians 5:9–13

> 5:9 **I wrote to you in my letter not to associate with sexually immoral persons—** [10] **not at all meaning the immoral of this world, or the greedy and robbers, or idolaters, since you would then need to go out of the world.** [11] **But now I am writing to you not to associate with anyone who bears the name of brother or sister who is sexually immoral or greedy, or is an idolater, reviler, drunkard, or robber. Do not even eat with such a one.** [12] **For what have I to do with judging those outside? Is it not those who are inside that you are to judge?** [13] **God will judge those outside. "Drive out the wicked person from among you."**

The earlier letter that Paul mentions (5:9) is something of a mystery. Evidently he had told the church to keep clear of flagrantly sinful people, and there is a passage in 2 Corinthians (6:14–7:1) that makes roughly this point. So some have wondered whether those verses could be part of his early "severe letter." We shall see later on how this suggestion connects with other theories about the make-up of 2 Corinthians. But it is possible that the "severe letter" has simply been lost.

Yet whatever Paul said in that earlier letter, it seems that some in Corinth misunderstood him. He meant to warn them—as he does here (5:11)—about the boundaries and discipline of their own church community. He wanted them to be watchful over one another's habits and conduct, and to refuse Christian fellowship to anyone whose life was a blatant denial of the gospel. Some at Corinth, however, thought he was referring to the church's contact with the wider community and that he expected them to break contact with their sinful neighbors. Yet they must not do that, Paul tells them (5:10). Christians are called to live in the world, to be salt for God's earth and for those who share it with us. We cannot fulfill that calling if we hide away from people whose lifestyles offend.

Judging the world is God's task. God knows better than we do, and we should leave God to deal with these issues in due time (5:12–13). The judgment for which Christians are responsible concerns one another's faithfulness. Paul does not quite say that what we bind on earth will be bound in heaven (Matt. 18:18), but he does imply that church members are accountable to each other for our walk with Christ. To handle that duty well, to negotiate our differences of opinion and perspective as we discern and travel the Christian road together, will always require patience, love, and skill. But it seems to be what Paul expected, as the next chapter confirms.

COURTS OF THE LORD?
1 Corinthians 6:1–8

> 6:1 When any of you has a grievance against another, do you dare to take it to court before the unrighteous, instead of taking it before the saints? ² Do you not know that the saints will judge the world? And if the world is to be judged by you, are you incompetent to try trivial cases? ³ Do you not know that we are to judge angels—to say nothing of ordinary matters? ⁴ If you have ordinary cases, then, do you appoint as judges those who have no standing in the church? ⁵ I say this to your shame. Can it be that there is no one among you wise enough to decide between one believer and another, ⁶ but a believer goes to court against a believer—and before unbelievers at that?
>
> ⁷ In fact, to have lawsuits at all with one another is already a defeat for you. Why not rather be wronged? Why not rather be defrauded? ⁸ But you yourselves wrong and defraud—and believers at that.

The switch of subject at the start of this chapter seems abrupt. After hearing about a vexing family issue, now we are off to the lawcourt. Yet the two issues are linked. Paul wanted the church to act as a responsible community and to deal with difficulty and dispute among its members. Up to now, they had not managed to do this. On one hand, they had ignored a pastoral scandal (5:1–2); on the other, they were asking secular courts to settle Christian quarrels (6:1). Paul believed, however, that their credibility as church required a different way. When issues started to divide and disturb them, they should learn how to settle these within the fellowship.

A number of ancient authors make it clear that courtrooms in a city like Corinth were unpleasant places. The scales of Roman justice were tilted, in favor of riches and rank, so it was mainly the wealthy who resorted to law. Men (it was generally men) brought their social and business rivalries into court. Without strict rules of evidence, speeches were often ill-tempered and vicious. You could not count on getting an honest jury. Yet, for all this, legal proceedings conferred a kind of prestige. Simply being there showed that you were a person of substance. Here was a chance to settle old scores, to attract attention by your rhetorical skills, and to gain ground in the struggle for status.

A few of the Christians in Corinth were familiar with this legal environment and had used the arena to challenge and confront one another. We never hear what their disputes were about. All we know is that Paul objected to Christian taking on Christian in a secular court. Obviously he was worried about the unity and peace of the church, but he does not say this outright. The arguments he uses relate quite directly to the legal issue. He makes five points.

1. He reminds his readers that Corinth's courts are corrupt. Words like "unrighteous" (6:1) or "wrong and defraud" (6:8) hardly reflect confidence in the law. Paul did not want Christians to use an unreliable judicial system against each other.
2. He challenges the church with the thought that Christ's people will "judge the world" and "judge angels" (6:2–3). This idea comes out of the Old Testament: when the Son of Man comes, judgment will be given "to the saints of the Most High" (Daniel 7:22). Over the years the church has linked this chapter in Daniel to the Ascension of Christ, and a saying in the gospels envisages Christians sharing in Christ's work of judging the earth (Matt. 19:28; Luke 22:30). So Paul reasons, from this thought, that if the Corinthians will share with Christ in judging the world, they really should be able to handle the day-to-day disputes that arise in their local church.
3. He urges the Corinthians to find arbitration within their fellowship, from someone who is "wise enough to decide" (6:5). This advice reflects Paul's Jewish background. For Israel's law authorized the appointment of judges in the nation (Deut. 16:18–20), and in New

Testament times the scattered Jewish communities of the Roman world had their own judges who would settle internal disputes without turning to secular authority. (One hears of similar arrangements today among some migrant groups in the West.) Paul was familiar with this custom, and he saw it as a model that Christians could adopt.

4. He uses family language. The NRSV has the word "believer" three times in 6:5–6 but with footnotes to explain that the Greek word really means "brother" or "sibling." In the ancient world, you would not take close relatives to court. Family disputes were settled by the head of the house. So Paul is saying in effect, "You are family. Now act as a family. Sort out your disputes among yourselves, and show a united front to the world."

5. Lastly Paul reminds the Corinthians that a courtroom can be a destructive place. Fortunes, careers, and reputations get taken apart. People get hurt. It would be better to put up with some wrong and unfairness than to trade blows with one another in such an unforgiving arena (6:7–8). This teaching resonates with Jesus' words about "turning the other cheek" and "going the second mile" (Matt. 5:38–42). For Jesus too knew how damaging a court case could be. Those who live by contempt and quarrel, he said, will find it a damaging and costly path (Matt. 5:21–26).

All this advice connects with the words in Paul's next paragraph, about Christian identity (6:11). A Christian is a person transformed, and our behavior should match the new nature Christ gives. This will work itself out in many different practical ways. In particular, any in Corinth who loved to litigate should learn a more peaceful and patient approach to life's disagreements—especially when fellow Christians were involved.

Obviously times have changed since Paul wrote, and the law works differently now. Yet there are a couple of strands of wisdom for our day in this text. Most directly, settling difficulties with one another as "brothers and sisters" is a good habit for Christians to cultivate. Handling conflict well can build trust rather than destroy it, and we need people in our churches and our society who can help us to do this. There is also a suggestion that—bad as the legal system in Corinth was—the law is meant to be a "righteous" and helpful thing. People who work today with codes and courts have a high calling—to keep these right, strong, and fair. Justice, when it is carried through honestly and truly, helps to realize and reflect the goodness of God in the world.

BODIES AND BELONGING
1 Corinthians 6:9–20

Past and Present
1 Corinthians 6:9–11

> **6:9 Do you not know that wrongdoers will not inherit the kingdom of God? Do not be deceived! Fornicators, idolaters, adulterers, male prostitutes, sodomites, ¹⁰ thieves, the greedy, drunkards, revilers, robbers—none of these will inherit the kingdom of God. ¹¹ And this is what some of you used to be. But you were washed, you were sanctified, you were justified in the name of the Lord Jesus Christ and in the Spirit of our God.**

This short section is a transition. The passages either side of it discuss very thorny issues. Members of the Corinthian church were taking one another to court (6:1–8); men in the congregation were visiting prostitutes (6:12–20). Paul deals with both issues head-on. In each case his advice addresses the specific problem.

However, these two issues had one feature in common. The people involved were following a Corinthian pattern of behavior rather than a Christian path. Their conduct might have been acceptable by local standards, but it did not represent the life of Christ, in whom they now believed. Paul looked on any Christian as someone with a new identity (2 Cor. 5:17), as a person called into a new way of being. How we behave should reflect who we are and the ways that God has renewed us in Christ. This is the point made in 6:9–11.

Matching words at each end of the paragraph highlight the contrast. The word "wrongdoers" (6:9) would more literally be translated "unrighteous." Then this echoes in the word "justified" (6:11), which means "set right" or "right with God." So the message of these verses is that, since the Corinthians have been "put right," let them not live as if they are "unright." That would both deny what God has done for them (6:11) and prevent them from discovering what God means to give them (6:9, 10).

The list of various kinds of "wrongdoers" in 6:9–10 is one of several such lists in Paul's letters. This list repeats the six behaviors named in 5:11 and adds four more. If we ask why these ten are included, rather than other sins, part of the answer may lie in the Old Testament. A number of the Ten Commandments (Exod. 20; Deut. 5) are reflected here. However, Paul may also be preparing the way for the next issue he intends to discuss in the paragraph ahead.

The lifestyle of many wealthy Greco-Roman men was notorious. Their banqueting culture offered plenty of opportunities for casual sex. It seems that some men in the Corinthian church had been part of that scene, and Paul was keen to dissuade them. Some of the sins that he lists here reflect the reputation these occasions had acquired. The verses that follow will address this group of men directly.

But first a couple of notes on individual words and phrases in these verses:

(1) The ending of this paragraph is one of several traces in the New Testament of an emerging belief in God as Trinity. To speak of salvation "in the name of the Lord Jesus Christ and in the Spirit of our God" (6:11) is to see the three Persons of the Godhead acting in concert and common purpose. At this early stage in the church's story, the Trinity was not an agreed-on and defined doctrine. Nonetheless, when this doctrine did take more formal shape, it drew heavily on material in the Gospels and Epistles. We shall return to some of these ideas when we get to 8:6.

(2) Finally, this is one of three texts in Paul to mention same-sex relationships. In 1 Timothy 1:10 the issue appears in a list, as it does here, and is said to be "contrary to sound teaching." In Romans 1:26–27 Paul takes a little longer to explain his views, and as a result it is often writers on Romans who consider most fully how Christians today might interpret his words. For example, in this Westminster Bible Companion series, David L. Bartlett's *Romans* comments on this question.

Reasons for Restraint
1 Corinthians 6:12–20

> 6:12 "All things are lawful for me," but not all things are beneficial. "All things are lawful for me," but I will not be dominated by anything. [13] "Food is meant for the stomach and the stomach for food," and God will destroy both one and the other. The body is meant not for fornication but for the Lord, and the Lord for the body. [14] And God raised the Lord and will also raise us by his power. [15] Do you not know that your bodies are members of Christ? Should I therefore take the members of Christ and make them members of a prostitute? Never! [16] Do you not know that whoever is united to a prostitute becomes one body with her? For it is said, "The two shall be one flesh." [17] But anyone united to the Lord becomes one spirit with him. [18] Shun fornication! Every sin that a person commits is outside the body; but the fornicator sins against the body itself. [19] Or do you not know that your body is a temple of the Holy Spirit within you, which you have from God,

and that you are not your own? [20] **For you were bought with a price; therefore glorify God in your body.**

Whenever people come fresh to Christian faith, there are old habits to unlearn if people's lives are to be true to Christ. This was certainly the case in Corinth. Some men in the church were visiting prostitutes. And the attitude of the surrounding society tolerated and even encouraged this sort of behavior.

It was quite common for dinners among wealthy men to lead on to casual sex. Indeed a host might arrange for prostitutes to be present, and the custom was reckoned entirely acceptable. Greco-Roman tradition operated a double standard. If a woman got involved in a premarital or extramarital relationship, she shamed her family and herself. Whereas young men, who generally married rather later in life than women did, had recourse to this sort of relationship during their bachelor years. Indeed the habit might continue; many married men too would find sex outside the home without any loss of honor or status.

Paul challenges this habit. His words are direct and carefully reasoned. In several ways he grounds his ethics in the gospel. What Christians do must be shaped by what God has done for us. Our living should be a response to the life of Christ within. That is the point made in 6:9–11, and it carries forward into the specific issue addressed here.

Not all of the words in 6:12–20 represent Paul's own opinion. Sometimes he quotes the Corinthians' views, or states what he thinks they believe, and then replies to the words he has just quoted. The effect is an imaginary conversation, going to and fro like a tennis match. So the NRSV puts quotation marks around three short portions of verses 12–13 to show that in these places Paul seems to be quoting.

The Corinthians' view was that they could behave just as they wanted: "All things are lawful for me." The body should be used as fully and freely as possible: "Food is meant for the stomach and the stomach for food." And sexual opportunities too were there to be taken, without inhibition. The body, after all, is only temporary. Use it while you have it.

That sort of attitude tends to see persons and their actions in isolation. "I'm an individual. Why shouldn't I?" is the watchword. There is no sense that anyone else might be involved or that our choices endure beyond the events of the moment. But Paul's response looks at a wider web of experience and consequence. "Not all things are beneficial." Deeds have effects. People live in relationships. He makes four main points:

1. Resurrection (6:13–14). For a Christian, the future should shape the present, and the future is that our bodies will share the risen life of Christ. (Paul says more about this in chapter 15.) So although our present bodies are perishable, there is something about our bodily life that will turn out to be permanent. We should use our bodies now in ways that are worthy of the destiny God promises.
2. Relationship (6:15–18). A Christian belongs to Christ. We are like limbs of his body. (There will be more about this in chapter 12.) So it would be wrong to establish a physical union that denied our identity as Christians. Sex forms deep bonds; it affects people profoundly. The wrong kind of sexual liaison will mess up badly the Christian's contact with the Lord.
3. Residence (6:19). God's Holy Spirit lives within a Christian. We have heard Paul call the church a temple and a dwelling place for the Spirit (3:16). Now we see the individual Christian in that role. Our bodies are a venue for the Spirit to occupy. So a Christian's body is sacred space and is not to be treated carelessly or casually.
4. Redemption (6:20). The final verse describes Christians as a people ransomed, bought and set free by God. Perhaps there is an echo of the exodus in this ransom language, but the main reference is surely to the saving death of Jesus. What God has done for us and given for us sets a claim and command on our living: that we should be holy people.

For all of these reasons, Paul explains, a Christian should avoid casual sex. Our faith does not ask us to ignore our bodies but to take them seriously and to honor God in the ways we use them. Obsession with the body is not a Christian virtue; there is more to life than health and beauty. But neglect and abuse of the body are not faithful either. Our physical self is an important aspect of the life we share with Christ, and it deserves care and respect.

You may notice that Paul says nothing in these verses about the exclusive claims and loyalties of marriage. That might have seemed an important and relevant point, but Paul does not mention it. A possible reason is that he may have been addressing not only husbands but also any unmarried men in the Corinthian church who were behaving in this way. A second possible explanation may emerge from chapter 7. There it seems that a group of Corinthians was so keen to be spiritual that they were renouncing sex altogether, even within their marriage relationships. If some homes in the church were feeling the strain of this abstention, Paul may not have wanted to base his advice too heavily on the claims and comforts of marriage. In chapter 7 he will try to clear up the Corinthians' misunderstandings about marriage. But first he has been concerned to underline that extramarital sex is not a Christian option. The relationships we make with our bodies should reflect the relationship we have with Christ.

MARRIAGE, SINGLENESS, AND CHRISTIAN FAITH
1 Corinthians 7:1–40

Some themes from chapters 5 and 6 run on into chapter 7. This too is about relationships, and about handling them properly and faithfully. It seems natural and logical that all this material should come together in one corner of the letter.

Yet the mood shifts in this chapter, in two ways. For here Paul starts to respond to questions that the Corinthians have put to him—"the matters about which you wrote" (7:1). Earlier we saw him dealing with concerns that were "reported," presumably through personal contact (1:12; 5:1). Now, it seems, he is addressing a topic the church has raised with him by letter.

The second switch of perspective in this chapter is that Paul has just been trying to curb the free-and-easy relationships into which some Corinthians have entered. He has written to restrain them (6:12–20). Then suddenly the situation has turned inside-out. It seems that some married people in the Corinthian church were restraining themselves. They decided to avoid having sex, as if faith somehow raised them above the realm of physical desire. From libertarianism (people exercising their desires with too much freedom) we have now run into asceticism (people denying their desires, because of their faith). It is odd that these two attitudes should exist side-by-side in Corinth, but apparently they did. In the Introduction we discussed some theories about why this might be. Here in chapter 7 we find Paul counselling a very confused church.

So we should not think that this chapter gives a complete Christian view on sex and marriage. Many big themes are simply not discussed here. There is not much, for example, about raising children. Paul does not even tell married people to love one another. He is addressing particular issues rather than trying to cover every base. This is a pastoral letter to people with questions and problems, not a wedding sermon.

However, the chapter does bring big principles into view. In two significant ways Paul's writing is balanced and symmetrical. One balance is that he deals carefully with both marriage and singleness. He sees both as legitimate Christian options and callings. Both are settings in which faithful and fruitful living is possible. So we shall read about entering into marriage, about living as married people, and about allowing marriage to end. Equally, the chapter covers the experience of becoming single, the life of a single person, and the transition from singleness into marriage. Neither group is ignored, or overlooked, or overshadowed by the needs and experiences of the other.

A second symmetry is between women and men. Equality in marriage was not to be taken for granted in the ancient world, yet several times Paul makes a point of addressing both genders in similar terms (7:2, 3, 4, 10–11, 12–13, 14, 16, 28, 32–34). He regards both as responsible to each other and to God. In separate Christian discipleship and in shared human partnership, women and men are each called to commitment, faithfulness, and mutual respect.

Several times in this chapter Paul advises, "Stay the way you are. Do not fret to change your circumstances. Bloom where you are planted." Sometimes the advice seems quite pragmatic: accept what life has given you, and serve God there. Yet this pragmatism is rooted in a belief that circumstances are not the most important thing about a person. We are not here simply to be married or to be single; we are called to be Christ's. Our relationships are rarely perfect. Yet very often the right way forward will be to serve the Lord where we are and to love the people God has given us.

We go on to look at the chapter a section at a time. It falls into six sections:

1. Addressing a question about sex within marriage (7:1–7)
2. Advice to the single and widowed (7:8–9)
3. Advice to the married (7:10–16)
4. Digression: in general, serve God where you are (7:17–24)
5. Advice to those thinking of marrying (7:25–38)
6. Summing up (7:39–40)

Sex and Marriage
1 Corinthians 7:1–7

7:1 Now concerning the matters about which you wrote: "It is well for a man not to touch a woman." [2] **But because of cases of sexual immorality, each man should have his own wife and each woman her own husband.**

> ³ **The husband should give to his wife her conjugal rights, and likewise the wife to her husband.** ⁴ **For the wife does not have authority over her own body, but the husband does; likewise the husband does not have authority over his own body, but the wife does.** ⁵ **Do not deprive one another except perhaps by agreement for a set time, to devote yourselves to prayer, and then come together again, so that Satan may not tempt you because of your lack of self-control.** ⁶ **This I say by way of concession, not of command.** ⁷ **I wish that all were as I myself am. But each has a particular gift from God, one having one kind and another a different kind.**

Some married couples in the Corinthian church seem to have ceased having sex together. Possibly they felt that faith raised them above mere biology. For in Christ "there is no longer male and female" (Gal. 3:28). So what better way to express this than to give up sexual activity? But Paul was skeptical. He quotes the slogan, "It is well for a man not to touch a woman" (7:1). If this was their ideal, he questions whether it is a good maxim for marriage.

Some people, Paul says, are called to single living, and this way of life is their "gift" from God (7:7). But those whose "gift" has been to marry should honor the sexual aspect of their marriage. A wife should "have" her own husband; the verb implies the sharing of bed and body. The husband too should "have" his wife (7:2). A married couple belong to one another, and in physical intimacy they express this belonging (7:3–4).

Paul also knew that if sex were not offered in marriage, it was likely in a place like Corinth that one of the parties (probably the man) would seek it outside the home (7:2, 5). It was better to be realistic. If couples wished to abstain from sex and concentrate more fully on prayer, let them agree to do so, but this should be for a set period only (7:5).

Paul never suggests, however, that sex is ungodly in itself. He does think sex outside marriage is wrong, but within marriage he affirms it as part of the commitment each partner owes and offers to the other. Certainly he favors celibacy (another word for single living). He thinks all Christians might serve God better if they were single "as I myself am" (7:7). But, as he explains later, this preference for celibacy is not directly to do with sex at all. There is a more practical reason—that singleness allows clear and undivided priorities and a fuller focus on the work of the Lord.

Singleness and Marriage
1 Corinthians 7:8–9

> **7:8 To the unmarried and the widows I say that it is well for them to remain unmarried as I am.** ⁹ **But if they are not practicing self-control, they should marry. For it is better to marry than to be aflame with passion.**

So Paul encourages widows to think seriously about remaining single. Remarriage was normally expected in the Roman world, and it was often swift, especially when a woman was widowed young. But Paul asks those who find themselves single to ask whether their gift and calling might now be to remain alone (7:8). He knew, however, that some would fall in love again. This, rather than the pressures of social convention or expectation, would be a reason for remarrying (7:9). We shall find much more about the situation and needs of single people later in this chapter (7:25–38).

Separation and Marriage
1 Corinthians 7:10–16

> 7:10 **To the married I give this command—not I but the Lord—that the wife should not separate from her husband** [11] **(but if she does separate, let her remain unmarried or else be reconciled to her husband), and that the husband should not divorce his wife.**
> [12] **To the rest I say—I and not the Lord—that if any believer has a wife who is an unbeliever, and she consents to live with him, he should not divorce her.** [13] **And if any woman has a husband who is an unbeliever, and he consents to live with her, she should not divorce him.** [14] **For the unbelieving husband is made holy through his wife, and the unbelieving wife is made holy through her husband. Otherwise, your children would be unclean, but as it is, they are holy.** [15] **But if the unbelieving partner separates, let it be so; in such a case the brother or sister is not bound. It is to peace that God has called you.** [16] **Wife, for all you know, you might save your husband. Husband, for all you know, you might save your wife.**

These verses are directed to married people. We saw in 7:1–7 that some married couples in Corinth had given up sex. Now it seems that some Christians there had thought of ending their marriages entirely, possibly for the same sort of reason. If faith made gender irrelevant, should not Christians release themselves into a more "spiritual" pattern of life?

Paul writes to prevent this. He tells his readers not to initiate divorce nor even to separate (7:10–11). The guiding principle is that marriage is meant to be permanent, and when Paul says "not I but the Lord" (7:10), he means that this teaching comes from Jesus himself. The relevant Gospel passages are Matthew 5:32 and 19:3–9, Mark 10:2–12, and Luke 16:18; what we have here from Paul is a fifth version of this teaching.

The process of oral transmission, which handed on Jesus' teaching in the decades before the Gospels were written down, has led to some differences of detail among these five passages. Yet they have a striking consistency, against the cultures and customs of the times. In the Greco-Roman world divorce was easy and common, and marriages were often ended for purely selfish reasons. For example, serial remarriage was one way to climb the social ladder. Christians by contrast were to be a distinctive people, who nurtured their marriages and aimed to go the distance together. Jesus' teaching spoke of a more patient and permanent kind of love than Corinth was used to.

A particular issue that strained some marriages in Corinth appears in 7:12-13—the tension that arises when one partner comes to Christian faith and the other does not. Suddenly the home is divided, and taking separate paths into the future may seem the least painful way forward. Paul speaks to this concern in 7:14-16. He cannot quote Jesus on this (7:12), but his basic advice is to stay in the marriage, if possible. A Christian should not initiate a break-up. If the partner is determined to leave, then the Christian spouse is also free to move on (7:15). But nothing will be gained, and much might be lost, by a Christian walking out.

Indeed, says Paul, Christians should realize that their life radiates something of Christ, and the influence of this may be strongest in the home. Christ's presence in one person will enrich and affect the lives of others. Holiness is infectious. God often reaches into people's lives through those around them (7:14). The resistance and unbelief of a spouse may mellow and melt in the course of time (7:16).

These verses have offered no simple advice for the bad times in a marriage. But they do manage to blend ideals and realities, and this balance is an important one for Christians to hold. Like Jesus and like Paul, we know that marriage is meant for life, and we encourage one another to respect this and to aim for it. We offer practical help and care when love and trust become strained. When healing is no longer possible, we seek to deal constructively with the situation that results and the separate lives that remain to be lived. And when mistakes have been made, we try to work toward forgiveness for one another and for ourselves.

Circumstance and Service
1 Corinthians 7:17-24

> 7:17 However that may be, let each of you lead the life that the Lord has assigned, to which God called you. This is my rule in all the churches. [18] Was anyone at the time of his call already circumcised? Let him not seek to remove the marks of circumcision. Was anyone at the time of his call uncircumcised? Let him not seek circumcision. [19] Circumcision is nothing, and uncircumcision is nothing; but obeying the commandments of God is

everything. ²⁰ **Let each of you remain in the condition in which you were called.**
²¹ **Were you a slave when called? Do not be concerned about it. Even if you can gain your freedom, make use of your present condition now more than ever.** ²² **For whoever was called in the Lord as a slave is a freed person belonging to the Lord, just as whoever was free when called is a slave of Christ.** ²³ **You were bought with a price; do not become slaves of human masters.** ²⁴ **In whatever condition you were called, brothers and sisters, there remain with God.**

On several occasions in this letter, Paul digresses. Part way through a complex pastoral discussion, he changes the subject. This is not absent-mindedness. It is a deliberate method. The digression serves to highlight a principle, which Paul can then take up and apply to the original issue. We shall meet digressions of this kind in chapters 9 and 13. Another is here.

Paul has just urged married people to remain in their marriages (7:10–16). Shortly he will encourage engaged couples to stay as they are rather than rushing to marry (7:25–38). So here in the middle is the overall principle: "lead the life that the Lord has assigned" (7:17); "remain in the condition in which you were called" (7:20); "there remain with God" (7:24). In general, Christians should stay put. Serve the Lord where you are and as you are.

The principle is illustrated from two spheres of life—race and social status. First comes race. A Gentile man who becomes a Christian need not take on Jewish circumcision. A male Jew who believes in Jesus should not try to erase this sign of his Jewishness (7:18). Neither circumcision nor the lack of it makes one a better Christian; grace does not depend on race (7:19). So although Christian faith gives us many new brothers and sisters, it does not deny our genes, our ancestry, or our birth. It invites us to serve Christ amid the background, the kin, and the community that we inherit.

Paul then makes the same point in relation to slavery—whatever your status, whether slave or free, you can serve Christ in the situation you have. Yet slavery and race are different sorts of issues: one is a natural gift, the other a human imposition. So, as an aside, Paul looks at what a slave should do, if the chance of freedom comes. What he says about this, at the end of 7:21, is hard to translate. I think the meaning shown in the NRSV footnote (and in some other Bible translations, like the RSV and NIV) is probably right: given the chance of freedom, the slave should take it and welcome it.

Paul never challenges slavery as an institution in the public way that many nineteenth-century Christians in America and Britain did. The church in New Testament times was too small and marginal a group to mount a major political protest over anything. Yet some of his writings, including this passage, do start to undermine the custom that allowed one person to own another. For Paul, living with slavery might be a condition a person cannot change. If it is, then serve Christ there. But it does not truly determine or identify a person.

Every Christian is simultaneously both slave and free. Our lives are bought with a price (7:23). As a ransomed people, we are both released by Christ and owned by Christ. The person whom the world counts free is bound forever to the service of the kingdom. The one whom the world reckons a slave belongs more truly and deeply to Christ than to any human bond. As church we live by the dignity of the gospel, rather than by the definitions and divisions of earthly role and rank. That is the reason Paul invites Christians to serve God with confidence wherever they are.

Single-Minded
1 Corinthians 7:25–38

> 7:25 Now concerning virgins, I have no command of the Lord, but I give my opinion as one who by the Lord's mercy is trustworthy. 26 I think that, in view of the impending crisis, it is well for you to remain as you are. 27 Are you bound to a wife? Do not seek to be free. Are you free from a wife? Do not seek a wife. 28 But if you marry, you do not sin, and if a virgin marries, she does not sin. Yet those who marry will experience distress in this life, and I would spare you that. 29 I mean, brothers and sisters, the appointed time has grown short; from now on, let even those who have wives be as though they had none, 30 and those who mourn as though they were not mourning, and those who rejoice as though they were not rejoicing, and those who buy as though they had no possessions, 31 and those who deal with the world as though they had no dealings with it. For the present form of this world is passing away.
>
> 32 I want you to be free from anxieties. The unmarried man is anxious about the affairs of the Lord, how to please the Lord; 33 but the married man is anxious about the affairs of the world, how to please his wife, 34 and his interests are divided. And the unmarried woman and the virgin are anxious about the affairs of the Lord, so that they may be holy in body and spirit; but the married woman is anxious about the affairs of the world, how to please her husband. 35 I say this for your own benefit, not to put any restraint upon you, but to promote good order and unhindered devotion to the Lord.

³⁶ **If anyone thinks that he is not behaving properly toward his fiancée, if his passions are strong, and so it has to be, let him marry as he wishes; it is no sin. Let them marry.** ³⁷ **But if someone stands firm in his resolve, being under no necessity but having his own desire under control, and has determined in his own mind to keep her as his fiancée, he will do well.** ³⁸ **So then, he who marries his fiancée does well; and he who refrains from marriage will do better.**

Much of this material is aimed at engaged couples. Girls were betrothed young in the Roman world and were often married in their early teens. Betrothal was a serious and formal bond, but it seems that some in the Corinthian church were hesitant about going forward to marriage. So although he has no saying of Jesus to help him, Paul recognizes his pastoral duty to the church and gives what guidance he can (7:25). His counsel here reiterates what he said in 7:8–9.

"Virgins" (7:25) are young marriageable women, although later we see that Paul speaks more directly to the men involved (7:36–38). The man, who was generally older than his bride, would be likely to take the lead, whether in marrying or in deferring marriage. Yet the basic point for both parties is exactly what Paul has just said (7:17–24): Stay where you are, and serve God within your situation (7:26). For marrying is not wrong (7:28), but singleness will probably prove a better choice (7:37–38).

Paul offers two arguments for this. One is the danger of living a divided and distracted life (7:32–35). A married Christian may be pulled in two directions: Can I give myself fully to the work of the Lord? Or shall I prioritize the well-being of my family? Paul obviously recognized this dilemma. Perhaps he had once been married himself. It is curious, however, that he should want to "spare" his people the "distress" of domestic life (7:28), and this language may shed light on his second reason for advising as he does.

That second reason is the mood of urgency and unrest in these verses—of present crisis, pressured times, and a changing world (7:26, 29–31). This sense of stress clearly influenced Paul's thinking. So what was he talking about? What was causing the stress, and why must it affect people's domestic plans? There are two main suggestions.

One possible cause is eschatology—the sense that time is moving toward a moment of crisis and climax. In 7:29 Paul speaks of a foreshortened perspective on life. So, although he does not say so directly, he may have in mind the return of Christ and the Christian hope that all creation will then be gathered in salvation and final judgment. This hope gave

Paul great energy for the work of the gospel. But it put earthly ties into shadow. All the institutions of this world are only temporary. Why marry, he might have thought, when Christ is coming?

An alternative explanation is based in history. The "present crisis" (7:26; "present" is a better translation than "impending") may be a particular event. Indeed the late forties and the fifties of the first century were a period of severe famine around the Mediterranean (Acts 11:28). Rome was always fed; the capital had first claim on the empire's harvest. But cities in the east could not always protect their supplies, and Corinth ran into serious grain shortage on at least three occasions. Many people surely suffered badly. If Paul had all this in mind, he may simply mean that a time of famine is not a moment to take on new commitments. People with family responsibilities will find a long lean spell hard to bear.

These two lines of insight may connect, if a particular event (hunger, perhaps) had sharpened Paul's sense that history is moving toward a crisis. The famines of these years may have seemed to him a signpost to greater change, a foretaste of the woes that would, like labor pains before birth, usher the kingdom of God into history. Paul felt he lived in critical times. He wanted the Christians he served to see their lives too within the context of a pressing divine purpose. The world is not permanent, and its fragilities and stresses are reminder of that.

So Paul dissuades the young men and women of the Corinthian church from hastening into marriage. Yet, as in 7:9, he realizes that some will want to marry, and he has no wish to prevent them. He clearly thinks that sex should be enjoyed within, not outside, the security of the marriage relationship (7:36).

Bound and Blessed
1 Corinthians 7:39–40

> 7:39 **A wife is bound as long as her husband lives. But if the husband dies, she is free to marry anyone she wishes, only in the Lord.** [40] **But in my judgment she is more blessed if she remains as she is. And I think that I too have the Spirit of God.**

These last two verses round off what has gone before. Marriage should be taken seriously. Widows may choose whether and whom to remarry. There is no hint here of the Jewish custom that expected a widow to marry her husband's brother (Deut. 25:5–6). But this freedom is qualified in two ways. If she marries, let her do so "in the Lord": a Christian woman should choose a Christian husband. And, as Paul said in 7:8, she might do even better to remain "as she is."

Paul has been giving the best counsel he can, in the face of serious confusions. "I think I have the Spirit" (7:40), he says. Guiding other people's marriages is not an exact science. Several times in the chapter he has left scope for discretion, decision, and flexibility. And we still cannot be sure of how much his advice was shaped by circumstances. What would he have said, once the famine finally lifted? Would his case for singleness have been quite so strong then? I do not know.

Yet I do hear insights in this chapter that stand the test of time: the encouragement to Christians to have some sense of our own gift and calling, to be realistic about the choices we make and the circumstances in which we make them, to respect both marriage and singleness, and not to change our situation unless we can do so carefully and confidently. In it all we remember that our truest and fullest identity is given in Christ.

4. Other Gods in Town
1 Corinthians 8:1–11:1

These three chapters are all about one topic. How should followers of Jesus conduct themselves in a society that is religious but not Christian? How do you connect with your local community if much of its life is animated by religious beliefs that you do not share? How do you maintain Christian integrity in a multifaith world?

In the Greco-Roman world, religion was normal. Shrines and statues were everywhere. Religious rites and ceremonies were woven into many aspects of private and public life, and all of this raised questions for the church. The Corinthians may have sought Paul's advice about this matter. For he starts with the words, "Now concerning . . ." (8:1)—the same formula he used earlier to take up an issue they had asked about (7:1).

These concerns still arise in many lands where Christians are a minority faith. In some places solutions or strategies are handed down from one generation to another. You face the challenge, you hold your convictions, you steer between isolation and compromise on a path that your parents or your fellow church members have already mapped and made. But the Christians in Corinth had no precedent to guide them. Everything was very new. It would take them time to work out how to handle these issues. It was almost inevitable that they would disagree and divide over what to do.

For Roman Corinth was a city of many temples, with many gods and goddesses to worship. The boundary between religion and the rest of life—business contacts, social events, and so on—was harder to draw than in some modern and more secular lands. For example, services in the various temples often led on to feasts. Guests would gather for food and friendship, in dining rooms on the temple premises. These rooms could also be booked for private celebrations, professional dinners, or club meetings.

This last point may seem very familiar. Many church congregations today hire out rooms for local business or community events. So what was different when a temple in Corinth did so? Food is the answer—the link between socializing and sacrifice. For a good deal of Greco-Roman worship involved animal sacrifice, but when an animal was offered up in worship, only a portion of the carcass was actually burnt. In a token way the whole animal had been presented to the god, yet the bulk of the flesh was still available for cooking. So now this meat might find its way to the city market. Or it could be cooked in the temple kitchens if there was a dinner party to cater for.

So if you accepted an invitation to a meal at a temple, you had a good idea where the meat had come from. It had been offered in sacrificial worship, and in theory it belonged to the god on whose territory you were sitting. For a Christian, that raised questions: How might attendance at this event mesh with my loyalty to Jesus? Will my faith suffer? Ought I to refuse the invitation? Or is my Christian life strong enough to withstand any challenge?

A complicating aspect of all this, in Paul's time, was the so-called imperial cult—the formal worship of the Roman emperor. In this era it was a growing feature of public life in many corners of the empire. It was a way for provinces to show their loyalty to Rome, and Corinth promoted it keenly. So civic events, local holidays, and even sports meetings included religious ceremony with a sacrifice in a local temple and a meal to follow. The top people in Corinth would be there. It would be a sign of rank and status to be invited. But again Christians would face questions: Does it clash with my faith? Or do my duties as a citizen, my standing in the community, and my circle of friendships oblige me to attend?

In these chapters Paul works gradually around the angles of the matter. As with chapter 7, on marriage and singleness, there were several cases and situations to consider and important principles to outline. Careful explanation rather than instant direction is the policy he adopts.

THE PROBLEM: ONE PERSON'S MEAT
1 Corinthians 8:1–13

These verses speak of a Christian "eating in the temple of an idol" (8:10)—attending a meal that followed a sacrificial service. Some church members in Corinth were glad to be there. They had "knowledge" (8:1, 10, 11). If other people thought the occasion had religious resonances, they reckoned to know better. They knew the deities of Greece and Rome were not real gods (8:4). So the event was only a dinner. The food was only meat.

They were confident to attend, to mix with friends, and to maintain their place in the social networks of the town.

Paul, however, reckoned that the pressures and dynamics of the situation were more complicated than this. He was uneasy about Christians participating so readily. As a first move, he asks these confident Christians to consider how their conduct might affect and influence others in the church. He asks them to blend knowledge with love.

Idols and Israel's One God. A key idea that runs through this chapter is the contrast between God and idols, the claim that other gods in other nations do not compare in any way with Israel's God. This sort of contrast appears quite frequently in the Hebrew Old Testament (e.g., Isa. 44:6–20), and in New Testament times the Greek word "idol," which could mean "shadow" or "phantom," helped to make the point. Israel's God stood in a category alone. Other gods might have a visible face, but they were not real.

Paul uses the word "idol" often in this chapter (8:1, 4, 7, 10). He surely means to impress on his readers that the gods of Greece and Rome are hollow; they have no substance. So he does not reflect at all on the motives of the people who worship these gods. His point is that a Christian, who knows Israel's God through Jesus, will not expect to find any comparable reality in other deities.

The classic Old Testament statement of this belief was called the *Shema* (Hebrew for "hear"). You may recognize it. Indeed you may have come across two different translations of it. "Hear, O Israel: The Lord is our God, the Lord alone" says the NRSV (Deut. 6:4). But in some English versions the ending reads, "the Lord is one," which matches the original Hebrew more tightly. In Judaism this verse was regularly used as a little creed.

Paul takes up this text, with its claim that God is one, and uses it as the hub of this chapter. A couple of times he emphasizes the point it makes: "no God but one . . . one God, the Father" (8:4, 6). For when the Shema says "one," it claims that Israel's God is unique. There are no rivals. No other being compares or competes. This God is responsible for all creation (8:6): "one God, the Father, from whom are all things and for whom we exist."

Some of the Corinthians would have agreed with Paul gladly. They had "knowledge," they would have assured him. They knew that "there is no God but one" (8:4) and that "no idol really exists" (8:4). So they were free to eat in a Greco-Roman temple. If the gods were not real, the worship could not harm them. They would attend, mix, and dine without any anxiety at all.

To address this issue, Paul interprets and adapts the Shema in two ways. One is rooted in the Old Testament text (8:1–3). The other comes out of the beliefs and convictions of the New Testament church (8:4–6).

Knowledge and Love
1 Corinthians 8:1–3

> 8:1 **Now concerning food sacrificed to idols: we know that "all of us possess knowledge." Knowledge puffs up, but love builds up.** [2] **Anyone who claims to know something does not yet have the necessary knowledge;** [3] **but anyone who loves God is known by him.**

The Shema makes a strong link between belief and love. As a statement of belief, it looks for response and relationship. For the ancient text goes on, "You shall love the LORD your God with all your heart . . ." (Deut. 6:5). Jesus called this the greatest of God's commands (Mark 12:29–30). And for Paul, too, the surest knowledge of God comes through loving God (8:3). Belief alone can be sterile. Knowledge may mislead badly (8:2).

For on its own, says Paul, knowledge inflates people (8:1). It turns us in on ourselves and makes us think of our own claims and rights. It tends to produce the sort of pride, competitiveness, and rivalry that blighted church life in Corinth (4:6, 18; 5:2). But love opens people out. It moves us to consider others. It "builds up" (8:1) both the neighbor and the body of Christ.

So Paul reminds the Corinthians of their need to show love. The Christian life is lived in relationship. Love binds Christians to God, and this same love for God connects us to each other. None of us is meant to fly solo as a Christian. The choices we make and the courses we take should reflect our belonging together. We are one body in Christ. And Christ, Paul goes on to say, is Lord of all creation.

Christ and Creation
1 Corinthians 8:4–6

> 8:4 **Hence, as to the eating of food offered to idols, we know that "no idol in the world really exists," and that "there is no God but one."** [5] **Indeed, even though there may be so-called gods in heaven or on earth—as in fact there are many gods and many lords—** [6] **yet for us there is one God, the Father, from whom are all things and for whom we exist, and one Lord, Jesus Christ, through whom are all things and through whom we exist.**

The second move that Paul makes in using the Shema is to say that Jesus shares in God's nature and work. The two halves of verse 6 are exactly symmetric:

| one God ... | from whom are all things | and for whom we exist, |
| and one Lord ... | through whom are all things | and through whom we exist. |

This symmetry is surely deliberate. God is unique, says Paul, and yet Jesus shares with his Father in this uniqueness. He does not compare or compete with God as if he were separate. He communicates and connects as one who is not separate, and this has been so from the beginning. All God's creation came into being through him, and through him God's church has its life (8:6). God's creative work of shaping the world and God's re-creative work of saving the church have Jesus at their very heart.

This is surely one of the New Testament's most emphatic claims about the identity of Jesus and his relationship to God. But it does not stand entirely alone. A number of texts (as we mentioned on 6:11) pave the way for the church's belief in God as Trinity. This verse (8:6) is part of that larger picture. It speaks of Father and Son working intimately together from the beginning. They are equal in intent and achievement. Together they stand distinct and apart from all other beings. Admittedly some verses in 1 Corinthians show Jesus in a servant role in relation to the Father (3:23; 11:3; 15:24, 28). Yet his service is exercised within the godhead as part of the life of God. And here in 8:6 Paul uses the Shema, which sets God above and apart from all other beings, to show Jesus in the closest possible association with his Father as Lord of "all things" and of the church.

All of this will shape a balance between knowledge and love in the advice Paul is about to give. For the relationship between Jesus and his Father brings love into the foreground. It shows the cross as God's sign of love for the world (Rom. 5:8). To say that the world has its life and meaning through Jesus (8:6) is to recognize that love, as well as knowledge, must shape the way his people behave. The Christian cannot ignore the person "for whom Christ died" (8:11). One way that we assess the rightness of an action is to consider its effect on sisters and brothers. Paul will pursue that concern in the verses ahead.

Custom and Conscience
1 Corinthians 8:7

> 8:7 It is not everyone, however, who has this knowledge. Since some have become so accustomed to idols until now, they still think of the food they eat as food offered to an idol; and their conscience, being weak, is defiled.

So now Paul returns to the vexed question of the serving of idol-meat. He reminds Corinth's more confident church members that "not everyone" (8:7) will reflect on the issue in the way they have done. A key word is "conscience" (8:7, 10, 12). In English this word has a moral flavor—sensitivity to right and wrong. However, this is not quite the sense of the Greek word. A truer translation might be "consciousness"—an awareness of the factors and dynamics involved in a situation. What powers are present; what forces are active; what elements and energies must I reckon with?

Consciousness, Paul reminds his readers, is shaped by experience. Our past gives us lenses for looking at life, and these will color our perceptions of any new situations we meet. Here it seems that some Christians in Corinth had experienced the world of Greco-Roman religion in ways they could not easily forget. In Christ they had become new people; but still they carried old memories. If they were to eat idol-meat, the encounter would feel intensely religious, and this might cloud and confuse their commitment to Christ. They could not say, "It's just meat." Something in their past would tell them it was more.

Paul was concerned for these "weak" sisters and brothers. He knew that their faith might be disturbed, and even destroyed, by the behavior of more confident Christians. So this whole chapter is a warning to those who thought themselves strong. What I know is not the only standard that should guide me. Love requires me to look sideways, at other members of the church, and at the effect I have on them.

Freedom and Family
8:8–13

> 8:8 "Food will not bring us close to God." We are no worse off if we do not eat, and no better off if we do. ⁹ But take care that this liberty of yours does not somehow become a stumbling block to the weak. ¹⁰ For if others see you, who possess knowledge, eating in the temple of an idol, might they not, since their conscience is weak, be encouraged to the point of eating food sacrificed to idols? ¹¹ So by your knowledge those weak believers for whom

Christ died are destroyed. [12] **But when you thus sin against members of your family, and wound their conscience when it is weak, you sin against Christ.** [13] **Therefore, if food is a cause of their falling, I will never eat meat, so that I may not cause one of them to fall.**

These verses now set out explicitly the point toward which Paul has been working. Food of itself is not the issue (8:8). There is no great spiritual benefit in attending a dinner and no big loss in staying away. The larger issue is pastoral. If other Christians seem "weak" (8:9, 11), that is no reason to ignore them. Indeed weak people need even greater consideration to prevent them falling (8:9, 13).

An important word in this section is "liberty" (8:9). This is not the usual Greek word for political freedom or freedom from slavery. It is freedom in the sense of "rights"—the right to act in certain ways. In the next chapter Paul will talk of his own rights as an apostle and will use this same word several times (9:4, 5, 6, 12, 18). So I wonder if some Corinthian Christians had spoken of their "right" to dine in a temple. They might have meant that conscience gave them the "right" to do this. Or possibly their civic status or membership in a business guild granted the "right" to attend a big event. But whatever "right" they had in view, Paul was not impressed. Rights are wrong if they end up hurting a neighbor—especially if the neighbor belongs to the family of faith.

For, as we have seen before (in 6:5–6), Paul regarded the church as family. Three times here he uses a word that means "brother or sister" (8:11–13). The NRSV shows this meaning in 8:12—"members of your family"—and mentions it in a footnote in the two adjacent verses. Christians belong to Christ (8:11, 12). In him we are sisters and brothers.

So the Christian's freedom is always constrained by love. Christ's love for me commits me to loving others, and sometimes this limits my options or curbs my choices. Relationships are always like this. Yet love is a surer freedom than rights. It reflects the life of Christ.

THE PATTERN: SERVICE AND SACRIFICE
1 Corinthians 9:1–27

In this chapter Paul pauses the discussion of idol-meat to talk about his own example and practice as a Christian. The pause has a purpose. He wants to help the Corinthians think more carefully about their behavior. He wants to teach them to balance rights and relationships, just as he does, and to take seriously the claims of the gospel when they make their choices and decisions. So this chapter sets out some patterns of Christian conduct. Then chapter 10 will give advice about putting the patterns into practice.

Chapter 9 falls into three main sections. First Paul sets out his rights as a pastor and missionary—the material help and support he could ask from the church (9:1–14). Then he steps back and explains that in practice he does not exercise these rights. He wants to spread the gospel as freely and widely as possible. And he will only be able to do this if he does so generously and humbly without standing on dignity or insisting on being rewarded (9:15–23). Finally and briefly, he describes the Christian life as a discipline, like the intense training regime of an Olympic athlete. Paul takes his commitment to Christ seriously, and he wants others to do so too (9:24–27).

The Rights of an Apostle
1 Corinthians 9:1–14

> 9:1 Am I not free? Am I not an apostle? Have I not seen Jesus our Lord? Are you not my work in the Lord? ² If I am not an apostle to others, at least I am to you; for you are the seal of my apostleship in the Lord.
>
> ³ This is my defense to those who would examine me. ⁴ Do we not have the right to our food and drink? ⁵ Do we not have the right to be accompanied by a believing wife, as do the other apostles and the brothers of the Lord and Cephas? ⁶ Or is it only Barnabas and I who have no right to refrain from working for a living? ⁷ Who at any time pays the expenses for doing military service? Who plants a vineyard and does not eat any of its fruit? Or who tends a flock and does not get any of its milk?
>
> ⁸ Do I say this on human authority? Does not the law also say the same? ⁹ For it is written in the law of Moses, "You shall not muzzle an ox while it is treading out the grain." Is it for oxen that God is concerned? ¹⁰ Or does he not speak entirely for our sake? It was indeed written for our sake, for whoever plows should plow in hope and whoever threshes should thresh in hope of a share in the crop. ¹¹ If we have sown spiritual good among you, is it too much if we reap your material benefits? ¹² If others share this rightful claim on you, do not we still more?
>
> Nevertheless, we have not made use of this right, but we endure anything rather than put an obstacle in the way of the gospel of Christ. ¹³ Do you not know that those who are employed in the temple service get their food from the temple, and those who serve at the altar share in what is sacrificed on the altar? ¹⁴ In the same way, the Lord commanded that those who proclaim the gospel should get their living by the gospel.

Two key ideas highlight the message and layout of this whole chapter. Paul mentions them in the first few verses and takes them up again later on. The first of these words comes at the very start: freedom.

Paul is "free"; he is "an apostle"; he has "seen Jesus" (9:1). For him, freedom, apostleship, and vision belong together. His words about seeing Jesus refer to his Damascus vision and to the commission that came to him there. For vision led to apostleship: seeing Jesus was the heart of the experience that launched Paul's ministry and sent him to the nations (Acts 26:17–18). And this made him free: because his mission began with a personal encounter, Paul had a kind of independence. No one controlled his ministry. He could make his own choices and decisions and determine his own way of living as he went about his work.

Yet, as we see later, Paul has chosen to turn his freedom into a kind of slavery. He has become a servant of the church (9:19). For him the only freedom that really counts is freedom to serve—to serve Christ, to share the gospel, and to support the churches. If he can do this, then he will consider himself truly and happily free.

The second key word is "rights." According to Paul, he might have sought a range of entitlements and benefits as he went about his ministry. He could hope to be fed by his churches; to travel with a wife, rather than alone (so presumably she too would be provided for); and to be paid for his ministry, so that he need not have to look for a job. Three times over he uses the word "right" (9:4–6).

Yet later he says that he has not used these rights (9:12, 15, 18). For Paul, the path of rights would sidetrack and divert his ministry. So he has set his rights aside and taken another way. The motive for it is all in the gospel and in the church's mission to the world. But before coming to this, Paul sets out six reasons why he might have claimed this support (9:5–14).

1. Christian precedent. Other traveling missionaries got these benefits (9:5–6). Some may well have been supported by the church at Corinth (9:12).
2. Illustrations from working life. People are paid for their work. Soldiers are fed and provisioned by the army. Shepherds and vine growers receive a share of the harvest they gather (9:7).
3. A verse from Scripture. Do not muzzle a threshing ox, said the Jewish law (Deut. 25:4). If a beast is treading corn to separate grain and husk, let it eat what it threshes (9:8–9). In Paul's time, this text was viewed as a guideline for all kinds of manual labor. Anyone who

works—on a farm, for example (9:10)—should be allowed to benefit from the job they do.
4. The results of his ministry. His work at Corinth, says Paul, should give him special credibility with the Christians there. Their faith was the fruit of his work. They were living proof that he was a true missionary of Christ (9:2). So it would be proper for them to support him (9:11).
5. A comparison with temple worship. Priests were fed from their work (9:13). When people brought animals as a sacrifice, part of the meat was given to the priest. The Jewish law prescribed this (Lev. 7:1–10; Num. 18:8–19), and similar practices were followed in Greco-Roman temples too.
6. A command of the Lord. Jesus told his disciples to expect food and shelter when they went about Galilee preaching (Luke 10:7). Obviously the church had remembered what Jesus said, and Paul thought the principle should apply to all traveling preachers (9:14).

For all these reasons, Paul believed he was entitled to material support. Like the farmer and the priest, the apostle should be able to live from his work. If rights mattered, Paul had plenty. Yet rights can be used wrongly. Other factors—responsibilities, service, neighbors' needs—must be considered too.

Freedom to Serve
1 Corinthians 9:15–23

> **9:15 But I have made no use of any of these rights, nor am I writing this so that they may be applied in my case. Indeed, I would rather die than that—no one will deprive me of my ground for boasting!** [16] **If I proclaim the gospel, this gives me no ground for boasting, for an obligation is laid on me, and woe to me if I do not proclaim the gospel!** [17] **For if I do this of my own will, I have a reward; but if not of my own will, I am entrusted with a commission.** [18] **What then is my reward? Just this: that in my proclamation I may make the gospel free of charge, so as not to make full use of my rights in the gospel.**
>
> [19] **For though I am free with respect to all, I have made myself a slave to all, so that I might win more of them.** [20] **To the Jews I became as a Jew, in order to win Jews. To those under the law I became as one under the law (though I myself am not under the law) so that I might win those under the law.** [21] **To those outside the law I became as one outside the law (though I**

am not free from God's law but am under Christ's law) so that I might win those outside the law. ²² To the weak I became weak, so that I might win the weak. I have become all things to all people, that I might by all means save some. ²³ I do it all for the sake of the gospel, so that I may share in its blessings.

Paul signals what is coming in this section of the chapter, before he gets there. Two threads of thought run side-by-side in his mind, and the second comes into view before he has finished laying out the first. The first thread is that churches should be willing to support their pastors, and the second is that he will not claim this support. So midway through a list of reasons for offering support, he interrupts himself: "Nevertheless, we have not made use of this right . . ." (9:12). Only a little later (from 9:15) does he explain himself properly.

These are emotional verses. Paul was passionate about his work. He felt driven to preach. For him it was not a choice; it was calling and commission and compulsion (9:15–16). He was an enlisted man, a slave of Christ. So just to do this work would be no credit at all. The only credit, the only real satisfaction, would be if he could give something of himself to God by preaching without pay (9:17–18). Then he would add his generosity to God's goodness and would share through his own love the message of God's grace. Only in working this way would he feel truly rewarded.

So Paul felt an inner motivation about serving without payment. But he had an outward concern too. He did not want to "put an obstacle in the way of the gospel" (9:12). He aimed to make the good news as accessible as he could, so that people of all sorts and situations could receive it. So he adapted his ways to the culture and customs of the people he was trying to reach (9:19). When he mixed with Jewish people, he observed the ancestral laws, even though his life was not centered on law in the way it once had been (9:20). But among Gentiles he would follow Gentile ways and would not be bound by Jewish dietary rules (9:21).

In a similar way—and this is surely the most important of these points—he was ready to identify with weak people (9:22). He would respect the inhibitions and anxieties of those of tender conscience and would limit his own freedom accordingly. This, of course, is exactly what he asked the more confident Christians in Corinth to do. Their "liberty" was disturbing "the weak" (8:9), and Paul wanted them to curb their conduct, as he would do himself. He wanted them to copy him. And he was acting this way "for the sake of the gospel" (9:23).

You may notice that the argument is not quite rounded off. After writing about financial rights and then saying he will not claim these, Paul has not explained precisely how this will help the gospel. Maybe he takes this for granted: hearers surely respond to a message more readily if the preacher does not ask to be paid. Yet the main point Paul has in mind is broader than this: that Christ's gospel matters more to him than his own rights. He voluntarily sets his rights aside for the sake of the church, and he wants Christians in Corinth—especially the confident, assertive ones—to do the same.

There may also be one further factor in the situation unstated here. For we shall see later that Paul accepted gifts from other churches but did not ask for payment in Corinth (2 Cor. 11:7–11). This may perhaps arise from an issue we have already discussed—the rivalries and patronage system of this city (see comment on 1:10–17). For in this era traveling orators often received support from rich patrons as they went from place to place. Benefits flowed both ways: the orator got fed and lodged, and taking a popular speaker into one's home would enhance a host's standing in the town. So in the Corinthian church, wealthier members might have been glad to help their preachers in this way. It would boost their status among fellow Christians, to have a well-known pastor as houseguest. But Paul was wary. He did not want the patronage of a powerful family. Instead he worked at his trade (Acts 18:3). This may have lowered his prestige in the eyes of some. But it gave him opportunities to meet people of all sorts and conditions and the freedom to speak without fear or favor when he had strong views to share. All this, of course, is part of the liberty of the gospel.

Running Hard
1 Corinthians 9:24–27

> 9:24 **Do you not know that in a race the runners all compete, but only one receives the prize? Run in such a way that you may win it.** [25] **Athletes exercise self-control in all things; they do it to receive a perishable wreath, but we an imperishable one.** [26] **So I do not run aimlessly, nor do I box as though beating the air;** [27] **but I punish my body and enslave it, so that after proclaiming to others I myself should not be disqualified.**

In this section, the focus and emphasis shift a little. Paul has been speaking about sharing the gospel with others. But as he reflects on his own work, he starts to write about the demand and discipline that are always part of

Christian living. We have to be committed, not just for the sake of others, but also to sustain our own walk with Christ.

Athletic metaphors are common in Paul's letters (Phil. 2:16; 3:12–14; Col. 4:12). The ancients enjoyed sport, and Corinth hosted the famous Isthmian Games every two years, with running, wrestling, and various other events. A lot of honor attached to winning, and top athletes took their training very seriously. Christians, says Paul, must be equally committed. We do not compete with one another, as athletes do, but holy living is still a strenuous task, and the Christian cannot be casual.

So the image of physical exercise and effort runs right through this paragraph. Yet Paul's point is not just about bodily discipline (even though this must sometimes be part of Christian living). Rather he is reminding the Corinthians not to take their spiritual well-being for granted. They must be watchful and active in the Christian race, or they may miss their destination. This thought continues into the first part of chapter 10, where Paul remembers a journey of a previous era, the Exodus.

A PRECEDENT: THE EXODUS AS EXAMPLE
1 Corinthians 10:1–13

> 10:1 **I do not want you to be unaware, brothers and sisters, that our ancestors were all under the cloud, and all passed through the sea,** [2] **and all were baptized into Moses in the cloud and in the sea,** [3] **and all ate the same spiritual food,** [4] **and all drank the same spiritual drink. For they drank from the spiritual rock that followed them, and the rock was Christ.** [5] **Nevertheless, God was not pleased with most of them, and they were struck down in the wilderness.**
>
> [6] **Now these things occurred as examples for us, so that we might not desire evil as they did.** [7] **Do not become idolaters as some of them did; as it is written, "The people sat down to eat and drink, and they rose up to play."** [8] **We must not indulge in sexual immorality as some of them did, and twenty-three thousand fell in a single day.** [9] **We must not put Christ to the test, as some of them did, and were destroyed by serpents.** [10] **And do not complain as some of them did, and were destroyed by the destroyer.** [11] **These things happened to them to serve as an example, and they were written down to instruct us, on whom the ends of the ages have come.** [12] **So if you think you are standing, watch out that you do not fall.** [13] **No testing has overtaken you that is not common to everyone. God is faithful, and he will not let you be tested beyond your strength, but with the testing he will also provide the way out so that you may be able to endure it.**

Paul has not mentioned idol-meat directly in chapter 9 and will not do so again until 10:14. But he still has this issue in mind. His argument is progressing gradually, and the mood and tone are starting to change. Chapter 10 develops a concern that was not nearly so obvious in 8 and 9.

In chapter 8, Christians who went to meals in temples were reminded that this might disturb others whose "conscience is weak" (8:10). Then in chapter 9 Paul spoke of his own example. He had not insisted on rights and entitlements and nor, he implied, should the Corinthians. All of this material has a single message: be careful for the Christian lives of others.

Only very late in chapter 9 did the focus shift. Now there was a more personal emphasis: be careful for your own Christian life. Christians must show discipline and commitment in order to "receive the prize" (9:24) and "not be disqualified" (9:27). Our journey with Christ requires stamina and some sacrifice. It matters to travel with purpose; otherwise we may miss the mark entirely. This theme continues into the early part of chapter 10.

Here Paul reflects on the Exodus of old (10:1–10). Israel's way from Egypt to the promised land was strewn with temptations. The people made some bad mistakes, and the consequences were grim. But, says Paul, these are not just past events. They "occurred as examples" (10:6), and they "happened . . . to instruct us" (10:11). It is vital to learn from them. Amid the complexities and compromises of a multifaith society, Paul was keen that the Corinthians should not take God's goodness for granted.

So to start with, he summarizes the Exodus story and likens it to the life of the church. For God blessed Israel with experiences that were something like Christian sacraments (10:1–4). To start with there was a kind of baptism. As the people journeyed a cloud led them forward. Then as they waited to cross the sea, it moved behind them to ward off the pursuing Egyptian army (Exod. 14:19). So they were safely covered, "under the cloud." They "passed through the sea" (10:1) and were saved. It was, in a way, like being baptized "in the cloud and in the sea" (10:2).

After this baptism, there was a sort of Communion. God gave the people "spiritual food and . . . drink" (10:3–4). Manna came down from heaven for them to eat (Exod. 16). Water spurted from the rock when they were thirsty (Exod.17; Num. 20). Some Jewish accounts of the Exodus spoke of the rock following Israel through the desert. Yet as Paul takes up this thought (10:4), he says that "the rock was Christ." For him, every sign of God's grace, even in the distant past, was a shadowy anticipation of Jesus. The Exodus generation had been dealing with him as the Corinthians must do.

It seems that Paul is warning the Corinthians against too cozy a view of the sacraments. They might think of their baptism or the church's Communion as some sort of safety net, a way of fending off any spiritual danger. But sacraments do not work like that. Israel had sacraments but still came to grief on the road (10:5). So if the Corinthians try and test God's patience, they too might struggle to finish their Christian journey (10:6). Indeed Paul will say later that Communion is actually dangerous if we are not serious about following Jesus (11:17–34).

To make the point really clear, Paul recalls a series of disasters from the Exodus years. Idolatry is his main concern—worshiping other gods. That was the issue at Corinth, and it reminds him of Israel's involvement with the golden calf (Exod. 32, in 1 Cor. 10:7). Then he goes on to recall three unhappy episodes from the book of Numbers (Num. 25, 21, and 14, in 1 Cor. 10:8–10) before urging his readers again to apply the lessons to their own lives. They are the ones "on whom the ends of the ages have come" (10:11). They live in the crucial era of human history, the age of the gospel. All of God's work in the Old Testament looks forward to this.

The section closes with a word of assurance. Vigilance, humility, and care are necessary Christian virtues. There is no doing without them (10:12). But even in times of trial, the Christian need not be afraid. God knows what we can handle and will give us wisdom and help when the heat is on (10:13). With this confidence in view, Paul is ready to speak more directly and firmly about the temples and temptations of Corinth.

THE PRACTICALITIES: TEMPLES AND TABLES
1 Corinthians 10:14–11:1

Sacrifice and Sharing
1 Corinthians 10:14–22

> 10:14 **Therefore, my dear friends, flee from the worship of idols.** [15] **I speak as to sensible people; judge for yourselves what I say.** [16] **The cup of blessing that we bless, is it not a sharing in the blood of Christ? The bread that we break, is it not a sharing in the body of Christ?** [17] **Because there is one bread, we who are many are one body, for we all partake of the one bread.** [18] **Consider the people of Israel; are not those who eat the sacrifices partners in the altar?** [19] **What do I imply then? That food sacrificed to idols is anything, or that an idol is anything?** [20] **No, I imply that what pagans sacrifice, they sacrifice to demons and not to God. I do not want you to be partners with demons.** [21] **You cannot drink the cup of the Lord and the cup of demons. You**

cannot partake of the table of the Lord and the table of demons. ²² Or are we provoking the Lord to jealousy? Are we stronger than he?

These few verses present a sharp challenge to the Christians in Corinth. The sentences are short, the language crisp, the choices plain, and the message unmistakable. Avoid the worship of other gods. Above all, steer well away from sacrifices. The message here recalls what Paul has just said about the Exodus generation: avoid idolatry (10:14); do not provoke the Lord (10:22). And it follows through on the assurance he gave at the end of the last paragraph—"God . . . will also provide the way out" (10:13). "Therefore . . . flee" (10:14).

The tone of these verses contrasts quite strongly with Paul's earlier writing, in chapter 8. There the main problem with eating in a temple was that you might injure another person's faith (8:10–11). But here the language is more direct. The concerns are intense, personal, and firsthand: don't desire evil (10:6); be careful not to fall (10:12); do not provoke God (10:22). So why the difference?

It looks as if the subject matter may have shifted. Paul is not talking about quite the same sort of event as he was earlier. Chapter 8 speaks of dinners that followed sacrificial services, and these meetings over dinner would not be as overtly and intensely religious as the worship itself. So Paul states the danger indirectly too, and he asks his readers to think about how their conduct affects other people. In contrast, this middle part of chapter 10 speaks of the central acts of pagan worship—sacrifices and the sharing of some of the meat in the sanctuary as part of the ceremony. About these occasions Paul gives the very strongest guidance. He regards these events as the spiritual equivalent of playing with fire. Christians must stay right away. Any involvement at all would deny and endanger their relationship with Christ.

Here, I am sure, we hear the heartbeat of Paul's concern on this issue. He regarded the whole realm of Greco-Roman worship as dangerous territory. He would prefer Christians to avoid it entirely, both the ceremonies themselves and the associated meals. But he has had to work gradually 'round to saying this. He allows for the fact that different sorts of occasion raise different concerns. He takes time to explain himself. That is why his argument has taken so long to get to this point.

Paul's main concern is that meals create community. Eating in worship brings you into fellowship with the god you honor. He gives a couple of examples. The first is that the church's Communion service creates fellowship with Jesus. When we take his body, in Communion bread, we are joined together as his body in the church (10:16–17). The second is that Israel's Old Testament worship required God's people to "eat . . . in the presence of the Lord" (Deut. 14:26). There they became "partners in the altar" (10:18). And in a similar way, sacrificial worship in a pagan temple will create fellowship—not with a nonexistent idol (10:19), but with "demons." Paul repeats this noun, four times altogether (10:20–21).

For Paul, although an idol was hollow and insubstantial, worshiping an idol was not an empty act. There were spiritual forces—"demons"—to reckon with. The Greeks thought of these as go-between beings, minor spirits that bridged the gap between gods and humans. Whenever the Bible mentions them, it does so in derogatory terms: beside Israel's God, demons were small and shallow. Yet they were also deceptive; they could lead the faithful astray. To offer them worship would be to waste your praise and to wound your life. It would also risk the severe and salutary judgment of a jealous God (10:22).

So Paul puts a sharp challenge before the Corinthians. The central acts of Greco-Roman worship are not neutral or empty. They are a dangerous denial of the claims of Israel's God. A Christian has no business at all to be there. Even if you are invited, even if friends will be present, even if attendance will enhance your image and status in the town, you should stay away. You cannot link yourself to other spiritual forces and expect your relationship with Christ to remain secure and unscathed.

Nonetheless, in a town like Corinth, the links between pagan worship and ordinary life were intricate and involved. The lines of contact were not always clear to see, and this in itself would cause concern and doubt for some Christians. So in the final part of this chapter Paul talks about the daily routines of living, commending a lifestyle and a frame of mind that are alert but not unnecessarily anxious.

Of Meat, Markets, and Meals
1 Corinthians 10:23–11:1

> 10:23 **"All things are lawful," but not all things are beneficial. "All things are lawful," but not all things build up.** [24] **Do not seek your own advantage, but that of the other.** [25] **Eat whatever is sold in the meat market without raising any question on the ground of conscience,** [26] **for "the earth and its fullness are the Lord's."** [27] **If an unbeliever invites you to a meal and you are disposed to go, eat whatever is set before you without raising any question on the ground of conscience.** [28] **But if someone says to you, "This has been**

offered in sacrifice," then do not eat it, out of consideration for the one who informed you, and for the sake of conscience— ²⁹ I mean the other's conscience, not your own. For why should my liberty be subject to the judgment of someone else's conscience? ³⁰ If I partake with thankfulness, why should I be denounced because of that for which I give thanks?

³¹ So, whether you eat or drink, or whatever you do, do everything for the glory of God. ³² Give no offense to Jews or to Greeks or to the church of God, ³³ just as I try to please everyone in everything I do, not seeking my own advantage, but that of many, so that they may be saved. 11:1 Be imitators of me, as I am of Christ.

Was it the Corinthians who had said, "All things are lawful"? Again Paul quotes the slogan and once more he queries it (10:23, as in 6:12). Again (as in 8:1), the need to build one another up must curb and condition the exercise of Christian freedom (10:24).

Corinth had a permanent public meat market controlled by the city authorities. A good deal of the meat sold there came from temples around the city and had been previously offered in sacrifice. How, then, were Christians placed when they went shopping? Might they purchase idol-meat without knowing? Would this matter, and what could they do about it?

Paul's answer is based on "conscience"—or, better, on "consciousness" (see comment on 8:7). Your awareness affects your decisions. If you knew where the meat had come from, that might be an issue. But if you do not know, it is simply meat. God created it, and the Christian may be grateful (10:25–26). In the same way, when you are invited out to dinner, simply accept the food as food (10:27). Do not ask where it comes from. Eat and be glad. Paul has no wish to stop Christians mixing with unbelievers (5:10).

All of this liberates the Christian to live confidently in a multifaith society. What I don't know about, I don't need to worry about. Unless eating is obviously linked to pagan worship, it is all right. But the situation changes if another person knows something about the provenance of the meat and comments on this (10:28). It is not clear whom Paul has in mind as the sort of person who might point this out: Would it be an unbeliever, even the host; or a fellow Christian, who has a sensitive "conscience"? Either way, this new information alters the situation. Someone has been aware enough to speak and will notice how the Christian reacts. For that person's sake (10:29), it is better to abstain.

The final verses sum up. The Christian is free to enjoy God's creation thankfully and cheerfully (10:30). The Christian is also bound to consider other people's needs, fears, and salvation (10:32–33). It is in balancing those two principles and in knowing the right time and situation for each that we give glory to God (10:31). For the God who made all things is also the God who gave his Son (8:6). In the gospel, creation and costly love belong together. Only by living in love do we truly honor our creator. Christians are called to copy the pattern of Christ and to hand it on (11:1).

Values and Questions. The argument in these chapters has been long and involved. Yet we end where we began: knowledge must be supplemented by love (8:1) and freedom by concern for the well-being of others (10:24, 33). Teaching about this balance fills most of the three chapters (8:1–9:23 and 10:23–11:1). The needs of the weak, the advance of the gospel, and the family of Christ take priority over the rights, preferences, and freedoms of the individual.

In the midst of this, the central section of these three chapters contains sharp words of challenge. Christian living must be disciplined if we are to keep on track and to travel with intent (9:24–27). We can trust God, but we should not trifle with God (10:1–13). This means that Christians should not get entangled in the worship of other gods (10:14–22).

These questions, about coexisting with neighbors of other faiths and handling the expectations that arise remain very much alive for churches in some parts of the world. For example, one recent writer (Newton, 1998) compares these chapters to a present-day setting in Asia, where Christians negotiate regularly the complexities of a multifaith society. Even so, this teaching may seem a little distant if we live in the Christian yet secular West. How, then, might it apply in our context?

I find three big issues in these chapters, each of which puts a question to our Christian living and practice and all of which require thought and care in relation to a range of issues and actions. One is fellowship—the needs of other Christians. The question here is, How might another person's faith be strengthened or weakened by what I do? The second is evangelism—the advance of the gospel. How does my way of life help or hinder my neighbor's openness to the good news? The third is belief—the faith of the church. How can my contacts, commitments, and conduct express my faith in Jesus as Lord? These three questions cross cultures and continents; they ask to inform our Christian witness wherever we live, amid whatever pressures and opportunities we meet.

5. The Church and Its Worship
1 Corinthians 11:2–14:40

In the West we are used to Christian worship. When we gather to praise God, we can use patterns and material that are much older than we are. Although our worship may change with the years and the generations, we have never needed to devise it all from nothing. There is a tradition to work with. But the Christians in Corinth could not do this. Although some of them once belonged to the Jewish synagogue, the two groups had now separated. And the Gentile members of the church did not have even this background. So the church had to find its own way and develop patterns and customs that would nurture their identity as the body of Christ. Where would they meet and when? What would they do? Who would lead? The situation was all very new, and good habits would take time to form.

These chapters take us into that formative era. They show us a fuller picture of early Christian worship than we find anywhere else in the New Testament. They also highlight some of the mistakes, conflicts, and difficulties of those days. We see Paul addressing three main issues—gender, gathering, and gifts.

First he writes about our human identities as male and female—the gender roles that we inherit in creation and live out in society (11:2–16). How should these shape our involvement in church life and worship? Then he talks about meeting for Communion services (11:17–34). How can Christians be truly united at the Lord's table when we belong to a divided and deeply unequal world? Thirdly, he thinks about the spiritual gifts that church members offer and how these can nurture the life of the whole fellowship (12:1–14:40).

GRACE AND GENDER
1 Corinthians 11:2–16

> 11:2 **I commend you because you remember me in everything and maintain the traditions just as I handed them on to you.** ³ But I want you to understand

that Christ is the head of every man, and the husband is the head of his wife, and God is the head of Christ. [4] Any man who prays or prophesies with something on his head disgraces his head, [5] but any woman who prays or prophesies with her head unveiled disgraces her head—it is one and the same thing as having her head shaved. [6] For if a woman will not veil herself, then she should cut off her hair; but if it is disgraceful for a woman to have her hair cut off or to be shaved, she should wear a veil. [7] For a man ought not to have his head veiled, since he is the image and reflection of God; but woman is the reflection of man. [8] Indeed, man was not made from woman, but woman from man. [9] Neither was man created for the sake of woman, but woman for the sake of man. [10] For this reason a woman ought to have a symbol of authority on her head, because of the angels. [11] Nevertheless, in the Lord woman is not independent of man or man independent of woman. [12] For just as woman came from man, so man comes through woman; but all things come from God. [13] Judge for yourselves: is it proper for a woman to pray to God with her head unveiled? [14] Does not nature itself teach you that if a man wears long hair, it is degrading to him, [15] but if a woman has long hair, it is her glory? For her hair is given to her for a covering. [16] But if anyone is disposed to be contentious—we have no such custom, nor do the churches of God.

This half-chapter has been something of a storm-center in the last few decades. As various churches have asked fresh questions about gender and ministry and have turned to Scripture for guidance, this has been one of the main texts to consider. Yet it is not an easy passage. In some places it is hard to know quite what Paul meant. And many details of the argument reflect the customs and perceptions of a world quite different to ours. So if we wish to make worthwhile sense of the passage (as I believe we can), we must try to understand the background to Paul's writing. First we look at some words he uses, then at some cultural issues, and finally at how he weaves his argument together.

Words and Meanings. The nouns "man" and "woman" also did duty in ancient Greek for "husband" and "wife." So when we meet these nouns, their meaning will depend on whether Paul is thinking about marriage (as he may be in 11:3) or about creation (in 11:8–9).

The word "head" also takes more than one meaning in the text. There is an obvious literal meaning—the upper part of the human body. So a head could be covered by a hood or veil (11:5) or indeed by long hair (11:15).

But Paul also uses this word as a metaphor for people's relationships (in 11:3). What did he mean by this? The English use of "head" to mean "leader, person in authority" was not very common in ancient Greek. So a meaning like "source" or "origin of life" may be more likely in this verse.

Then, whatever "head" means in 11:3, the next couple of verses play on the double meaning of this word. The covering (or not) of a person's physical head has to reflect the relationship of "headship" in which their life is set. If a man covers his head while praying, he dishonors his "head," who is Christ. But when a woman leaves her head uncovered, she dishonors her "head," her husband (11:4–5).

Indeed words that signal honor and shame crop up a number of times: "disgrace" (11:4, 5, 6), "degrading" (11:14), and "glory" (11:15). This same Greek word for "glory" is translated as "reflection" earlier in the passage (11:7), but it may well have overtones of honor there too. So honor and shame figure large in this passage, just as they did in the whole social structure of the Greco-Roman world.

The ancients judged a person's worth in quite formal ways. Honor was a matter of reputation and respect; it was accorded by custom, by neighbors, and by the community. So it was vital to meet cultural expectations, to adhere to convention, and to observe the role and relationships that went with one's situation in life. To break one's social mold would give rise to shame rather than honor. And we shall see that the issue of honor and shame contributes to Paul's advice in these verses.

Gender, Custom, and Covering. Paul's chief concern in this passage is that Christian women should cover their heads to pray. In traditional communities of the time, married women were expected to cover their heads in public as a sign of modesty and respectability. So why might some Corinthian women not have done this? Here are three theories:

1. A religious explanation. In some Greek religious movements women would take part without the usual head-covering. They quite literally let their hair down, perhaps in ecstasy or enthusiasm, as if to ignore the measured expectations of tradition and honor. Possibly some Christian women in Corinth were acting like this in church, setting aside the signs and customs of female subservience because of their new identity in Christ.
2. A matter of trend and style. In this period an increasing number of upper-class Roman women were claiming the right to make their own decisions and to shape their own pattern of living. This included breaking with custom in matters of attire and behavior. Corinth, as a top provincial city, was greatly influenced by Roman ways. So even within the church, it is possible that the wealthier and

more fashionable women paid little regard to the styles and rules of tradition and convention.
3. *An issue of place.* There were no church buildings in this era. Christians gathered in members' homes. So when the church met for worship, there was a blurring of the distinction between public and private space. In a sizeable Greek house with its vestibule open to the street, the worship was publicly visible. People could see what Christians were doing and could perhaps even wander in (14:23). At the same time, some women in the fellowship might feel that they were in a familiar domestic setting. "This is my own front room," they might think; or "I'm visiting a friend's home, a house I know well." They might not see the point of adopting formal public attire, even though they were taking part in a meeting of the church.

Each of these theories aims to relate our knowledge of ancient culture to what Paul has written. Yet none is absolutely compelling, and we still do not know for certain what motivated these Corinthian women. Yet clearly Paul urges on them a more conventional mode of dress. He also writes of men and of their attire. Indeed he mentions men at every stage of his argument. This surely helps to frame and complement his teaching to the women. But he may have a more direct concern too.

For male head-covering was a factor in the wider culture. Men who led ceremonial worship of the Greco-Roman gods often did so with covered heads. Friezes and statues show people praying or offering sacrifice with their toga pulled up over the head like a hood. If Christian men in Corinth were covering their heads in worship, Paul may have felt that this matched too neatly the style of the city's imperial and pagan religion.

Culture, Creation, and Christ. Now we are ready to follow through this passage and to trace the advice that Paul gives. Three different but interlocking sets of ideas about gender roles and relations appear one after another in the course of the text.

1. ***Culture.*** Ancient peoples regulated gender relations in various ways. As we mentioned above, there was a tradition of married women covering their heads in public. In a world that was very conscious of honor and shame, proper attire was one way to uphold the good name of husband and family. So this is where Paul begins (11:5), by connecting the matter of female head-dress to the honor of her "head." It would be socially and culturally shameful, he says, to pray with head uncovered—almost as crazy and off-beat as shaving off her hair (11:6).

2. ***Creation.*** Paul now supports the point he has just made by turning to the creation stories in Genesis. When he speaks of woman being created "from man" and "for the sake of man" (11:8–9), he is drawing on Genesis 2. There the woman comes to life from the man's body to meet his need for companionship (2:18–23). Paul also mentions the word "image" (11:7), which echoes Genesis 1. But he does not pursue the idea that male and female share God's image together (1:27). When he speaks in directly egalitarian terms, he roots this in Christian experience rather than in creation.
3. ***Christ.*** There is a new world "in Christ," of fellowship and unity. Women and men belong in this on the same basis through faith. Elsewhere Paul had written, "there is no longer male and female; for all of you are one in Christ Jesus" (Gal. 3:28). And here he speaks of mutual dependence: "in the Lord woman is not independent of man or man independent of woman" (11:11). Each needs the other. Neither ought to act as if the other were not there or did not matter.

Amid these three frames of insight, Paul spells out how he wants the Corinthians to behave. The word "ought" is a signal, and (as we saw in chapter 7) there are balancing commands to men and women (11:7, 10). A man, says Paul, "ought" to pray with head uncovered (11:7). In doing this he indicates and honors his direct commitment to God. He both reflects and seeks God's glory.

By contrast, a woman who speaks in worship "ought to" wear on her head "a symbol of authority" (11:10). But Paul's words were simpler than this. He did not write "a symbol of"; notice the NRSV footnote. He wrote the single word "authority," which we came across in chapter 9, meaning "a person's right." So this verse actually says that a woman should wear "authority" or "right" on her head.

This may mean that a woman covers her head—blanking out, as it were, the metaphorical "headship" of her husband—in order to claim the "right" to speak directly to and for God. Alternatively it may imply that she speaks from within her proper role and so retains the "right" to her honor. By covering her head, she visibly observes the social code that links her to her husband, even as she raises her own voice in Christian worship. I think this alternative reading of the verse is more likely to be correct.

For the passage ends by underlining the points Paul has made. These practices are "proper" (11:13), he says; they are "natural" (11:14); all the churches observe them (11:16). These three little postscripts suggest to me that Paul is advocating quite a traditional approach to female attire.

He wants the church to conduct itself honorably—that is, conventionally—and not to court notoriety and disrepute.

Incidentally, the phrase "because of the angels" (11:10) is impossibly obscure. Even the most learned commentators do not know what it means. One reasonable suggestion is that angels were thought of as guardians of the roles and order of creation. This thought would link the verse with those that precede it. Many big commentaries consider numerous possible interpretations of the phrase.

Mixed Voices. In closing, we should emphasize that this half chapter does not ask if women should pray and prophesy. It assumes they do and discusses how they should do so. Later in the letter women are told to be quiet in church (14:34–35), but there is no hint at this stage of Paul silencing the women of Corinth. He presumes that they speak in worship, and this is rather a novelty within his cultural background. In Jewish synagogues of the day women did not pray and prophesy. In this early Christian church they evidently did.

So perhaps Paul was less misogynistic and more egalitarian than has often been thought. He started a church in which women could speak. Now in this passage he has asked them to do so in ways that would not ignore their marital commitments and social context. Honor and custom were important to him, because these affected the reputation of the church in wider society.

We shall not make a modern feminist out of Paul. But we shall have heard him well if we find ourselves asking some of his questions in our own day. How can men and women contribute together to the life of the church, trusting and learning from one another? How can we reflect in worship the voices, graces, and gifts of both genders? And amid the perceptions and concerns of our present cultures, how can we represent the new life of Christ without causing unnecessary suspicion or offense?

SHARING THE SUPPER
1 Corinthians 11:17–34

Most church congregations today do not celebrate Holy Communion in the course of a shared meal. We might do so occasionally, perhaps during Holy Week, but it would not be a regular arrangement. Communion is part of the formal order of worship. If members eat a meal together, this is a separate event with a clear divide between.

In Corinth, however, things were different. The church met in members' homes, in a place where food was often shared with family and guests. Worship and eating were two aspects of one gathering, and there was no obvious boundary between. Supper and the Lord's Supper merged into one, and this caused big problems in the church—not of doctrine, but of fellowship, unity, and mutual care. And this difficulty may have been rooted in the house church.

House Church. Not many members of the Corinthian church were wealthy (1:26). But the better-off families had the largest houses, and these were natural places for the church to meet. Archaeology can tell us about houses of this kind and about the sort of layout that was common in affluent homes of the period.

An outer courtyard, called an atrium, would lead to a triclinium, an inner dining room. Although the triclinium could be large, it was quite an intimate room. It would be furnished with couches for diners to recline as they ate, normally for no more than about ten people. If more than that number were eating together, they would need to overflow out into the atrium, which was more sparsely furnished and where there was room for a few dozen people to gather.

We do not know how many people belonged to the church at Corinth. The epistle mentions seven names, and Romans (16:21–23), which was written from Corinth, gives us seven more. If we reckon that most of these had families, then estimates range from about thirty members upwards. A meeting of thirty or forty people could certainly get into one home. But if numbers were much greater than this, then the church would have had to meet in several groups (as the church in Rome did at this period). Either way, there were more than enough Christians in Corinth to overflow the capacity of a typical triclinium.

So when the Christians met, who would sit in the inner triclinium? Probably the richer members of the church, the host's equals and friends, would be invited inside. They were used to eating in this sort of setting. They had more leisure and would be able to arrive early. Whereas the larger group out in the atrium would be made up of people from lower down the social scale. Once we connect that suggestion to another custom of this period, we see more clearly why Paul writes as he does.

Some Greek and Roman writers tell of a curious habit they encountered at big dinner parties. The host and his closest friends were served large portions of costly food with good wine to drink. Friends of lower status were offered smaller quantities and poorer quality, while any freedmen present (former slaves, and not so well off) got scantier fare altogether.

So when Paul talks of a church divided (11:18) and of some members eating well while others went hungry (11:21), this may be the background against which he writes. Poorer members were out in the atrium and the rich in the triclinium. Servants in the house served the best food, as they usually did, to the company in the triclinium and poorer fare to the others. Alternatively, it may have been a bring-and-share, but there were those who had little to bring and found that no one shared much with them. It would not help if some were delayed in arriving; many slaves and people in menial work would not be able to control their hours. Meanwhile others were able to "go ahead with their own supper" (11:21). And in the midst of all this, the memory of Jesus got mislaid or at least very badly misunderstood.

Not the Lord's Supper
1 Corinthians 11:17–22

> 11:17 **Now in the following instructions I do not commend you, because when you come together it is not for the better but for the worse.** [18] **For, to begin with, when you come together as a church, I hear that there are divisions among you; and to some extent I believe it.** [19] **Indeed, there have to be factions among you, for only so will it become clear who among you are genuine.** [20] **When you come together, it is not really to eat the Lord's supper.** [21] **For when the time comes to eat, each of you goes ahead with your own supper, and one goes hungry and another becomes drunk.** [22] **What! Do you not have homes to eat and drink in? Or do you show contempt for the church of God and humiliate those who have nothing? What should I say to you? Should I commend you? In this matter I do not commend you!**

Paul wrote earlier about "divisions" in the church (1:10). A quarrelsome fellowship, with its members vying for power and allying themselves with different leaders, gave him no pleasure at all. But the "divisions" of which he writes now (11:18) are different to those of the opening chapters. The church was dividing along lines of wealth and status; the haves were separating from the have-nots. This denies, says Paul, the true meaning of the sacrament: "it is not really the Lord's supper" (11:20). To partition the fellowship in this way "shows contempt for the church of God" (11:22), because it overlooks and despises some of the people who make up the church.

Earlier Paul commended the Corinthians (1:4–7; 11:2), but here he is very critical of them (11:17, 22). He hates the thought of the church separating like this. There are bound to be "splits," he says sadly (11:19), between those who are "genuine" and those whose faith is shallow and inert. But he would rather the church's worship showed a greater sense of unity. When the church meets he wants there to be care, love, and respect. Then Communion will start to mean what it ought.

"The Lord's Death, until He Comes"
1 Corinthians 11:23–26

> 11:23 **For I received from the Lord what I also handed on to you, that the Lord Jesus on the night when he was betrayed took a loaf of bread,** [24] **and when he had given thanks, he broke it and said, "This is my body that is for you. Do this in remembrance of me."** [25] **In the same way he took the cup also, after supper, saying, "This cup is the new covenant in my blood. Do this, as often as you drink it, in remembrance of me."** [26] **For as often as you eat this bread and drink the cup, you proclaim the Lord's death until he comes.**

These verses are used in many churches, to introduce Holy Communion. Similar passages, telling of Jesus sharing bread and wine with his friends, appear in the Last Supper scenes in three of the Gospels (Matt. 26:26–29; Mark 14:22–25; Luke 22:15–22). So although the versions differ a little (Luke's wording being the closest of the three to Paul's), the memory of the event was evidently passed down in the early church and was surely recalled often when Christians met to break bread. Paul speaks of himself as a link in this chain of tradition, handing on words that came originally from Jesus (11:23).

By using these words, Paul portrays Jesus as host of the church's Communion service. The meal does not belong to the person in whose home the church meets nor to those who paid for the food. It is the Lord's Supper, and it binds the church together in his company and under his leadership. When we share the bread of Christ's "body" (11:24), we become one body in the sharing (10:16–17).

The Communion cup too is a sign of unity. The idea of "covenant" (11:25) both recalls God's ancient relationship with Israel (Exod. 24:8) and gives that idea a new focus in Jesus. So when Christians share Communion, both bread and wine speak of our responsibility to one another. We are called to be one people with our history and our hope in Jesus.

For Communion points both backward and forward—back to the church's founding and on to its future (11:26). The elements of bread and wine "proclaim the Lord's death"; they speak of flesh and blood that are separated in sacrifice. Yet this memory goes hand-in-hand with hope: one day Jesus will be fully and finally vindicated. As his own Last Supper looked forward (Luke 22:16, 18), his people still celebrate Communion "until he comes." The sacrament declares that the church was born in sacrificial love and is beckoned by promise. With this identity and destiny, we dare not live carelessly.

"Discerning the Body"
1 Corinthians 11:27–34

> 11:27 **Whoever, therefore, eats the bread or drinks the cup of the Lord in an unworthy manner will be answerable for the body and blood of the Lord.** [28] **Examine yourselves, and only then eat of the bread and drink of the cup.** [29] **For all who eat and drink without discerning the body, eat and drink judgment against themselves.** [30] **For this reason many of you are weak and ill, and some have died.** [31] **But if we judged ourselves, we would not be judged.** [32] **But when we are judged by the Lord, we are disciplined so that we may not be condemned along with the world.**
>
> [33] **So then, my brothers and sisters, when you come together to eat, wait for one another.** [34] **If you are hungry, eat at home, so that when you come together, it will not be for your condemnation. About the other things I will give instructions when I come.**

Paul's warnings not to eat and drink "in an unworthy manner" (11:27) and to "examine yourselves" (11:28) before Communion have made some Christians very anxious and introspective. This has been quite a big issue in the Presbyterian tradition (to which I belong). We wonder whether we are good enough to come to the table, for we know well that we are not nearly as holy as we ought to be. This anxiety has made many fine people cautious about coming to Communion, and in many ways it is a proper concern. The Lord's table is no place for presumption or pride. Yet Paul's accent in these verses is more corporate than individual. He is concerned for the church as a whole fellowship.

When he speaks of "discerning the body" (11:29), Paul wants the Corinthians to be more serious about their unity in Jesus. Those who take the body of Christ are themselves one body in Christ. Yet the Christians in Corinth were acting as splintered fragments rather than as a single fellowship. To "discern the body" would mean recognizing this unity, reckoning with the presence of Christ in brothers and sisters, and meeting one another in a spirit of service and love.

For Communion is a place of judgment (11:29). It shines the light of Christ's coming, and the judgment that this will bring, onto the life of his people. In Corinth many church members were sick; some had died (11:30). We do not know the circumstances. Yet clearly Paul saw a link between division at the table and exposure to the stresses of life. For him this was not an individual issue—"you sinned, so you are sick"—but a more corporate concern—"the body is dysfunctional, so some of its members are sick."

Today we are wary about looking for connections between sickness and sin. Holiness and health rarely link in straightforward ways. Yet we may still ask if there are connections between Communion on one hand and the pressures and adversities of living on the other. Surely those Christians who care well for each other, for whom Communion is truly an occasion of love and support, will be better able to face the changing winds of fortune. They are less likely to be casualties of hard times. Together in Christ, they will offer one another some strength and shelter.

So, says Paul, "wait for one another" (11:33). The Corinthians are to eat together. This would be the opposite of the situation when "each of you goes ahead with your own supper" (11:21). Indeed the verb translated "wait" often means "welcome" or "treat as a guest": as guests, the poor should share in the fare of the rich so that all can meet as one body. The unity and love of the people of Christ visibly contradict the divisions and distinctions of the world.

How, then, might this relate to your congregation or mine? Is this passage about the local fellowship itself and the disparities of wealth and status among the members? Or could it also speak to situations where one local church is richer than another? What of those towns and cities where church-going divides people by social class so that Christ's poorer followers are unseen by the rich, even though they live in adjacent streets? And what of the fact that most Christians in the West are far wealthier than sisters and brothers in other lands? Can we acknowledge these neighbors' needs at our Communion tables? If we do not, is it really the Lord's Supper that we are sharing?

The strong language of these verses was never meant to stop Christians coming to Communion. But it is meant to bring us to the table in a right attitude. So maybe the deepest meaning of Paul's word about self-examination (11:28) is that the prospect of this sacrament should always humble us, unite us, and challenge us to new ways of service and care. If it does all of this, then we are probably ready to receive it.

This theme of unity in worship will follow us into the chapters ahead.

GIFTS AND THE BODY (1): ONE IN THE SPIRIT
1 Corinthians 12:1–31

This third slice of teaching on the church's worship runs through three chapters. It includes some of Paul's most profound and best-known writing, about the body of Christ and about the nature and importance of love. There is also instruction on various spiritual gifts—teaching that many Christians have found joyfully liberating, although others have felt bemused or even alienated by it. It may be that the church in Corinth had the same mixture of feelings about some of these gifts.

The issue Paul addresses in these chapters is the way that gifts of speech were used in Christian worship. Some Christians in Corinth were expressing their faith with vigor and conviction, even though others could neither understand nor join in. But Paul wanted the church's worship to benefit all the members. So before talking about the worship service itself (chapter 14), he sets the whole issue of Christian gifts and service within a broader theological perspective. Reflecting on the Spirit (12:1–11), on the body of Christ (12:12–31), and on the call to love (13:1–13) helps to show why God's gifts have been given and how Christians should use them.

Many Gifts, One Spirit
1 Corinthians 12:1–11

> 12:1 **Now concerning spiritual gifts, brothers and sisters, I do not want you to be uninformed.** [2] **You know that when you were pagans, you were enticed and led astray to idols that could not speak.** [3] **Therefore I want you to understand that no one speaking by the Spirit of God ever says "Let Jesus be cursed!" and no one can say "Jesus is Lord" except by the Holy Spirit.**
> [4] **Now there are varieties of gifts, but the same Spirit;** [5] **and there are varieties of services, but the same Lord;** [6] **and there are varieties of activities, but it is the same God who activates all of them in everyone.** [7] **To each is given the manifestation of the Spirit for the common good.** [8] **To one is given through the Spirit the utterance of wisdom, and to another the utterance of knowledge according to the same Spirit,** [9] **to another faith by the same Spirit, to another gifts of healing by the one Spirit,** [10] **to another the working of miracles, to another prophecy, to another the discernment of spirits, to another various kinds of tongues, to another the interpretation of tongues.** [11] **All these are activated by one and the same Spirit, who allots to each one individually just as the Spirit chooses.**

This chapter is about "spiritual things" or "spiritual matters"; the NRSV wording "spiritual gifts" (12:1) is a slight over-translation. The Corinthians and Paul seem to have had different ideas about "spiritual things" and about the Holy Spirit's work. Some in Corinth judged spirituality by its outward expressions and maybe even by the emotion they could feel in worship. But Paul tells them to use a different standard. Even pagan worship could evoke strong emotional experiences, and some of the

Corinthian Christians had been involved in that scene (12:2). Now that phase of their lives is over. Strong feelings are not a reliable way to detect the Spirit. The key issue is a person's attitude to Jesus.

The first and basic sign of the Spirit's presence is Christian belief. The little formula "Jesus is Lord" (12:3) crops up in a few places in the New Testament (Rom. 10:9; 2 Cor. 4:5; Phil. 2:11). Indeed it may be one of the earliest creeds—a crisp and potent declaration of the church's faith. Like a few other passages in this letter (2:2; 8:6; 15:3–4), it is a condensed but very far-reaching statement of Christian belief. If you can say this, says Paul, your very confession of faith is a sign of the Holy Spirit's work (12:3), which means that all Christians have the Spirit, for all call him Lord. Church life should reckon with this and recognize the Spirit's presence in every member of the fellowship.

So we should expect variety in church life, for people vary. Indeed variety is one sign of the Spirit's work. In making this point, Paul chooses his words with care. No longer does he speak of "spiritual things" (*pneumatika*, 12:1); that idea was problematic in Corinth. Now he talks about "gifts of grace" (*charismata*, 12:4), acts of service (12:5) and the lively works of God (12:6). From the whole of the Trinity ("Spirit . . . Lord . . . God"), to the whole of the church ("to each", 12:7), come varied signs and seals of love. All Christians are gifted with the Spirit's generous life; everyone is a servant with something to offer to the rest; each is an agent of God, bringing heaven's active love into the world. We should not say that some Christians can give and others cannot or that some are called to serve while others merely receive. The church is a dynamic, animated fellowship, where every member shares some aspect of the life of Christ, for the good of all (12:7). Paul goes on to list a few of the Spirit's gifts (12:8–10).

The New Testament letters include several lists of spiritual gifts (1 Cor. 12:8–10, 28–30; Rom. 12:6–8; Eph. 4:11), and the detail of these lists varies quite a lot. It seems that there was no fixed list of gifts, recognized and used in all the churches. Rather each of these lists is a sample of what the Spirit can do, with particular gifts being listed according to the needs and situation of the people addressed.

The gifts mentioned here are mostly gifts of speech (12:8–10). Paul was concerned for the Corinthians' worship and about the use of tongues and prophecy in their meetings. So it is not surprising to find this list ending with prophecy, the weighing of prophecy, tongues, and the interpretation of tongues (12:10). In this situation, prophecy and tongues are Paul's main concern. The other five gifts that he mentions (wisdom, knowledge, faith, healing, and miracles) were surely important to him—he repeats some of them a little later (12:28–30)—but he does not really discuss them in these chapters.

We should not, then, think of the nine gifts in 12:8–10 as a fixed and eternal checklist—as if to say, "without these no congregation will truly know the life of Christ." That sort of approach would overlook Paul's emphasis on the variety and freedom of the Spirit's work (12:11). Instead I think the text invites us to think more openly and broadly about how receptive and sensitive we can be to the Spirit. What is God doing in our local church, among sisters and brothers, and in my own Christian service? How do we allow and expect each member to contribute? How willingly do we each seek the good of all? And how might we respond more faithfully to the gentle and generous presence of the Spirit of Jesus?

Many Parts, One Body
1 Corinthians 12:12–31

12:12 For just as the body is one and has many members, and all the members of the body, though many, are one body, so it is with Christ. [13] **For in the one Spirit we were all baptized into one body—Jews or Greeks, slaves or free—and we were all made to drink of one Spirit.**

[14] **Indeed, the body does not consist of one member but of many.** [15] **If the foot would say, "Because I am not a hand, I do not belong to the body," that would not make it any less a part of the body.** [16] **And if the ear would say, "Because I am not an eye, I do not belong to the body," that would not make it any less a part of the body.** [17] **If the whole body were an eye, where would the hearing be? If the whole body were hearing, where would the sense of smell be?** [18] **But as it is, God arranged the members in the body, each one of them, as he chose.** [19] **If all were a single member, where would the body be?** [20] **As it is, there are many members, yet one body.** [21] **The eye cannot say to the hand, "I have no need of you," nor again the head to the feet, "I have no need of you."** [22] **On the contrary, the members of the body that seem to be weaker are indispensable,** [23] **and those members of the body that we think less honorable we clothe with greater honor, and our less respectable members are treated with greater respect;** [24] **whereas our more respectable members do not need this. But God has so arranged the body, giving the greater honor to the inferior member,** [25] **that there may be no dissension within the body, but the members may have the same care for one another.** [26] **If one member suffers, all suffer together with it; if one member is honored, all rejoice together with it.**

[27] **Now you are the body of Christ and individually members of it.** [28] **And God has appointed in the church first apostles, second prophets,**

third teachers; then deeds of power, then gifts of healing, forms of assistance, forms of leadership, various kinds of tongues. [29] Are all apostles? Are all prophets? Are all teachers? Do all work miracles? [30] Do all possess gifts of healing? Do all speak in tongues? Do all interpret? [31] But strive for the greater gifts. And I will show you a still more excellent way.

Paul writes often of the church as a body (Rom. 12:5; Eph. 4:16; Col. 1:24). Indeed the body was a well-known image in ancient thought. Orators and writers used it, in varied ways: as a metaphor for society, with the members performing different roles; in a bid to unite competing political factions in a city; or even as a way to think about the universe as a whole. With Paul the image is certainly not an abstract idea. He uses it practically and pastorally, to speak about the interdependence of the various limbs and organs. Each needs the others. None can be ignored or neglected.

Indeed with Paul the body image is deeply personal in character. To talk of the body is not a metaphor only but also a description of the church's intimate relationship with its Lord. We are the body of Christ (12:12, 27). His Spirit animates us, his life flows among us, and his gifts enable us. We encounter the life and love of Jesus through one another.

This starts at baptism, where the Spirit joins Christians to Jesus and to each other (12:13). There we meet as equals across the boundaries and barriers of race and status. The water washes away the distinctions and separations of a divided world and gives us a common mark of identity as one body in Christ. We may not be very good at living this, but it is part of the deep truth about who we are. The final image in the verse—being "made to drink of one Spirit" (12:13)—then repeats, in a parallel way, this reference to baptism. For the verb "make to drink" can be used for watering a field or garden; here it speaks of the pouring of the Spirit's life onto a person in Christian baptism. And this is a blessing that Christians share. Paul uses the word "all" three times. All Christians belong to the body (12:12); all are baptized (12:13); all have received the Spirit (12:13). Each, then, must reckon with the membership and contribution of all the others.

The next verses develop the metaphor in more detail. The body is one yet varied in its makeup. So a diverse church, argues Paul, need not turn diversity into division (12:14). No one need think they cannot belong or do not fit in; those who think themselves odd often have a special contribution to make (12:15–16). And no one should despise or ignore the input of others; even the confident and capable can only represent a fraction of the diverse life of Christ (12:17–21). A monochrome church, with all its members alike, would be a poor image of the Spirit's work. Indeed those whom the church and the world often overlook—the church's "weaker," "less honorable," "less respectable," and "inferior" members (12:22–24)—may embody most fully the presence of our Lord.

In wording these last verses, Paul uses a number of words that suggest social status or the lack of it. He surely had in mind the snobbery and elitism of Corinth, the way that some Christians tended to despise others, and the power games that spilled over from the wider community into the church. He wanted the Corinthian Christians to outgrow these attitudes and to love one another. The weak need special care and respect (12:23–24). Only as we give one another this honor is the church true to its nature and calling. Only then can we truly learn to feel for one another and to hurt and laugh together as a single body (12:25–26).

After planting this message firmly in his readers' minds—that Christians depend on one another—Paul turns again to consider particular gifts (12:28–30). The selection here differs from the one he gave previously (12:8–10), but as in that earlier list, tongues is the last gift that he mentions. Indeed we see this twice, first in a list of eight gifts and ministries (12:28) and again when tongues and interpretation round off a series of seven rhetorical questions (12:29–30). Tongues, we shall see, has been an issue in Corinth. And while Paul does not disparage this gift, he is concerned that the Corinthians are using it wrongly.

We noticed earlier how Paul's language shifted from talking of "spiritual things" (12:1) to "gifts of grace" (*charismata*, 12:4). Now he speaks of tasks that God has "appointed" (12:28). This gives a sense of divine strategy and of gifts and services that connect and coordinate as the church spreads and grows. First come apostles to carry the gospel to new places and bring churches into being; then prophets to speak God's wisdom and teachers to explain the faith; mighty works and gifts of healing, to reveal the compassion and risen life of Christ; practical help and leadership (the same word that is used for steering a ship), to guide and sustain the life of the church; and last, tongues.

Each of these gifts, says Paul, is assigned to some Christians but not to all (12:29–30). The Spirit allots differently to each one (12:11). So the church is like a jigsaw; each member must look to the others and connect with what God is doing through them. My gift or yours may offer something vital to our fellow Christians, which they could not discover or do for themselves. So it matters that gifts are used wisely. For some gifts will help people very readily; others will only do so if we handle them with care. Seeking the "greater gifts" and following the "more excellent way" of love (12:31) will give the church a sense of priorities. For the detail of how Paul wanted this to work in practice, we must wait until chapter 14.

GIFTS AND THE BODY (2): ALL YOU NEED IS . . .
1 Corinthians 13:1-13

This chapter is probably Paul's best-known piece of writing. Its cadences are lyrical, its wording simple yet profound, and its insights into human nature searchingly perceptive. As we read, the lines strip away our pretenses and show us ourselves as we are and as we might be. No wonder this chapter is read often at weddings, for marriage too is a setting where partners may start to see their own personalities with a new and disconcerting clarity. But the context in 1 Corinthians has little to do with any wedding service. This chapter is part of Paul's pastoral teaching on the use of spiritual gifts.

We see this from the words that frame the chapter on either side. Directly beforehand Paul writes, "strive for the greater gifts" (12.31), and immediately afterwards he says, "strive for the spiritual gifts, and especially that you may prophesy" (14:1). Evidently Paul has a sense of priority. He uses words like "greater" and "especially," because he believes that some spiritual gifts are more beneficial than others. The guiding principle is that "Love builds up" (8:1). So if we pursue love (14:1), we will rate most highly those gifts that strengthen and encourage other people. Any gifts that do not do this must be used with caution. Getting to that practical point (in chapter 14) is the aim of this chapter on love.

For this is one of Paul's digressions. In the midst of a long pastoral discussion he has turned aside to explore a new and important principle, which he will then apply to the original issue. He did the same in 7:17-24, and again in chapter 9. So this present digression on love both breaks the flow of Paul's writing on gifts and fits the context and concern within which he writes. Indeed it connects quite tightly to the situation in Corinth. For tongues and prophecy are mentioned in 13:1-2 and 13:8-9; the attitudes and behavior criticized in 13:4-5 seem very Corinthian; and Paul's concern about his readers' spiritual maturity (3:1; 14:20) echoes in 13:11. This chapter—majestic and memorable as it is—fits very well within this letter.

Love Is Primary
1 Corinthians 13:1-3

> 13:1 **If I speak in the tongues of mortals and of angels, but do not have love, I am a noisy gong or a clanging cymbal.** [2] **And if I have prophetic powers, and understand all mysteries and all knowledge, and if I have all faith, so as to remove mountains, but do not have love, I am nothing.** [3] **If I give away all**

my possessions, and if I hand over my body so that I may boast, but do not have love, I gain nothing.

"All you need is love" is not quite the message. Paul's key point is that love is basic: this is the base on which everything else must rest, the vital ingredient to animate all of the church's life. Without water on the land, even the best seeds will not grow; without ink in the pen, the wisest words cannot find their way onto paper; and it is the same with love. Without it, nothing that we attempt for Christ will be of any real value. Love gives meaning and worth to everything else.

Whatever our gifts of speech (13:1), the depth and insights of our mind and spirit (13:2) or the sharing and service of our deeds and days (13:3), if we are loveless it is no use at all. We shall forge no true human bond or relationship, and our work will be all effort and no effect. Without love, neither the gifts that the Corinthians value so highly nor the sacrificial life that Paul lives for the gospel can find their true fulfillment and purpose.

Love Is Practical
1 Corinthians 13:4–7

13:4 Love is patient; love is kind; love is not envious or boastful or arrogant ^{5} or rude. It does not insist on its own way; it is not irritable or resentful; ^{6} it does not rejoice in wrongdoing, but rejoices in the truth. ^{7} It bears all things, believes all things, hopes all things, endures all things.

Paul starts and finishes this section by emphasizing the positive. Love embodies the fruits of the Spirit (Gal. 5:22)—patience, kindness, and a discerning and wholesome joy (13:4, 6). Love has resilience and stamina to hold the faith and press forward in hope, even when fortune and circumstance are testing and rough (13:7). Love has sinew and strength: it will be gentle and humble but never weak. Evidently love can be trusted. It is a practical and solid virtue—far more than a feeling.

Yet amid all of this, Paul also defines love with a string of negatives, from "love is not envious" through to "it does not rejoice in wrongdoing" (13:4–6). I think he names these qualities as a deliberate contrast to some of the attitudes and activities of the Corinthian church. For people there were "envious" (3:3), arrogant (literally "inflated", 4:6; 8:1; 13:4), and keen on getting their own way (8:7–12); some of their behavior had been indecent (6:15) and quarrelsome (6:1). All of this had its roots in the wider culture of their city. Whereas love, Paul might have said, gets its values from Christ rather than from Corinth.

Love Is Permanent
1 Corinthians 13:8–13

> 13:8 **Love never ends. But as for prophecies, they will come to an end; as for tongues, they will cease; as for knowledge, it will come to an end.** ⁹ **For we know only in part, and we prophesy only in part;** ¹⁰ **but when the complete comes, the partial will come to an end.** ¹¹ **When I was a child, I spoke like a child, I thought like a child, I reasoned like a child; when I became an adult, I put an end to childish ways.** ¹² **For now we see in a mirror, dimly, but then we will see face to face. Now I know only in part; then I will know fully, even as I have been fully known.** ¹³ **And now faith, hope, and love abide, these three; and the greatest of these is love.**

Paul's words about love's staying power and its capacity to endure (13:7) lead on to the claim that love is permanent. It does not fail, collapse, or dissolve (13:8); love abides (13:13). Other gifts, by contrast—even good and godly gifts—will have a shorter shelf life. One day Christ will come (15:24). His people will rejoice in his reign and see him "face to face" (13:12). Then the wisdom and perceptions of this age will be overtaken by the clear light of eternity. Tongues, knowledge, and prophecy will not be needed (13:8–10). We shall realize then that the speech, reasoning, and insights of today (13:11–12)—true and proper though they be—have been partial and provisional.

This is one reason that love matters so much. It has the currency of eternity in it. Along with faith and hope, love is one of the prime gospel virtues, and we meet this threesome often in the New Testament (1 Cor. 13:13; Col. 1:4–5; 1 Thess. 1:3). These three abide, Paul reminds his friends, and we too must go on nurturing and using them. Yet among the three, one stands out.

For faith lifts us beyond what we see today; but one day we shall meet the God we trust. Hope sustains us in this age; but in heaven there will be no need to look ahead. Love, on the other hand, is a taste of eternity. As it joins Christians to Christ and to one another, it introduces us now to the bonds and blessings of heaven. So we should cherish love and cultivate it as a habit of life. Indeed we should chase after it (the meaning of "pursue" in 14:1) in the decisions we take and the way we use our gifts. The gifts in themselves are temporary. The love with which we share them is permanent.

In all of this teaching, Paul is continuing a strong biblical tradition. Love was at the heart of Israel's relationship with God. It was commanded in the Shema (Deut. 6:4–5) as we noticed in chapter 8, and the Shema became the nation's most basic and widely used statement of faith. Then Jesus took this theme forward. He spoke of love for God and neighbor as Scripture's two great commandments (Mark 12:29–31). He also reminded his followers that "neighbor" is a wide category. Even someone you reckoned an enemy might show you God's love and claim some of yours (Matt. 5:44; Luke 10:29–37).

So love is a teaching and tradition for the church to sustain. By all means let us read chapter 13 at weddings. A couple could not find better words to guide and shape their life together. But let us also try to honor this text in the whole of our church life. In their context in 1 Corinthians, these verses are about how Christians do God's work together, about how we praise God together, and about the roles that we seek and claim in local church life. So when a church discusses worship, and members express their preference for one style or another; or when we think about how different interest groups can coexist within one congregation; or when we try to consider how the gifts and aspirations of every member can serve the good of all; then these are moments to heed Paul's words on love. For these were the sorts of difficulty and tension that caused him to write as he did.

GIFTS AND THE BODY (3): WITH SPIRIT AND UNDERSTANDING
1 Corinthians 14:1–40

Unwrapping the Gifts. After laying some foundations in chapters 12 and 13, Paul is ready to give the Corinthians practical guidance about using spiritual gifts in worship. Most of this long chapter concerns tongues and prophecy and the different ways in which these two gifts can help the church. So before we trace Paul's argument, we ought to ask what he meant by "tongues" and "prophecy." Both of these terms have been studied at length. Neither is entirely clear.

Tongues is the easier of the two to explain. Apart from 1 Corinthians it is mentioned in Acts (2:5–13; 10:46; 19:6) and in the postscript to Mark's Gospel (16:17). Tongues was speech, inspired and given by the Holy Spirit, but in a language unknown to the speaker. So on the Day of Pentecost (Acts 2) the apostles' preaching was heard in many languages, and this served both as a means of evangelism and as a witness to the many visitors who had come from other lands. But the tongues in Corinth may not be quite the same thing; for this speech seems to have been unintelligible to the hearers.

In our time, many Christians report that God has gifted them to speak in tongues, and some churches use and encourage this as part of worship. Usually it does not involve recognizable human language—it is in that respect more like 1 Corinthians 14 than Acts 2. Apart from this, however, we do not know how closely it parallels the Corinthian experience, and there seems no obvious way of finding out.

Some modern psychologists have asked if tongues of this sort could be an outlet for the unconscious, bringing to audible but undefined speech the deep recesses of the human mind. Our experience of God surely touches us at levels that we cannot fully explain or articulate. So might speech that bypasses our usual forms of language be a way of expressing this? Indeed might Paul himself have something like this in mind when he talks of the Spirit praying for us "in sighs too deep for words" (Rom. 8:26)? We shall explore this line of thought a little more in the course of 1 Corinthians 14.

What, then, of prophecy? In 1 Corinthians 14, prophecy is intelligible speech. Both speaker and hearers understand the words; in that sense it is conscious and rational, in a way that tongues was not. It seems to be prompted by God, but the speaker retains some responsibility and control (14:29–33). We find parallels of sorts in the Greek world—oracles, ecstatics, wandering teachers. But there are closer and stronger links in Jewish and early Christian tradition. Prophets were important figures in the Old Testament, and they are known in Judaism of the intertestamental period. Prophets are mentioned often in the New Testament—in the Gospels, in Acts, in several of the letters, and in Revelation. People called Jesus a prophet, and Christian prophecy was clearly a widely known phenomenon in the early church.

Yet a wide spread did not mean complete uniformity. The Old Testament prophets had been a varied lot, and New Testament prophecy too came in several styles and guises. Indeed there may be no watertight distinction between "revelation or knowledge or prophecy or teaching" (14:6). It is more likely that these sorts of godly speech merged into one another and even overlapped to some extent. So if some prophetic words were immediate and spontaneous (14:30), others may have been more thought out and considered. And just as there was a spectrum from the spontaneous to the deliberate, prophecy also reflected different levels of authority, credibility, and experience. The prophecies offered in Corinth may not always have had the secure and community-forming quality suggested in Ephesians (2:20; 3:5).

Yet the many expressions of Christian prophecy were meant to have this in common: they involved a person speaking for God, to other people, with a purpose. So prophecy is meant to be contextual, bringing a word from God to the needs of its own time and place. Prophets ought also to have a pastoral instinct; Paul writes of "upbuilding and encouragement and consolation" (14:3). Prophets should be open to God, to receive and share insights that would not be obvious to everyone (Acts 11:27–30). And they are servants, prepared to be tested by the church (1 Cor. 14:29; 1 Thess. 5:20–21). All of that should shape what we learn from this aspect of early church life.

There is no neat match, however, with any one task or ministry in today's church. Preaching is something like prophecy, when it brings pointed and prayerful insight into the situation and needs of a congregation or community; yet rarely do we test preaching in the ways that Paul advised in Corinth (14:29). The wise words of a pastor or spiritual director may carry a deep sense of God, and some would call this prophetic; but the setting is usually individual and private. And although Christian political comment is sometimes referred to as "prophetic," there are closer parallels to this in the Old Testament than in Corinth. And to Corinth we now turn.

In a Mirror, Dimly. As we shall see, this chapter includes three main pieces of instruction. So there may be a particular issue or problem behind each of these. To probe the text in this way is called mirror-reading—seeing in Paul's advice a reflection of the situation he is addressing. If he says, "Do not do X," we ask if people were doing it. When he says, "Do Y," we suspect that some of his readers had not done this. By listening to one side of a conversation, we try to understand the situation at the other end of the line. So this method is always rather speculative. Yet the questions it raises are natural ones to ask: why does he say this; what led him to speak in those terms; what sort of problem prompted that advice?

If we mirror-read this chapter, we might think, first, that some Christians in Corinth were using the gift of tongues rather lavishly in church worship. Paul tries to restrict this by insisting on interpretation (14:5, 13, 29). There may be a second concern around prophecy, with people using this gift in a chaotic or competitive way. Paul asks for order, patience, and the testing of what is said (14:30–33). And a third issue arises from a group of women in the church (14:34–35).

Leaving the third matter aside for the moment, we could relate the first two to a factor that has run right through this letter—the competitive and factional culture of ancient Corinth. Some church members, it seems, were asserting themselves, drawing attention to their gifts, and making much of their own contributions to worship. They were not taking much thought for other people but simply raising their own voices. The whole effect was somewhat wild and undisciplined. Many people were ceasing to find worship helpful. So Paul appeals for two values that the Corinthians had overlooked—concern for one another and a sense of order.

Balancing the Gifts
1 Corinthians 14:1–25

14:1 **Pursue love and strive for the spiritual gifts, and especially that you may prophesy.** ² **For those who speak in a tongue do not speak to other people but to God; for nobody understands them, since they are speaking mysteries in the Spirit.** ³ **On the other hand, those who prophesy speak to other people for their upbuilding and encouragement and consolation.** ⁴ **Those who speak in a tongue build up themselves, but those who prophesy build up the church.** ⁵ **Now I would like all of you to speak in tongues, but even more to prophesy. One who prophesies is greater than one who speaks in tongues, unless someone interprets, so that the church may be built up.**

⁶ **Now, brothers and sisters, if I come to you speaking in tongues, how will I benefit you unless I speak to you in some revelation or knowledge or prophecy or teaching?** ⁷ **It is the same way with lifeless instruments that produce sound, such as the flute or the harp. If they do not give distinct notes, how will anyone know what is being played?** ⁸ **And if the bugle gives an indistinct sound, who will get ready for battle?** ⁹ **So with yourselves; if in a tongue you utter speech that is not intelligible, how will anyone know what is being said? For you will be speaking into the air.** ¹⁰ **There are doubtless many different kinds of sounds in the world, and nothing is without sound.** ¹¹ **If then I do not know the meaning of a sound, I will be a foreigner to the speaker and the speaker a foreigner to me.** ¹² **So with yourselves; since you are eager for spiritual gifts, strive to excel in them for building up the church.**

¹³ **Therefore, one who speaks in a tongue should pray for the power to interpret.** ¹⁴ **For if I pray in a tongue, my spirit prays but my mind is unproductive.** ¹⁵ **What should I do then? I will pray with the spirit, but I will pray with the mind also; I will sing praise with the spirit, but I will sing praise with the mind also.** ¹⁶ **Otherwise, if you say a blessing with the spirit, how can anyone in the position of an outsider say the "Amen" to your thanksgiving, since the outsider does not know what you are saying?** ¹⁷ **For you may give thanks well enough, but the other person is not built up.** ¹⁸ **I thank God that I speak in tongues more than all of you;** ¹⁹ **nevertheless, in church I would rather speak five words with my mind, in order to instruct others also, than ten thousand words in a tongue.**

[20] **Brothers and sisters, do not be children in your thinking; rather, be infants in evil, but in thinking be adults.** [21] **In the law it is written,**

> **"By people of strange tongues**
> **and by the lips of foreigners**
> **I will speak to this people;**
> **yet even then they will not listen to me,"**

says the Lord. [22] **Tongues, then, are a sign not for believers but for unbelievers, while prophecy is not for unbelievers but for believers.** [23] **If, therefore, the whole church comes together and all speak in tongues, and outsiders or unbelievers enter, will they not say that you are out of your mind?** [24] **But if all prophesy, an unbeliever or outsider who enters is reproved by all and called to account by all.** [25] **After the secrets of the unbeliever's heart are disclosed, that person will bow down before God and worship him, declaring, "God is really among you."**

This whole section underlines, several times over, that prophecy is a more helpful gift than tongues. The opening verse picks up both the end of chapter 12, "strive for the greater gifts" (12:31), and the emphasis on love in chapter 13. The best gifts will always be those that strengthen other people. On this basis, prophecy is more useful than tongues (14:2–3). Tongues is a private hotline between the speaker and God. It helps the individual, but no one else benefits because no one else can understand it. Prophecy, on the other hand, is a shared experience. The speaker's words build up the whole church (14:4) and serve the fellowship in a way that tongues on its own cannot.

Paul makes these points very compactly in the first four verses. Then he explains and illustrates them more fully in the paragraphs that follow (14:6–19). He mentions musical instruments: without clarity they can neither entertain nor communicate (14:7–8). Language too: this will only bring people together if they understand one another (14:9–11). Prayer also must be clear if sisters and brothers are to gain from it and share in it (14:16–17).

Paul does not despise the gift of tongues. He regards it as a genuine communication with God and a meeting point with the Holy Spirit (14:2). He values it highly (14:18) and has no wish to ban its use (14:5). Tongues, says Paul, build up the one who uses it (14:4) by involving the person's "spirit" in prayer and praise (14:15). It comes from the unconscious and intuitive right side of the brain, we might say, rather than from the logical and formal processes of the left side. It is deeply personal but only in an individual way; it cannot be shared, because the words are not clear.

So only if tongues are "interpreted" is Paul happy for them to be used in worship (14:28). There is a spiritual gift, he says, of taking this speech and expressing its meaning in words that everyone knows (12:10, 30). Sometimes one person will interpret the words of others (14:27). On another occasion a speaker might offer an interpretation (14:13) by putting into clear and common speech prayers that had arisen in the depths of their own being.

Above all, Paul is concerned that the church be "built up" (14:3, 4, 5, 12, 19, 26). And this concern extends to newcomers in the services—possibly friends or relatives of members. Prophecy will be more effective than tongues in leading these people to faith (14:20–25). For if guests come in and see everyone speaking in tongues, they will realize that something strange is going on, but they will get no sense of what it might mean. There will be no real communication. Prophecy, by contrast, using words that come from God in the hearer's own language, will have a converting power. It will make God's presence clear and will enable visitors to see their own need of God (14:24–25). Prophecy produces believers; this may be the meaning of 14:22. A verse from Isaiah (28:11) underlines the point: people cannot be saved by words they do not understand (14:21).

When You Gather
1 Corinthians 14:26–33 and 14:36–40

> 14:26 **What should be done then, my friends? When you come together, each one has a hymn, a lesson, a revelation, a tongue, or an interpretation. Let all things be done for building up.** ^{27} **If anyone speaks in a tongue, let there be only two or at most three, and each in turn; and let one interpret.** ^{28} **But if there is no one to interpret, let them be silent in church and speak to themselves and to God.** ^{29} **Let two or three prophets speak, and let the others weigh what is said.** ^{30} **If a revelation is made to someone else sitting nearby, let the first person be silent.** ^{31} **For you can all prophesy one by one, so that all may learn and all be encouraged.** ^{32} **And the spirits of prophets are subject to the prophets,** ^{33} **for God is a God not of disorder but of peace.**
>
> **(As in all the churches of the saints . . .** ^{36} **Or did the word of God originate with you? Or are you the only ones it has reached?)**
>
> ^{37} **Anyone who claims to be a prophet, or to have spiritual powers, must acknowledge that what I am writing to you is a command of the Lord.** ^{38} **Anyone who does not recognize this is not to be recognized.** ^{39} **So, my friends, be eager to prophesy, and do not forbid speaking in tongues;** ^{40} **but all things should be done decently and in order.**

These verses lay out guidelines for worship in Corinth. There is no sense at all of a single individual controlling the event, nor of a set pattern of service to be followed. Neither is it clear how this teaching meshes with that given earlier on the Lord's Supper, although both passages begin by saying, "when you come together" (11:18; 14:26), so they may well refer to the same gatherings. One important theme, however, does bind the two passages—mutual care and respect. Both in eating and in the use of gifts, no Christian may ignore, despise, or dominate the rest. We worship as one body in Christ.

So there is a strong sense of openness to the Spirit. Yet openness is not anarchy. It is shaped by mutuality—the sharing of ministry—and by a concern for order. Every Christian will potentially have contributions to bring (14:26). Possibly some members in Corinth wanted to limit the input of others—even to silence those who lacked certain gifts. If this was so, Paul is more open than they were. He expects members to come with gifts and insights to share. Tongues may be used a little at a time if this can be interpreted. Otherwise tongue speakers should pray quietly (14:27–28). Prophets too should speak in turn and allow their words to be weighed by "the others" (14:29–32); this could refer to other prophets or perhaps even to the whole church. Paul thought of discernment as a gift (12:10). Here it tests and ratifies what the prophet has offered.

The whole effect is of "order" (14:40) and "peace" (14:33)—not inertia or rigidity—but a mood of respect and reverence that enables people to trust and support each other and to rejoice in God. This kind of worship, says Paul, is what other churches do (14:33). It would be odd if Corinth insisted on breaking this pattern (14:36). It would practically cut them off from the main stream of church life (14:37–38). And as Paul said at the very start, the Corinthians were part of a wide fellowship (1:2). They ought to learn from the insight and practice of other Christians.

What then can we learn from the church at Corinth? Surely their worship had many defects. But it gave many opportunities for the congregation to contribute (14:26) in a way that ours often does not. If the Holy Spirit is still at work in every Christian for the good of all (12:7), we might do well to ask whether more of the Spirit's work can be visible in our church services.

Women's Voices
1 Corinthians 14:34–35

> **14:34 women should be silent in the churches. For they are not permitted to speak, but should be subordinate, as the law also says. [35] If there is anything they desire to know, let them ask their husbands at home. For it is shameful for a woman to speak in church.**

We have left until last the most controversial portion of the chapter. Just as the first half of chapter 11 figures large in debates about gender and ministry, so do these two verses. One oddity is that Paul seemed content for women to pray and prophesy (11:5, 13), whereas these later verses seem to silence the women of the church. What, then, does he mean here? There are two main theories to consider.

One theory draws on insights from ancient manuscripts. We do not have Paul's original letter; only later handwritten copies, the earliest of these dating from about 200 CE. So when these later manuscripts do not agree (as happens in places), we have to work out Paul's original wording. And these two verses present a particular problem. In several manuscripts—as a footnote in the NRSV points out—they appear in a different location. They come after 14:40 rather than after 14:33.

Now, although scribes could make mistakes in copying, it would be unusual for such a large slice of text to be moved this far by accident. So something quite odd and unusual may have happened. Is it possible, perhaps, that these verses were not part of Paul's original writing at all but got added later by someone else? Then might some scribes, suspecting this but not being sure of it, have decided that they could not drop the verses but would shift them to the end of the chapter as a kind of postscript?

This theory has some able supporters, and it has three obvious merits. It explains the variation in the ancient manuscripts. It resolves the difficult contrast between 11:5 and 14:34, since it reckons Paul did not write 14:34–35 at all. And by plucking out verses 34–35 it effectively joins verse 33 to 36; and the line of thought in these two verses clearly connects. So this theory might be correct. If it is, then these two verses do not really belong in Paul's writing. We might decide to read him and to shape our views on gender and ministry without considering these two verses at all.

Now to the second theory. This reckons that 14:34–35 do come from Paul and regards these verses as an aside, within the context and instruction of chapter 14. Paul's concern, the theory suggests, is the weighing of prophecy. For the previous verses are all about prophecy, and Paul emphasizes the need for order (14:33). So he mentions a particular aspect of the matter—the conversations where prophecies were weighed and tested. In a traditional culture, it would have been unconventional (and so "shameful", 14:35) for a woman either to challenge her husband or to engage in public conversation with another man. It would be better for her to remain quiet than to get involved in this way. That very specific understanding of Paul's meaning would connect to the rest of the chapter and would also resolve the difficult comparison with 11:5.

This second theory would suggest, as we also saw in chapter 11, that Paul did not want the church to cause needless offense within wider society. Indeed in some ways the conservatism of the synagogue shapes his advice here rather than the more libertarian ways of certain Greek religious groups. Yet elsewhere he speaks highly of distinguished Christian service given by women. In Romans 16, which was written from Corinth, we meet Phoebe, Prisca, Mary, Junia, Tryphaena, Tryphosa, and Persis—all mentioned with honor for what they have done in the church. Within the customs and conventions of his time, Paul is quite an ally of women's ministry.

Part 3: People of the Resurrection: The Hope of the Gospel
1 Corinthians 15–16

6. Easter Gospel
1 Corinthians 15:1–58

This long chapter explains the church's belief in resurrection. Christ is risen, and his people will rise. Death may be the last enemy (15:26), but its sting has been drawn (15:54). We are an Easter people. So the chapter ends on a note of conviction and energy. Resurrection gives us hope, and hope is a mighty motivator amid the toils and duties of our days (15:58). Let Christ's people live with confidence and commitment: the future belongs to the Lord.

Yet as in every part of this epistle, there is a problem in the background. Some of the Corinthians said that "there is no resurrection of the dead" (15:12). So Paul writes to correct them and to put this central piece of Christian belief back into their picture of the gospel. We are not told why the Corinthians held this view. Here are two possible explanations.

One is that they looked on their spiritual experiences as some kind of resurrection, lifting them above the ordinary levels and limits of human existence. Among truly "spiritual" people, they thought, there was no need to talk of rising from the dead. They already had all the resurrection they needed. That outlook would connect pretty well with the problems we met in chapter 14 and the Corinthians' careless and assertive use of spiritual gifts. However, it does not match so well the tone of chapter 15, which is generally quite upbeat. As a whole, this chapter feels more like a counter to skepticism and doubt rather than an attempt to restrain the wrong kind of enthusiasm.

So I think another explanation is more likely: that the problem was caused by Greco-Roman views of the life to come. Few people in that world viewed death with hope. For them, death dissolved the link between soul and body, and while the soul might survive and enter some sort of future, this would be a poor and dim kind of existence. Philosophers of the time sometimes spoke of the body as a prison and longed for the soul's release into a purer and truer realm, but ordinary people looked at death with sadness and fear. A common Latin grave inscription read, *non fui, fui, non sum, non curo* ("I was not, I was, I am not, I care not"). Death was a void. And the Corinthians had recently lost some of their friends (11:30).

So, although Paul refers only briefly to these bereavements (15:18, and possibly 15:29), I suspect that they shape his purpose in this chapter. He sets out his argument with two aims—to encourage the sorrowing and to challenge the skeptical. As he did with the Thessalonian church, he is keen to help new believers who felt "uninformed about those who have died." He wants to prevent them grieving "as others do who have no hope" (I Thess. 4:13). Equally he tries to instruct and correct any who have been casting doubt on the thought of resurrection. He means to give the church confidence in this piece of Christian belief so that they will press on with courage and purpose.

For the chapter confronts the fear that the gospel might all be a waste—of time, of effort, and of trust. Several times over we meet the words "in vain." In the harsh face of death and grief, it can seem that all we have lived for is vanity and vapor. Yet the Corinthians' Christian life has not been a waste, says Paul—neither of God's grace (15:10), nor of his own labor (15:14), nor of their faith (15:2, 14, 17). Nor will their work for God be useless or wasted (15:58). They may serve the Lord in faith and without fear.

RESURRECTION FAITH: WHERE IT COMES FROM
1 Corinthians 15:1–19

> 15:1 **Now I would remind you, brothers and sisters, of the good news that I proclaimed to you, which you in turn received, in which also you stand,** ² **through which also you are being saved, if you hold firmly to the message that I proclaimed to you—unless you have come to believe in vain.**

The chapter starts by recalling the good news that Paul brought to Corinth. The language is positive, assuring and solid. This is a message, says Paul, which the church has "received." Now they should "hold firmly" to it. In this belief they "stand," and by it they "are being saved" (15:1–2). The heart of this good news is the resurrection of Jesus.

Later on Paul will explore the hope to which Christ's resurrection leads and the confidence this can give to his people (15:20–34). Then toward the end of the chapter, he will discuss the nature of the church's hope—what it means to speak of being raised with Christ (15:35–58). But here at the start, he looks back, to the Easter message as foundation for the whole of the Christian faith (15:1–19). Only by remembering the rising of Jesus will we be able to think clearly and wisely about our own.

"Of First Importance"
1 Corinthians 15:3–4

> 15:3 **For I handed on to you as of first importance what I in turn had received: that Christ died for our sins in accordance with the scriptures, ⁴ and that he was buried, and that he was raised on the third day in accordance with the scriptures,**

Earlier in the letter (2:2) Paul recalled the way that he focused on the cross of Christ, when he first preached in Corinth. Now he summarizes a little more fully the good news he brought. Two parts of the message were "of first importance" (15:3)—the crucifixion and the resurrection. For each of the two, Paul speaks about its source, its biblical roots, and its meaning.

- *Source.* These were not beliefs that Paul had devised or worked out for himself. They were the common property of the whole church. "I received them," he says, "and handed them on" (15:3). Paul had good opportunities in the years after his conversion to meet key people in the Jerusalem church (Acts 9:26–30; Gal. 1:18–2:2) and to hear about Jesus from those who had been with him. The beliefs of which he writes here surely reflect these early contacts, just as the memory of the Lord's Supper that Paul "received" and "handed on" (11:23) came through friends who had been there.
- *Biblical roots.* These two pillars of Christian belief were "in accordance with the scriptures" (15:3–4). But which Scriptures? Paul may have particular Old Testament passages in mind—possibly Isaiah 53 in relation to Christ's death and Hosea 6:2 for resurrection "on the third day." Later he will quote from the Psalms (8 and 110, in 15:25–26) and the prophets (Isa. 25:8 and Hos. 13:14, in 15:54–55), and some of these texts too may be in his thoughts as he starts this part of the letter. Yet he may also be making a more general point: that the cross and resurrection of Jesus fulfill abundantly the widest and deepest hopes of the Hebrew Scriptures. God is faithful and gracious; sin and sorrow shall not reign; the pardon and power of God will turn shame into joy and death into life.
- *Meaning.* For Paul the crucifixion of Jesus was more than a moment

in history. It was the hub of his faith, and he draws out its meaning in a variety of ways when he writes to his churches. But here he says simply, "Christ died for our sins" (15:3) and then moves on quite rapidly. The cross matters to him deeply, but for his present purpose, the meaning of the resurrection matters more; the rest of the chapter will explore this.

"He Appeared"
1 Corinthians 15:5–7

> 15:5 **and that he appeared to Cephas, then to the twelve.** [6] **Then he appeared to more than five hundred brothers and sisters at one time, most of whom are still alive, though some have died.** [7] **Then he appeared to James, then to all the apostles.**

As they shared the gospel around the Greco-Roman world, Christians spoke of the witnesses who had met the risen Lord. The church was keen to show that its faith was based on memory, experience, and record. Easter was not theory; it was event. So here Paul mentions five resurrection appearances. Two of these (15:5) can be matched to the Gospels (Luke 24:33–36). The others cannot (15:6–7). The most remarkable and intriguing appearance is the one with five hundred people, but we do not know any detail about this occasion. "James" probably refers to the Lord's brother, who went on to lead the Jerusalem church. And "all the apostles" is a group in which Paul places himself.

It is striking that no women are named, although faithful women appear in the Easter accounts of all four Gospels. Women saw the empty tomb and the risen Lord. But the formal witness of women was not rated in the ancient world. So when the Easter story was condensed for use in preaching and teaching, the summary majored on men. In the Gospels, by contrast, which preserved the church's memory and founding story, the role of the women is large and clear.

"Also to Me"
1 Corinthians 15:8–11

> 15:8 **Last of all, as to one untimely born, he appeared also to me.** [9] **For I am the least of the apostles, unfit to be called an apostle, because I persecuted the church of God.** [10] **But by the grace of God I am what I am, and his grace**

toward me has not been in vain. On the contrary, I worked harder than any of them—though it was not I, but the grace of God that is with me. ¹¹ Whether then it was I or they, so we proclaim and so you have come to believe.

Paul thinks of himself as "one untimely born" (15:8). His conversion was like the birth of a premature baby arriving in the world abruptly and far too soon. He lacked the preparation that others had, of acquaintance with Jesus and contact with the disciples. After this rushed entry into Christian faith, he needed a special measure of grace to sustain and strengthen him through the years (15:9–10). Yet God's grace had been sufficient. Paul worked hard. The Corinthians' faith came out of his ministry. His message of the risen Lord was the same gospel that was held and preached in the wider church (15:11). The Easter faith is common property, for all of Christ's followers. We are all resurrection people.

Yet Paul's description of himself as a child without a viable life of its own underlines his dependence on God. For the gospel takes seriously our human frailty. It is realistic about death. Christ "was buried" (15:4); he was truly dead. Of the five hundred witnesses "some have died" (15:6). Easter is about victory over death, not about ignoring it or side-stepping around it.

"If Christ Has Not Been Raised"
1 Corinthians 15:12–19

> 15:12 Now if Christ is proclaimed as raised from the dead, how can some of you say there is no resurrection of the dead? ¹³ If there is no resurrection of the dead, then Christ has not been raised; ¹⁴ and if Christ has not been raised, then our proclamation has been in vain and your faith has been in vain. ¹⁵ We are even found to be misrepresenting God, because we testified of God that he raised Christ—whom he did not raise if it is true that the dead are not raised. ¹⁶ For if the dead are not raised, then Christ has not been raised. ¹⁷ If Christ has not been raised, your faith is futile and you are still in your sins. ¹⁸ Then those also who have died in Christ have perished. ¹⁹ If for this life only we have hoped in Christ, we are of all people most to be pitied.

Up to now, Paul has staked out some common ground: the whole church remembers and preaches Easter. The Corinthians know this (15:11). Now he looks at the logic of this belief and at the difference Easter makes. "If Christ has not been raised" (15:14, 17), then the whole of Christianity falls: preaching and believing are useless (15:14); sin and guilt hang around like a bad smell, with no pardon to wash them away (15:17); the dead lie in their graves, the bereaved find no comfort (15:18), and those deluded souls who still try to live faithfully deserve only pity (15:19).

Putting these points more positively, Paul sees Easter as the central pillar of the church's life and faith. It offers the preacher a message, that Jesus is Lord. It gives meaning to the cross: if Jesus is risen, then his death is much more than tragedy or accident. It holds out hope to the dying and bereaved, for it shows God's power reaching into the grave. And it adds hope to faith: the future lies in God's hands.

So how can anyone say "there is no resurrection of the dead" (15:12)? If this were really true, it would mean that Jesus did not rise (15:13, 15) and make the entire gospel hopeless and hollow. Denying resurrection cuts two ways: it attacks the church's foundation story, and it devalues all our experience of the Lord. Paul could not see this as a valid Christian view at all. Both the logic of the good news and the testimony of the church pointed him in a very different direction.

RESURRECTION FAITH: WHERE IT LEADS
1 Corinthians 15:20–34

"For He Must Reign"
1 Corinthians 15:20–28

> 15:20 **But in fact Christ has been raised from the dead, the first fruits of those who have died.** [21] **For since death came through a human being, the resurrection of the dead has also come through a human being;** [22] **for as all die in Adam, so all will be made alive in Christ.** [23] **But each in his own order: Christ the first fruits, then at his coming those who belong to Christ.** [24] **Then comes the end, when he hands over the kingdom to God the Father, after he has destroyed every ruler and every authority and power.** [25] **For he must reign until he has put all his enemies under his feet.** [26] **The last enemy to be destroyed is death.** [27] **For "God has put all things in subjection under his feet." But when it says, "All things are put in subjection," it is plain that this does not include the one who put all things in subjection under him.** [28] **When all things are subjected to him, then the Son himself will also be subjected to the one who put all things in subjection under him, so that God may be all in all.**

The last paragraph was all hypothesis and supposition—full of "if." And it looked back, at the meaning of Easter in past and present. But now the mood and perspective change. The tone switches to strong affirmation—"in fact Christ has been raised" (15:20). And the focus moves forward. We look ahead, at where Easter leads and at the way it shapes the future.

For Paul believed in the Parousia—the second coming of Christ, as the church has called it. He looked for Christ's power and glory to be known in the world, spectacularly, fully, and finally. And this "coming" (15:23) is the central focus of these verses. This, for Paul, would be the great echo of Easter, sounding resonantly and triumphantly Christ's victory over sin and death. This is when the dead will rise, death will end forever, and God's reign will be complete, without rival, shadow, or challenge.

It sometimes seems today that these other aspects of hope—that the dead will rise and God will reign—matter more to the church than the coming of Christ. Yet for Paul, the personal focus on Christ was vital: his faith was based personally on Jesus, from beginning to end. So the promise of Christ's coming frames these verses. It sets the context in which they speak of God's kingdom and of the life Jesus gives to his people. Several Old Testament motifs help to outline these points.

- *Firstfruits*. The start of harvest was always a cause for rejoicing and praise (Lev. 23:10; Deut. 26:2, 10). Once again the earth was sharing its life. The early produce was a sign of God's faithfulness, the first installment of greater blessing to come. And this is how the church rejoices in the rising of Jesus. We greet Easter as the sign of a larger and fuller resurrection. As Christ is risen, so his people will rise (15:20, 23). He leads the way.
- *Adam*. Adam and Christ are two prototypes. Each is "the firstborn within a large family" (Rom. 8:29). Each founds and forms a great company of people and shapes the character of their living. So just as Genesis tells of Adam bringing death into the world (Gen. 3:17–19), Easter declares Jesus as the one who reverses that curse. Through his resurrection, his people find their risen life. He puts into motion a new hope and prospect for humanity (15:21–22).
- *Kingship*. The image of Jesus with "his enemies under his feet" (15:25) comes from Psalm 110:1. In Old Testament times this was a royal psalm, talking of Israel's anointed king; so there is a connection with the word "Christ." "Christ" is a kingly word. *Christos* is the Greek version of the Hebrew word *mashiah*, "the anointed one." And in these verses Christ's kingship is center stage. He will reign over all his enemies, even over death.
- *Humanity*. Reflecting on Psalm 110 leads Paul to Psalm 8. There is a resonance in the expression "under [one's] feet." For as Jesus

rules over his enemies (15:25, quoting Ps. 110:1), he embodies God's desire and design, that people too should rule the created world in wise and wholesome ways (15:27, from Ps. 8:6). As he offers back to his Father the authority given to him (15:24, 28), he fulfills in a new way the promise of Genesis 1, of a people made in God's image and looking to God in blessing and trust.

All of this, for Paul, is part of the church's Easter faith. Because of Easter, we celebrate Jesus as conqueror and look for his victory over all that destroys and damages God's world. He will rule over his enemies, and he means his people to rejoice in his reign.

And because of Easter, God gathers and forms a new and holy people. Paul's images of the future are richly corporate—harvest, Adam, humanity. In Christ there is a new creation (2 Cor. 5:17). His people become the community of servants and stewards God means us to be.

"If the Dead Are Not Raised"
1 Corinthians 15:29–34

> 15:29 **Otherwise, what will those people do who receive baptism on behalf of the dead? If the dead are not raised at all, why are people baptized on their behalf?**
> ³⁰ **And why are we putting ourselves in danger every hour?** ³¹ **I die every day! That is as certain, brothers and sisters, as my boasting of you—a boast that I make in Christ Jesus our Lord.** ³² **If with merely human hopes I fought with wild animals at Ephesus, what would I have gained by it? If the dead are not raised,**
>> **"Let us eat and drink,**
>> **for tomorrow we die."**
> ³³ **Do not be deceived:**
>> **"Bad company ruins good morals."**
> ³⁴ **Come to a sober and right mind, and sin no more; for some people have no knowledge of God. I say this to your shame.**

We noticed earlier in the chapter how Paul's argument deliberately oscillates. He shifts between comfort and challenge; he moves from strong assertion about the fact and meaning of Easter to hypothesis and query in the face of doubt and unbelief. So after the bright hopes of 15:20–28, he returns to the quizzical tone that we met in 15:12–19.

Paul makes three fresh points in these verses. Here are more ways, he implies, in which the church depends on the resurrection. He sets out each one provocatively as a question or a challenge to remind the Corinthians of how strongly this belief already shapes their lives.

- Why trouble with baptism (15:29)? This verse about "baptism for the dead" is notoriously obscure. It may mean, "What's the point of receiving baptism if it only washes our mortal bodies? If the dead are not raised, why bother to baptize our dying bodies now?"
- Why suffer for Christ (15:30–32a)? Paul's labors as an apostle only make sense in the light of Easter. His work is dangerous at times and is always intensely demanding, robbing him of safety, comfort, and security. Every day is a kind of dying. Why bear this, and why risk death, if there is no hope of resurrection?
- Why be good (15:32b–34)? If this life is all there is, why bother with godly conduct? Why discipline and restrain yourself in the face of temptation? You might as well feed the senses before you die. If we put this thought more positively, the point is that hope shapes your character. It gives you the nerve and courage to be holy. Without hope, it would be harder to cultivate an upright and moral way of life.

In making these points, Paul is addressing the skeptics in Corinth. He wants them to realize how much difference a resurrection faith makes and what it might cost them to live without it. He knows, however, that he must give some positive explanation too, to overcome their doubts and to help them resist the gloom and pessimism of their world. For our bodies can look a sorry sight when we die. Is it these weak bodies that will be raised? That is the issue to which Paul turns next.

RESURRECTION FAITH: WHAT IT MEANS
1 Corinthians 15:35–58

"How Are the Dead Raised?"
1 Corinthians 15:35–41

> 15:35 **But someone will ask, "How are the dead raised? With what kind of body do they come?"** [36] **Fool! What you sow does not come to life unless it dies.** [37] **And as for what you sow, you do not sow the body that is to be, but a bare seed, perhaps of wheat or of some other grain.** [38] **But God gives it a body as he has chosen, and to each kind of seed its own body.** [39] **Not all flesh is alike, but there is one flesh for human beings, another for animals, another for birds, and another for fish.** [40] **There are both heavenly bodies**

and earthly bodies, but the glory of the heavenly is one thing, and that of the earthly is another. [41] There is one glory of the sun, and another glory of the moon, and another glory of the stars; indeed, star differs from star in glory.

This part of the chapter starts with a question. When our bodily life eventually ebbs away, what is it that will be raised? Will it be the tired body with which we ended this life, which our friends then bury in the ground for the years and the elements to decay further? If it is, then any notion of resurrection seems bizarre and even pathetic. But if this is not the case, how can the church talk about personal resurrection? In what sense would the risen body still be me? That is the question Paul confronts: "How are the dead raised? With what kind of body do they come?" (15:35).

He starts by mentioning that life often changes form as it moves from one stage to another. Seed is a common example of this. It has to die before it can live in a new way (15:36–38). Admittedly that is not the language a scientist would use today, but it does fit the fact that we bury the seed to allow it to change. Then it rises up and lives again with a different kind of "body." So there is continuity between seed and plant. There is also change: they do not look the same. And that is Paul's point—continuity and change. If God can do this for plants, why not for people? "So it is with the resurrection of the dead" (15:42).

But before drawing that conclusion, Paul emphasizes that different kinds of life have different natures (15:39). Humans, animals, birds, and fish do not have the same "flesh"; the material of their bodies varies from one order of life to another. Something similar is true in the realms of space: the heavenly bodies have different kinds of "glory." Each has its own particular dignity and beauty (15:40–41). So surely, Paul suggests, life beyond death may not be like the bodily existence we know on earth. It will be truly ours; but it will not be the same.

"So It Is with the Resurrection"
1 Corinthians 15:42–44

> **15:42 So it is with the resurrection of the dead. What is sown is perishable, what is raised is imperishable.** [43] **It is sown in dishonor, it is raised in glory. It is sown in weakness, it is raised in power.** [44] **It is sown a physical body, it is raised a spiritual body. If there is a physical body, there is also a spiritual body.**

Paul's illustrations above have prepared the way for this next paragraph. We know, he has said, that different kinds of life involve different kinds of body; if that is true in ordinary living, surely it can also apply after death. So the kind of risen life to which Christians look forward will not be like the frail mortal frame that we inhabit now.

For the body that we "sow" in the grave is decaying, sorry and weak; that is how we are when our lives come to an end. But the body will be raised imperishable, glorious, and powerful (15:42–43)—solid, splendid, and strong. Rather than being a natural body, it will be "a spiritual body" (15:44).

The contrast, however, is not really between "physical" and "spiritual"; the NRSV's wording "physical body" (15:44) slightly misses Paul's point. For the Greek word translated "physical" is a word Paul used earlier to speak of "unspiritual people"—human nature, operating on its own—in contrast to "those who are spiritual" (2:14–15). So here this same word describes not the body's constitution but the source of its energy and life. The point is that our mortal body is animated by our own human resources; we are running on our own tank of gas.

Then in parallel to this, the word "spiritual body" does not mean "made of spirit." It means that the Holy Spirit will energize our risen body. Rather than our own nature animating us, God's Spirit will stir within us so that our resurrection body will be dense and rich with God's presence and power. A new act of creation will be involved, a remaking of human living by the breath of God. And with that hint of creation in mind, Paul again likens Jesus to Adam (15:45).

"The Image of the Man of Heaven"
1 Corinthians 15:45–49

> 15:45 Thus it is written, "The first man, Adam, became a living being"; the last Adam became a life-giving spirit. ⁴⁶ But it is not the spiritual that is first, but the physical, and then the spiritual. ⁴⁷ The first man was from the earth, a man of dust; the second man is from heaven. ⁴⁸ As was the man of dust, so are those who are of the dust; and as is the man of heaven, so are those who are of heaven. ⁴⁹ Just as we have borne the image of the man of dust, we will also bear the image of the man of heaven.

For Adam became "a living being." Paul is quoting from Genesis (2:7, in 15:45) and describing the old creation. Adam was "a living being," an animate personality. But Jesus, as "the last Adam," has risen to become "a life-giving spirit." His resurrection was not for himself only but for others. Because he has risen, many can share his life. They can be raised with bodies like his, bodies that are "spiritual"—enlivened and energized with the presence of God's Spirit (15:46).

We met a contrast between Adam and Jesus earlier on (15:21–22). There the counterpoint was death versus life—between mortal being that perishes and life that is raised up new. Now these later verses contrast two sources for these two phases of living: one stage of our being is fashioned from the dust of earth; the other is full with the glories of heaven (15:47–49). Just now we carry the image of the Adam of dust; dust we are and to dust we shall return. Yet in rising we shall bear the image of Christ; our life will be new and bright and strong.

So the "spiritual body" (15:44) to which Christians look forward need not mean "a nonphysical body." We do not slip away into a shadowy and ethereal existence—this was the common ancient view that Paul wanted to correct. But in Christ we rise to a fuller kind of bodily life than we live at the moment—not less physical, but more so. This is what Paul means by "the resurrection of the dead."

"Thanks Be to God, Who Gives Us the Victory"
1 Corinthians 15:50–58

> 15:50 What I am saying, brothers and sisters, is this: flesh and blood cannot inherit the kingdom of God, nor does the perishable inherit the imperishable. [51] Listen, I will tell you a mystery! We will not all die, but we will all be changed, [52] in a moment, in the twinkling of an eye, at the last trumpet. For the trumpet will sound, and the dead will be raised imperishable, and we will be changed. [53] For this perishable body must put on imperishability, and this mortal body must put on immortality. [54] When this perishable body puts on imperishability, and this mortal body puts on immortality, then the saying that is written will be fulfilled:
> "Death has been swallowed up in victory."
> [55] "Where, O death, is your victory?
> Where, O death, is your sting?"
> [56] The sting of death is sin, and the power of sin is the law. [57] But thanks be to God, who gives us the victory through our Lord Jesus Christ.
> [58] Therefore, my beloved, be steadfast, immovable, always excelling in the work of the Lord, because you know that in the Lord your labor is not in vain.

This last part of the chapter underlines and rounds off all that Paul has been saying. "Flesh and blood"—the perishable form of life we now have—"cannot inherit the kingdom of God" (15:50). As we are now, we cannot experience either the life of heaven or the kingship of Christ as fully as God intends. No more can you glue flowers or fruit onto a seed; it has to die and rise before it can fully live.

This brings Paul back to the matter of "when." He has already spoken of Christ's coming (15:23). Now he reflects again on what that day will bring. It will be a day of resurrection when the dead will rise and the living too will put on "the imperishable." "We will not all die" (15:51). Some will still be living—history will still be going on—when Christ appears. Indeed Paul writes as if he will be among that number. "We will be changed," he says (15:51, 52). In later writings he speaks frankly of the prospect of his own death (2 Cor. 4:16–5:5; Phil. 1:21–24), but here he looks forward vividly to the coming of Christ, as if he will be there to share the experience.

Yet Paul's main point is not about precise timing. It is that mortal flesh, whether living or dead, must be clothed with the resurrection life of Christ (15:53). As "a bare seed" (15:37) can only be clothed by rising, our natural bodies too are waiting to be wrapped in new life. One day they must be animated by the life of the Spirit. Only then will Christ's victory over death be full and final (15:54–55).

It is odd to find Paul referring so very briefly to "sin" and "the law" (15:56). These issues are important in his scheme of thought, and elsewhere he explains them at great length—most obviously in Romans 5–8. But here he takes no time at all to develop these ideas. He had probably taught the Corinthians something about them, and he simply alludes to them in passing.

Finally there is a strong upward beat, of confidence and praise (15:57–58). For Paul, resurrection is an energetic doctrine. It makes Christians assured and active as we go about God's work. It tells us that our "work is not in vain." Paul has stretched his readers' minds in this chapter and quite strenuously so; but his intention has always been pastoral, to settle their hearts and to stir them with courage.

So perhaps this chapter can enrich and inform our Christian lives too. For it reminds us how heavily our faith depends on Jesus and his rising. Easter is still the center and mainspring of the church's gospel. Further, the idea of resurrection takes our physical life seriously. Creation matters. God values our bodies. Death and resurrection can surely transform these, but there is no sense in this chapter that our physical being is simply discarded or that we live on as homeless souls. Third, this teaching invites us to live and to die in hope. A dull skepticism might shape the minds of many in our world today, as it surely did in Corinth. Yet the church walks to a different beat. We travel toward the dawn.

7. Plans and Personalities
1 Corinthians 16:1–24

This final chapter is full of personal news and greetings. As in several of Paul's letters, these last lines draw us into the complex web of relationships that linked the early churches. They introduce us briefly to a host of individual Christians in Corinth and elsewhere. And they let us see the warmth of Paul's concern for the men and women among whom he served. Although the chapter reads as a series of short, separate paragraphs, it falls broadly into two main portions. The first is mostly about Paul's own plans and projects and the second mostly about other people.

PAUL'S PROJECTS
1 Corinthians 16:1–9

"Concerning the Collection"
1 Corinthians 16:1–4

> 16:1 **Now concerning the collection for the saints: you should follow the directions I gave to the churches of Galatia.** ² **On the first day of every week, each of you is to put aside and save whatever extra you earn, so that collections need not be taken when I come.** ³ **And when I arrive, I will send any whom you approve with letters to take your gift to Jerusalem.** ⁴ **If it seems advisable that I should go also, they will accompany me.**

The collection was a major venture. It took up a lot of Paul's attention and effort over a period of years, and in many ways it summed up his life's work as a Christian missionary. The church in Jerusalem had fallen on hard times, and Paul asked the churches of his mission field to gather money for help and relief. He discusses the project in at least three of his letters (see also Rom. 15:25–31; 2 Cor. 8–9; and possibly Gal. 2:10).

Part of the motivation was straightforward Christian care for sisters and brothers in a tough situation. But the collection involved deeper issues too. There were many Gentiles in Paul's churches, and their style of Christianity was not very tightly tied to the law and customs of Judaism. Yet now Paul wanted these churches to acknowledge their spiritual debt to the mother church (Rom. 15:27). The faith had come to them from Israel. Jerusalem was the source and origin of the church's mission. This was a chance to say thank-you.

Surely Paul hoped that the gesture would help the Jewish Christians in Jerusalem to respect both his Gentile mission and the churches he had brought into being. If this happened, the collection would forge an important bond of fellowship, as well as helping the needy. It would enable scattered and diverse groups of Christians to affirm their unity in the love of Christ. It would make sense of Paul's work and show that his preaching among the Gentiles had not been a splinter movement. It would witness to the breadth and power of the gospel.

There is a parallel of sorts to this collection, in the annual levy that Jewish men paid to Jerusalem. From centers around the Jewish dispersion, consignments of money were sent year by year to support the worship and upkeep of the temple. There was also a well-established Jewish tradition of helping the poor. So in some ways the plan for this collection would have seemed quite natural to Paul. Yet the Gentile world had not the same traditions of almsgiving that existed in Judaism, and it certainly had no natural focus on Jerusalem. So in churches such as Corinth the project may have required serious advocacy. From the way Paul introduces the topic here, the Corinthians already know about his plans (16:1). These few sentences are a reminder rather than a full account of the matter.

Paul wants all in the church to be involved, not just the wealthier members (16:2). Each can give as their affairs prosper, and everyone's contribution matters. For Paul knew that gathering a worthwhile sum would depend on careful saving and giving. This would not be a matter he could fix quickly when he got to Corinth. Most people in ancient times lived quite near to the margins of economic survival, and even middle-status Christians would not have been able to dig quickly into well-lined pockets. Substantial giving would need sustained commitment and goodwill.

Once Paul arrives in Corinth, he says, he and the church can make plans to send the money to Jerusalem. The church should choose people to carry the gift (16:3). Their involvement would prevent any thought that Paul might misuse the collection. They would also represent the

Corinthian church when they handed over the money; the Christians in Jerusalem would see where this gift had come from.

In the event it seems that Corinth did contribute (for Paul refers to "Achaia" doing so; Rom. 15:26), but no one from Corinth traveled with the money. Acts does, however, show a little posse from several Gentile churches setting off with Paul to Jerusalem (20:3–4). They go as the escort and representative donors of his collected Gentile gift.

"I Will Visit You"
1 Corinthians 16:5–9

> 16:5 I will visit you after passing through Macedonia—for I intend to pass through Macedonia— ⁶ and perhaps I will stay with you or even spend the winter, so that you may send me on my way, wherever I go. ⁷ I do not want to see you now just in passing, for I hope to spend some time with you, if the Lord permits. ⁸ But I will stay in Ephesus until Pentecost, ⁹ for a wide door for effective work has opened to me, and there are many adversaries.

Meanwhile Paul's personal plans are taking shape. He is writing from Ephesus, on the eastern side of the Aegean Sea, and means to stay there a while yet. The work is proving tough but fruitful (16:8–9), as the longer account in Acts (19:1–41) also indicates. Once he leaves Ephesus, he will go north and west, around the shore of the Aegean. In the northern province of Macedonia he will visit his churches in Philippi and Thessalonica (16:5) before coming south to Corinth.

All of that will take time. Paul's reference to Pentecost suggests he is writing in the spring, and he may not reach Corinth until the traveling season ends at the onset of winter. This, he thinks, might be ideal. It will allow a long visit, without any urgent need to move on (16:6–7). Corinth will require plenty of help and care.

When Paul did get to Corinth—although it was probably not that same year—his months there were productive (Acts 20:2). He had time to write Romans and to dispatch it with Phoebe, who was from Cenchreae, just outside Corinth (Rom. 16:1). He also managed to complete his collection to take to Jerusalem at the Pentecost season (Acts 20:3–7, 16). Yet as he writes 1 Corinthians, his intentions seem quite open and undecided. He is not yet sure about accompanying the collection to Jerusalem; it may be right for him to go, or it may not (16:4). If other needs claim him, he will ask the Corinthians for support on the necessary journeys (16:6). In Corinth he was wary about accepting patronage (see comment on 9:15–23). But he will be glad for this church to support his gospel work elsewhere.

For earlier Paul reminded the Corinthians about the wide Christian fellowship to which they belonged (1:2; 11:16; 14:33). In this chapter he reinforces the point, mentioning Galatia, Jerusalem, Macedonia, and Ephesus. The early Christian network was very spread out, yet there were some strong bonds of concern and love. The Corinthians were part of this network—not a law unto themselves.

GOD'S PEOPLE
1 Corinthians 16:10–24

Friends and Journeys
1 Corinthians 16:10–12

> 16:10 **If Timothy comes, see that he has nothing to fear among you, for he is doing the work of the Lord just as I am;** [11] **therefore let no one despise him. Send him on his way in peace, so that he may come to me; for I am expecting him with the brothers.**
> [12] **Now concerning our brother Apollos, I strongly urged him to visit you with the other brothers, but he was not at all willing to come now. He will come when he has the opportunity.**

Although Paul was a strong character, he was a keen team worker too. He valued friendships, and he needed helpers if the churches he founded were to prosper. So he was glad to see the gifts and abilities of colleagues develop and grow. In these verses we see that he tried to arrange for others to help the church in Corinth while he was busy in Ephesus. For although he could guide the church by writing, Paul obviously felt that they needed more support than a letter alone could give. He wanted them to have some personal ministry and care too.

So Timothy would come, "to remind you of my ways" (4:17). Timothy often traveled with Paul. He is mentioned in many of the letters, and although he was not a forceful or imposing personality, Paul trusted him deeply. So he comes to Corinth as Paul's agent and envoy—"doing the Lord's work, as I am"—and Paul asks that he be treated with warmth and respect (16:10).

Apollos, too, was a trusted colleague. Problems may have arisen when some church members in Corinth preferred his ministry to Paul's (see comment on 1:12–17). But Paul was keen to stress the links between the two men (3:6; 4:6). The tone in this present section suggests that people in Corinth were keen to have Apollos visit again. Paul too expects Apollos to be a helpful presence in Corinth and would be glad for him to get there as soon as possible (16:12).

References to "the brothers" are a mystery (16:11, 12). The neatest explanation in 16:12 is that these "brothers" are Stephanas and his companions (16:17), who had come from Corinth to visit Paul. Now they will carry this letter back to Corinth, although it appears that Apollos will not travel with them. This explanation, however, will not help with 16:11; we do not know which "brothers" are meant there. Paul's networks of acquaintance and help were surely wider and more complex than we know about. This is not the only time that he refers to friends in rather cryptic terms (2 Cor. 8:16–24).

Strength and Love
1 Corinthians 16:13–14

> 16:13 **Keep alert, stand firm in your faith, be courageous, be strong.** [14] **Let all that you do be done in love.**

Some other New Testament letters include a compact set of maxims near the end—brief commands about Christian character and behavior (Col. 4:2–6; 1 Thess. 5:12–22). The selection here (16:13–14) is very condensed, yet as with the opening prayers in Paul's letters, there are links between the body of the letter and these closing exhortations. Paul is not merely firing off a few improving thoughts; he is offering advice that fits the local situation.

- "Stand firm" echoes the language of the previous chapter, on resurrection. Christians "stand" "in the gospel" (15:1) and "in . . . faith" (16:13). Their hope makes them "steadfast" and "immovable" (15:58).
- "Love" is also a vital theme for Corinth (16:14). It "builds up" (8:1) and "abides" (13:13) and will be the key to resolving a host of pastoral difficulties. Indeed some of the Christians have been practical examples of this, as Paul outlines in the next verses.

People to Respect
1 Corinthians 16:15–18

> 16:15 **Now, brothers and sisters, you know that members of the household of Stephanas were the first converts in Achaia, and they have devoted themselves to the service of the saints;** [16] **I urge you to put yourselves at the service of such people, and of everyone who works and toils with them.**

> [17] **I rejoice at the coming of Stephanas and Fortunatus and Achaicus, because they have made up for your absence;** [18] **for they refreshed my spirit as well as yours. So give recognition to such persons.**

Stephanas and his family were the first Christian converts in Corinth, and Paul himself had baptized them (16:15; 1:16). Now they—or to be precise, Stephanas and two other men—we do not know quite how these three are connected—have visited Paul in Ephesus. They may not be the same group as "Chloe's people" (1:11), but they probably passed on to Paul some of the information reflected in this letter.

As Paul sends these men back—probably carrying this letter with them—he commends them to the church. He picks out three matters for comment—the "service" (16:15) of the Stephanas family, their hard work (16:16), and the encouragement his visitors have given to him and to others (16:18).

- The word for "service" is *diakonia*, which often refers to humble and useful duty, without any obvious honor or glamor. Paul calls himself and Apollos *diakonoi* (3:5). Diaconal work need have no special status or kudos; it finds its dignity in being useful to others, rather than in prominence or praise.
- Paul often speaks of "hard work," both his own efforts (1 Thess. 2:9) and those of others (Rom. 16:6, 12). He looked on Christian ministry, with all the commitments and strains involved, as a tough and demanding task; indeed this is a major theme in 2 Corinthians. So he was glad when others too were willing to work hard in the life and care of the church.
- Paul rated the gift of encouragement highly (Phlm. 7). When he was separated by distance or difficulty from people he loved, occasional contacts meant much to him. He was restless when contact and communication were broken and refers often to the sense of refreshment that company and good news could bring (Rom. 1:11–12; 2 Cor. 2:13; 7:5–7; 1 Thess. 3:1–7).

With all this in view, Paul urges the Corinthians to accept the leadership of people like Stephanas (16:16, 18). Amid the chaotic and competitive moods of Corinth, leaders like this would be a steady and supportive influence on all around. Indeed characters of this kind still contribute massively to the well-being of our churches; we too should honor them and try to be like them.

Christian Greetings
1 Corinthians 16:19-20

> 16:19 **The churches of Asia send greetings. Aquila and Prisca, together with the church in their house, greet you warmly in the Lord.** [20] **All the brothers and sisters send greetings. Greet one another with a holy kiss.**

The closing lines of the letter emphasize the rich network of relationships to which the Corinthians belong. They tell of the grace of Christ (16:23) and of Paul's love for his friends in Corinth (16:24) and carry the greetings and good wishes of other Christians and churches (16:19-20). Five times over Paul uses the word "greet" or "greeting" (16:19-21).

"The churches of Asia" (16:19) refers to the Roman province of that name, reaching inland from Ephesus into what is now western Turkey. Paul was presently based in the provincial capital and surely knew of other Christian groups in the area. At this early stage in church history, these would be quite small and scattered.

Among Paul's Christian contacts in Asia, Prisca and Aquila (16:19) were especially dear to him. The three had sewn leather in Corinth (Acts 18:3-4, 18, 26), and Paul later recalled with warm appreciation their courage and contribution in the work of the gospel (Rom. 16:3-4). Both in Ephesus, from where Paul writes to Corinth, and later in Rome, they gathered a group of Christians to meet in their home (Rom. 16:5). Now this little fellowship sends "greetings" to brothers and sisters in Corinth.

The "holy kiss" (16:20) is mentioned several times in New Testament letters (Rom. 16:16; 2 Cor. 13:12; 1 Thess. 5:26; 1 Pet. 5:14). This was a common way in Greco-Roman culture to greet relatives or close friends. Its use by the churches shows that they thought of one another as family. Indeed all through this letter Paul uses family language to address the Corinthians (3:1; 15:50, for example), as he does when he speaks of the church in Asia (16:20).

His Own Hand
1 Corinthians 16:21-24

> 16:21 **I, Paul, write this greeting with my own hand.** [22] **Let anyone be accursed who has no love for the Lord. Our Lord, come!** [23] **The grace of the Lord Jesus be with you.** [24] **My love be with all of you in Christ Jesus.**

Finally Paul takes the pen from the scribe to sign off (16:21). His remark about some people being "accursed" (16:22) may grate amid the warmth and kindness of these last greetings. Yet it has a purpose. There were strong personalities in the Corinthian church, and Paul cared enough to leave them with a serious challenge. If any in Corinth (or indeed today) treat the church and their fellow Christians in ways that are merely manipulative and self-serving, then they are living at odds with the gospel. Such people have no right to ask for God's blessing or to expect it.

"Our Lord, come!" (16:22) is a little prayer. It is actually an Aramaic expression, *Marana tha*, although included here in a Greek letter. Paul surely expected the Corinthians to recognize the words. Probably he had taught them to use this prayer, perhaps when they celebrated Holy Communion, "until he comes" (11:26). Its origin was in the earliest days of the church. For Aramaic was the language of Jewish people in the Holy Land, and this prayer must come from Christians there. They called Jesus *Mare* (Master) as he went about among them. After the resurrection they acclaimed him as Lord and prayed for his coming again, and the prayer quickly became part of a widely used church tradition.

And at the very end, even when the talking has been tough, it is often possible to check out with a genuine word of goodwill. The letter finishes (16:23–24) with the Lord's grace and a pastor's love.

Second Corinthians

Introduction to the Second Letter to the Corinthians

STRESS AND SERVICE

"Second Corinthians was the last of Paul's letters that I really got to know." So said my colleague. "Now I see why this was. It's a letter about stress. It comes out of a difficult situation in Paul's life. And when I ran into a time of stress myself, this letter started to speak to me in all sorts of deep and important ways."

For me too, this letter speaks to some deep and fragile places in Christian experience. It is not easy reading, but it is realistic, honest, and profoundly spiritual. It tells of God's call to serve the gospel through thick and thin, to be the best we can be for Christ and for other people, even when life is hurtful and tough. It reminds us that those Christians who reveal the risen life of Jesus most clearly are often those who have to live in the shadow of the cross. And it assures us that even the most painful experiences of our living are within range of God's grace. God can sustain and strengthen us, even there.

So if your life is going well, if the sun is shining on you, and all your fields are fruitful, this letter may not meet your mood. But for most of us, the time will come when we need Scripture of this kind. When the storms rage around us and thorns pierce and pain our hearts, writing like this will help us to draw on God's grace. It will give us fresh courage for service in the midst of stress. It will speak to us too in deep and important ways.

Before we turn to the letter itself, we look at how it came to be written.

A NEW SITUATION

Turning from 1 Corinthians to 2 Corinthians is rather like leaving the room in the middle of a TV program, then coming back a few minutes later. The main characters in the story are the same, but the sequence of events has moved on. You find people responding to one another in new ways. Relationships have obviously changed, and it takes a little while to work out why.

The most obvious difference between the two letters is a change in tone. Paul is less confident than he was before. In 1 Corinthians he has plenty of advice to give. He seems sure of his own role and leadership in the church: although far away from Corinth, he is still trusted by many of the Christians there. So in the first letter his pastoral counsel flows freely. On a host of issues he sets out his insights and tells the Corinthians what to do. In 2 Corinthians, by contrast, his bond with the church seems tense and fragile. We watch him trying to retrieve and repair a pastoral relationship that has fallen on bad times. He has to defend and explain himself in a new way.

There are several reasons for this change. All of them reflect the fact that time has moved on, and new events and factors have come into play. There are five points to explore.

Clash and Challenge

One issue that affected relationships was Paul's own dealing with the Corinthians. His first letter to Corinth had been written from Ephesus, a few days' sail from Corinth across the Aegean Sea. People traveled to and fro fairly readily. Christians in particular were keen to sustain a lively network of contact and friendship. (See, for example, our comments on 1 Corinthians 16:10–20.) So the possibility of an occasional pastoral visit to sort out a problem or to monitor and encourage the well-being of the church was never very far from Paul's mind.

Indeed he did visit, shortly before writing this second letter, and the encounter was not a happy one. The memory it left behind was of clash and challenge rather than comfort or care. Paul's words—"pain, punishment, sorrow" (2:1–7)—clearly show this unease. All of this then made him wary about visiting again in a hurry (2:1). So he had written instead, a letter of "many tears," yet full with "abundant love" (2:4), and although this letter did some good (7:8–9), it also caused criticism. Some people in Corinth had expected a further visit and were angry when Paul just sent a letter. How could they trust a man like that? So while visiting Corinth had been a difficult experience, staying away caused difficulties too. A new set of suspicions and strains arose, which would surely take time and effort to resolve. Second Corinthians is part of the resolution.

Gathering Gifts

A second major concern in this letter is money. Earlier Paul had reminded Corinth of his plan to gather a gift for poor Christians in the Holy Land (1 Cor. 16:1–4). He wanted the Corinthians to put money aside week by week to be ready for the time when it would be taken to Jerusalem along with contributions from several other Gentile churches.

By the time Paul comes to write 2 Corinthians, this matter too has moved forward. The collection project is maturing, other churches are doing their bit, and the time for shipping the money is coming nearer. In two ways, then, Paul must appeal to Corinth: for their generosity to help make the collection as substantial as possible; and for their trust, if they are to put their money into his hands. An ally in achieving these aims will be a friend and fellow worker named Titus.

Titus and the Team

The New Testament shows Paul as such a strong character that we might easily overlook his emphasis on teamwork. Regularly he worked with companions and friends and depended on others to do God's work with him. In his dealings with Corinth, Titus was an important colleague. This man (who appears first in Galatians 2) had visited Corinth more recently than Paul. Indeed it appears that Paul had sent Titus with the so-called "tearful letter" to try and repair the difficult situation that Paul's own visit had brought about. Evidently Titus's mission achieved some success, and this gave Paul welcome assurance about his own relationship with the church (7:5–16). More than that, Titus also made progress with the collection, and this too heartened Paul (8:6).

So by the time Paul writes 2 Corinthians, Titus is about to return to Corinth with two companions (8:16–24) to carry forward the collection and to prepare the way for Paul's next visit (9:1–5). Indeed Paul too hopes to travel with company. For as he writes to Corinth from Macedonia, in northern Greece, he speaks of having recently arrived there (7:5), of the generosity of local Christians (8:1–5), and of friends from Macedonia who may come with him to Corinth (9:4).

All of this enables us to make sense of much of the letter. Chapters 1–7 serve to retrieve and reestablish Paul's pastoral bond with the Corinthian church in the aftermath of his difficult visit. Chapters 8 and 9 speak of the collection, which is the project immediately ahead. Thus the letter talks both of work that Titus had already done in Corinth and of a task he had yet to complete. So as Titus and his little band make their way to Corinth, we may reasonably suppose that they carry this letter with them, as a commendation.

The final topic in the letter is, then, Paul's own visit, for which Titus's good work would pave the way, and chapters 10–13 have this very clearly in view (10:2; 12:14; 13:1). But even as Paul looks forward to coming to Corinth, he is anxious to discuss a new and difficult issue, which makes the prospect of his visit rather unsettling.

"A Different Gospel"

A group of newcomers have arrived in Corinth. It seems likely that Paul heard about them through Titus. For they call themselves Christians (11:13, 23), they talk of Jesus, and they have gained the friendship and trust of believers at Corinth. So Titus is likely to have met these people, spent time in their company, and told Paul about them. Yet their version of the good news seems rather different to Paul's, and Paul fears for the well-being of the church he has founded.

We do not know these "opponents" very well. This is partly because our information comes at one remove. We never see them at work nor hear them speak for themselves. We do not know their names. What we can glean comes through Paul's writing. But even he may not have ever met these people. So we, like him, must make what we can of the information we have.

Clearly the newcomers have had some influence in the Corinthian church, and Paul feels uncomfortable about this. He thinks of them as secondhand missionaries, trespassing on his territory (10:12–18), which in itself makes him suspicious and skeptical. But a deeper cause of his unease is his anxiety about their message and the impression they have given of the Christian life. He fears that they "proclaim another Jesus" (11:4).

One sign of the problem is a concern with image and style. The newcomers criticize Paul for being "weak and contemptible" (10:10). Their own manner is more forceful, even aggressive (11:20). And this may be why Paul has a lot to say in this letter about the cross of Christ. He believes that humility and vulnerability are a normal part of Christian service. True Christian leaders should know something of the cross in their own experience (4:7–12), and he does not find this in what he hears about the incomers.

They were confident, to be sure, of their Jewish ancestry (11:22); perhaps they had stronger links than Paul to the church in Jerusalem.

They—one of them, at least—must have been a gifted speaker; this gave them leverage to decry and despise Paul's abilities as an orator (10:10). Possibly they talked of mystical powers, or of miracles they could do; this may be why Paul recalls a vision of his own (12:1–4) and the "signs" he performed in Corinth (12:12). But the heart of the gospel—Jesus crucified (1 Cor. 2:2)—was less obvious in the opponents' life and message.

So when Paul writes about "super-apostles" (11:5; 12:11), he is surely being ironic. He does not really rate the newcomers as spiritual supermen. In his view something vital is missing from their ministry: they put too much emphasis on power and personality; they forget that God can work through human weakness. Paul fears that the Corinthians are being duped and offered a shallow and superficial version of the faith. So this letter is an attempt to set the record straight, to remind the church of the gospel Paul had taught, and to help them to think more deeply about the cross of Christ.

Once we understand this, we start to see how this concern shapes 2 Corinthians as a whole. For although these opponents only appear clearly in the final chapters, they cast a shadow over earlier sections too. Paul knows that other voices are being heard in Corinth, and another version of the gospel is abroad. So as he reviews his own dealings with the church and writes about the collection, he aims to contrast two very different styles of ministry. He justifies and defends the sort of leadership he offers and underlines those aspects of the Christian message that he reckons most important.

For him this is more than a personal issue. It is a spiritual and pastoral concern too. The Christian life, for him, is a thing of paradox: strength through weakness; life out of death; affliction and glory; joy in the midst of sorrow; and in the cross and resurrection, a wounded healer. Paul aims to reflect this gospel in both his words and his deeds; he fears that the opponents do not reflect it at all.

Coming to Town

Alongside this concern for the Christian message, Paul returns again and again in this letter to reflect on his own relationship with the Corinthians. Although he canceled one visit (2:1), he still means to come and see them (9:4), and this will be his third spell in Corinth (12:14; 13:1). There was a long initial stay in the city (Acts 18:1–18), then a second difficult visit (2 Cor. 2:1); he hopes that his third coming will be happier.

For Paul's heart is open wide to the Christians at Corinth (6:11–13). He loves them and wants to build them up (12:20). So he hopes to come in peace, with the accent on love, support, and encouragement. Yet if need be, he will be ready for a showdown, whether with the incomers (10:2) or with members of the church whose Christian lives have fallen out of line (12:19–13:4). At the time of writing, however, Paul does not know what he will meet and how he will need to react, and this uncertainty about the situation gives the whole of his letter an emotional and rather jagged quality.

Which takes us back to where we came in. The relationship between Paul and the church in Corinth has moved on and become tense and fragile in some new ways. Paul is uncomfortable about the situation, about his own distance from the church, and about the various tensions that make it hard for him to help as readily and effectively as he would like. As a result, the writing is restless. It is full of energy and passion, but it does not flow as smoothly as some of his other letters. There are awkward turns of phrase, and occasional jolting and abrupt changes of subject. The tone and style reflect the content.

Some modern readers, however, have explored other possible reasons for this uneven kind of writing.

ONE LETTER OR MANY?

More than any other letter in the New Testament, 2 Corinthians has given rise to a host of "partition theories." Could it represent, people ask, more than one original letter? Could several short letters—or parts of letters—have been retained in Corinth for a number of years, until church members forgot that these separate pieces of papyrus did not really belong together? Paul's relationship with the church was both lively and difficult; there might have been many pieces of correspondence. Indeed at least two stern letters seem to have vanished—the one mentioned at 1 Corinthians 5:9, and the tearful letter of 2 Corinthians 2:4. Might one or both of these be present in some way within what we now call 2 Corinthians? Might this second letter really consist of several letters, not just of one?

A hypothesis of this kind is often set out along these lines:

1. Chapters 10–13 are higher temperature writing than we find earlier in the letter. Paul's tone has become less conciliatory and more threatening. He discusses the opponents more directly than before.

Introduction

So does this last section of the letter really belong with the rest? Could it be the so-called "severe letter" (2:9; 7:8) that preceded the writing of chapters 1–9? Or alternatively, might chapters 10–13 be a later writing than 1–9, reflecting troubles that Paul did not know about when he drafted those calmer earlier chapters?

2. Chapters 8 and 9 seem very different from the rest of the letter. They talk about money, which is scarcely mentioned anywhere else. They too might not belong either with 10–13 or with 1–7.
3. Within chapters 1–7 are a couple of jarring discontinuities. Between 2:13 and 2:14 Paul shifts quite sharply from specific personal memories to a much more general account of the nature of his ministry; then later, between 7:4 and 7:5, he transitions again, from appeal back to personal memories. Yet if we pluck out 2:14–7:4 and join 2:13 to 7:5, the resulting seam is quite smooth. The language matches—restlessness, Titus, and Macedonia with the themes of discipline and repentance just a few verses away (2:5–11; 7:9–12). So have two documents become tangled? Could a longish reflection on ministry (2:14–7:4) have found its way into the midst of another letter that was primarily based on personal reminiscence?
4. Finally a clutch of verses in 6:14–7:1 stands out from its surroundings, whereas 6:13 and 7:2 seem to connect quite well with one another. By the same sort of argument used above, is this a slice of rogue text that has ended up (perhaps quite accidentally) in a place where it did not originally belong?

All of this would give us material from at least four letters plus a further stray fragment. (The numbers here reflect the four points above, and are for notation only; they need not imply this as the order of composition.)

Letter 1: 10–13
Letter 2: 8 and 9
Letter 3: 1:1–2:13 and 7:5–16
Letter 4: 2:14–6:13 and 7:2–4
Fragment: 6:14–7:1

Several of the big commentaries consider these ideas in more detail. Yet in recent years a growing number of commentators have moved away from this sort of hypothesis to the simpler idea that 2 Corinthians gets its jagged and uneven character from the emotional and stressful situation in which it was written. It should be clear from the last few pages that I too shall work with this simpler notion. So it is right to outline briefly some reasons for not following the four lines of argument set out above.

1. Certainly chapters 10–13 are angrier and more direct than the early chapters. In these four chapters we see the opponents more clearly and explicitly than we have done earlier. Yet Paul's writing about ministry in the first half of the letter does seem to anticipate and address some of the concerns and challenges that these newcomers to Corinth have raised. Much of what he says in the early chapters makes better sense in the context of his anxiety about the opponents than it would as a simple defense of his own ministry.
2. The section about the collection has quite strong links to chapters on either side. For chapter 7 speaks of Titus coming from Corinth to Macedonia, and in chapter 8 we hear of Titus going back to Corinth. Chapter 9 talks of Paul coming to Corinth too, a little later. Then Paul's visit, and the situation he will find when he comes, is a recurring theme of chapters 10–13.
3. The section from 2:14 to 7:4 is not a detached exposition of Paul's ministry. It speaks particularly about his relationship with the church at Corinth and about his credibility there; we can see this, for example, at 3:1; 4:5, 12; 5:11–13; 6:11–13; 7:2–4. So this section fits quite well in the midst of chapters (1, 2, and 7) that recount Paul's dealings with Corinth and his pastoral love for the Christians there. The shifts at 2:13/14 and 7:4/5 are not abrupt changes of subject; they are adjustments of angle within a connected and coherent discussion.
4. The short section from 6:14 to 7:1 is dense and complex in itself, and it does stand out from the verses on either side—partly because the language is so intensely challenging. Yet it sits within a part of the letter that is full with appeal and exhortation, as Paul urges his readers to repair their relationship with him and with God (5:20; 6:1; 6:13; 7:2). We can certainly make some sense of the warning language of these verses by hearing it within this context.
5. Beyond this, we may note that there is no manuscript evidence for partitioning 2 Corinthians. The manuscripts of the letter that survive from the ancient world show no indication of the fractures outlined above. So the simpler notion, that this is a single letter, will be a working basis for the pages ahead. The credibility of taking this view—apart, of course, from the fact that simple hypotheses have a certain natural credibility—will need to be worked out in the course of the commentary.

Introduction

MAPPING SECOND CORINTHIANS

Here, then, is an outline of the letter, along the lines that we shall explore and explain it:

2 Corinthians 1–7	**Paul's ministry: a call to trust**	
1:1–11	Comfortable words	
	1:1–2	Saluting the saints
	1:3–7	God of comfort
	1:8–11	Pressure and prayers
1:12–2:13	Difficult days	
	1:12–22	Changed plans
	1:23–2:4	"I did not come"
	2:5–13	Moving on
2:14–5:10	Confidence and integrity	
	2:14–3:6	"Sufficient for these things"
	3:7–4:6	Spirit of glory: the face of Jesus Christ
	4:7–5:10	Hope of glory: suffering and renewal
5:11–7:16	Repair and reconciliation	
	5:11–21	God and reconciliation: the cross of Christ
	6:1–7:4	Paul and reconciliation: "open your hearts"
	7:5–16	Corinth and reconciliation: grief and comfort
2 Corinthians 8–9	**Collecting for the saints**	
8–9	A call to contribute	
	8:1–15	Opportunity for giving: as others have given
	8:16–9:5	Occasion for giving: Titus's visit and Paul's
	9:6–15	Objects of giving: sharing and praise
2 Corinthians 10–13	**Challenge to Corinth**	
10–13	A call to discern and decide	
	10:1–18	Facing the critics

11:1–12:13	"A little foolishness"
12:14–13:13	Coming to Corinth

There is less variety in this second letter as a whole than we found in the first. In that earlier letter Paul worked steadily through a series of issues, exploring problems, urging Christians to respond appropriately, then moving on to the next topic. Here, by contrast, most of the chapters revolve around the pains and joys of a pastoral relationship. There are tighter connections of theme across the letter as a whole. Fewer issues are raised, but there is more intensity and depth in the writing. And perhaps for this reason, the letter speaks to deep places in us.

LISTENING TO SECOND CORINTHIANS

Service

Much of Second Corinthians concerns Christian leadership. Anyone who holds responsibility in the church can find wisdom here about the nature of the task and about how we view our work and ourselves. The main point is that strength often comes through weakness. The times that strain us, the difficulties that hurt us, and the situations that threaten to overwhelm us can be gifts from God. At these moments we are most likely to draw close to Christ and to discover more deeply the reality and power of his cross and resurrection. And when we do this, our work will gain and grow.

Humility and vulnerability are part of church leadership. An inflated self-image can be like a screen between us and Christ; it deflects God's grace, and we have no true spiritual resource either to live by or to offer. Too much desire to be resourceful and resilient can deceive and destroy us. If we serve the gospel in any capacity, we need to know that this task is really too great for us and that we are not good enough for it. When we know this, "the life of Jesus" will be seen "in our mortal flesh" (4:11), and we can give of our best, humbly, honestly, and hopefully.

Suffering

Pain and weakness isolate people. When we suffer, we cannot be as active as we used to. Our friendships lose some of their energy, and even our faith can wither if it is not nourished as before. Suffering can be a lonely and arduous place in which to live. Yet 2 Corinthians takes a deeper view:

when Christians suffer, there is more going on than meets the eye. For suffering does not isolate you, is the message—not from God; nor from other Christians, because you need their prayers more than ever; and certainly not from fruitful service. Bruised and burdened people can be healers among us; often they are rich in grace and strength and wisdom; the church should value its hurting saints.

Speech

Some of the language in Second Corinthians is tough and direct. Paul is taking a stand over issues that concern him deeply. He feels the need to speak boldly and frankly, and in doing so, he gives us an insight into his personality and his own fragility. Perhaps there is a message here about the times that we meet difficulty or disagreement in church life.

Straight talking can be important, especially when—as with Paul—we find that people misunderstand us or misjudge our motives. Yet when we talk straight, we take a risk. We disclose ourselves and we open wounds within us, sometimes more fully than we intend. And this can be a difficult situation to handle.

The wisdom of 2 Corinthians is that we need sure spiritual roots if we are to handle situations of conflict and vulnerability well. A deep relationship with Jesus can give us the security and steadiness to respond wisely to criticism, to speak constructively as well as directly, and to transform dispute into reconciliation. It can bring us, in times of stress, closer to the cross. This may be a costly and demanding path to take, but it will enable people to see Christ in us. And it will give us strength, even when we are at our weakest and most perplexed, to bear the demand and to speak with integrity, care, and love.

Spirituality

Spirituality is the mesh of faith and experience—the way that God's reality shapes our living—and 2 Corinthians sets out a spirituality of power and paradox. It speaks about a God made known through crucifixion and resurrection, about grace that shapes us from within rather than crushing and overpowering us, and about new creation welling up from the broken places of human living. It speaks of Christ's cross as the mainspring of Christian experience as well as the hub of Christian doctrine. It offers a vision of a church that embodies the good news it tells.

For God has entered our humanity and shared our frailty. Out of the poverty of the cross, God has given generously (8:9). Through the fear and anger that crucified Jesus, God reshapes the world with love (5:14). From the place of hurt, sin, and death, God has brought a word of reconciliation (5:20–21). And to a church struggling to discover its identity in a fractured world, God invites us to "carry the death of Jesus, that his life too may be made visible in us" (4:10, adapted).

We go forward to explore these themes in the course of this study.

Part 4: Paul's Ministry: A Call to Trust
2 Corinthians 1–7

8. Comfortable Words
2 Corinthians 1:1–11

SALUTING THE SAINTS
2 Corinthians 1:1–2

> 1:1 **Paul, an apostle of Christ Jesus by the will of God, and Timothy our brother,**
> **To the church of God that is in Corinth, including all the saints throughout Achaia:**
> ² **Grace to you and peace from God our Father and the Lord Jesus Christ.**

We have heard most of these opening words already. These lines match the start of 1 Corinthians (1 Cor. 1:1–3) almost exactly, and there is quite a full comment on that earlier passage (see pp. 19–20). At the start of this second letter, only two details are new—the references to "Timothy our brother" and to "the saints throughout Achaia."

Timothy's name appears at the start of Paul's letters to Philippi, Colossae, Thessalonica, and Philemon, as well as here. On this count he is Paul's most constant companion and coworker. They first met in Lystra in central Turkey. Timothy's mother was a Christian and Paul recruited the young man to help in his mission work (Acts 16:1–3). Before long their journeys led to Corinth (Acts 18:5). So the Corinthians knew Timothy, and Paul was able to use him as an envoy and deputy there (1 Cor. 4:17; 16:10).

By the time of 2 Corinthians, a year or two after the first epistle, Timothy and Paul are together, and their names are bracketed at the head of the letter. Yet this is not really a joint composition. Paul slips quickly and often into the first-person singular (1:13, 19, 23). Indeed even when he reverts to "we" (2:14; 3:1; 4:1), he often seems to be speaking particularly about himself. Timothy may be acting as scribe, but the intense mental energy in the writing is Paul's. Paul was the one who brought the gospel to Corinth (Acts 18:1–4; 1 Cor. 2:1), he is the one who has fallen out with the church there, and he is the one whose relationship with them needs to be restored.

The Roman province of Achaia covered the southern half of Greece. So as in 1 Corinthians (1:2), Paul's opening words remind the church at Corinth that they belong to a larger fellowship. Indeed as the chief city in Achaia they have some duty to model and sustain wholesome and healthy church life for the sake of others.

GOD OF COMFORT
2 Corinthians 1:3–7

> 1:3 **Blessed be the God and Father of our Lord Jesus Christ, the Father of mercies and the God of all consolation,** [4] **who consoles us in all our affliction, so that we may be able to console those who are in any affliction with the consolation with which we ourselves are consoled by God.** [5] **For just as the sufferings of Christ are abundant for us, so also our consolation is abundant through Christ.** [6] **If we are being afflicted, it is for your consolation and salvation; if we are being consoled, it is for your consolation, which you experience when you patiently endure the same sufferings that we are also suffering.** [7] **Our hope for you is unshaken; for we know that as you share in our sufferings, so also you share in our consolation.**

The start of 1 Corinthians includes a thanksgiving prayer for the church (1:4–9). In this second letter the opening prayer has a rather different emphasis: Paul gives praise for all that he himself has learned in his walk with God. The verses are thick with repetition. We can hardly miss the point: in the midst of "affliction" (1:4, 6, 8) and "suffering" (1:5, 6, 7), we have a "God of all consolation" (1:3).

This word "console" or "consolation" appears ten times in five verses. It is the same word that John's Gospel uses for the Holy Spirit—"the Comforter," according to the King James Bible (John 15:26). Here, as in John, it speaks of God's wise and steady presence, offering support and confidence in times of adversity. The language recalls the resonant words of Isaiah, "Comfort, O comfort my people" (40:1), which point on to God's sure and tender company (40:9–11) and to strength in times of strain (40:27–31).

These few verses set the tone for almost everything that follows in the letter. Paul has learned that the Christian road can be arduous and painful. There is an overflow from "the sufferings of Christ" (1:5) into the lives of

Christ's people. Now Paul wants the Corinthians to reckon with this too and to realize that God can enter the hard and hurtful places of their living.

For comfort is God's nature (1:3). Comfort comes in Jesus, who spreads his peace as surely as we share his pain (1:5). And comfort is given to pass on (1:4, 6). Those who receive God's consoling love have a gift to offer to others in trouble. People who have discovered God's care can often enter deeply and sensitively into the sorrows of friends. They know what to say and when to be silent. They understand how to support and how much of the experience they can share.

It can be tough to trust in Christ's good news when you are dealing with trouble in your own life. Yet we all meet times of distress, and all Christians are called to represent Jesus to the people around us. How can we be signs of good news in bad times? Paul's answer—learned the hard way—is that suffering is not a barrier to Christian service (1:6). Indeed we may reveal Christ more truly to others when we have known him in our hardships. Paul goes on to tell how this became real in his life.

PRESSURE AND PRAYERS
2 Corinthians 1:8-11

> 1:8 **We do not want you to be unaware, brothers and sisters, of the affliction we experienced in Asia; for we were so utterly, unbearably crushed that we despaired of life itself.** [9] **Indeed, we felt that we had received the sentence of death so that we would rely not on ourselves but on God who raises the dead.** [10] **He who rescued us from so deadly a peril will continue to rescue us; on him we have set our hope that he will rescue us again,** [11] **as you also join in helping us by your prayers, so that many will give thanks on our behalf for the blessing granted us through the prayers of many.**

There must have been a real trauma in Asia. Paul spent a long time in the province, mainly in the city of Ephesus (Acts 19:10), and something that happened there brought him right to the limit of his own resources (1:8). We do not know what it was. Paul says cryptically that he "fought with wild animals at Ephesus" (1 Cor. 15:32), and Acts tells of a riot there. But even language like "wild animals" and "sentence of death" (2 Cor. 1:9) may not be meant literally; and Paul himself was not caught up in the worst of the rioting (Acts 19:30–31). So the event is a mystery. Yet the reason he mentions it is clear.

For this episode in Asia had given Paul new insight into the cross and resurrection of Christ. He felt he was taken from the realm of death and brought back to life. He had been drawn, in a deeper and more intimate way than before, into the death and risen life of Jesus. From now on he would look to God with new confidence and courage (1:9–10). More than this, he would depend more consciously and gratefully on the prayers of friends (1:11).

For Paul believed that prayer, like comfort, is meant to be infectious. Praying is not for yourself alone, but it regularly draws you more fully into the life of God and of your neighbor. So when we pray for other people, we share in the troubles and trials of their living. And when others are blessed, our prayer comes back to us and rises again to God in thanks and praise. Three times in this letter Paul speaks of giving thanks to God: when prayer for friends is answered (1:11); when the grace of the gospel reaches new places and people (4:15); and when Christians share financially with one another (9:12). Worship, the surest sign of the church's love for God, rises when Christians offer loving service—as we support one another in trouble, as we speak and share the good news, and as we meet needs with our gifts.

9. Difficult Days
2 Corinthians 1:12–2:13

CHANGED PLANS
2 Corinthians 1:12–22

These verses look back at a journey Paul never made. The big project in this phase of his ministry was collecting money from Gentile churches to take to Jerusalem. So in 1 Corinthians he reminds the church to start saving (16:1–4) and tells them about his travel plans (16:5–7). He would visit his churches around the Aegean Sea—both to gather the collection and as a kind of pastoral farewell—first going north from Ephesus into Macedonia and then southward to Corinth. But after writing 1 Corinthians, he changed this plan.

The reason was that a problem cropped up in Corinth, and Paul traveled swiftly from Ephesus to try to sort it out. But the problem could not be settled quickly, and once he got back to Ephesus, he decided he ought to visit Corinth again as soon as possible. So he altered the plan for his main journey to allow two further stops in Corinth. He would sail west from Ephesus to Corinth, go north from there to Macedonia, and come south to Corinth again afterward (1:16). But before making this journey, he changed his mind again and reverted to the original route, canceling one projected visit to Corinth (1:23; 2:1) and going to Macedonia first.

As he now writes this letter from Macedonia, he realizes that questions have been raised in Corinth about his integrity and goodwill. Christians in the city who liked him would be disappointed that he had postponed a planned visit; any who resented him would find a new reason to complain. So in this letter Paul has some repair work to do. He must defend his character and his care for the Corinthian church, and this he does in the present section. Then the verses that follow (1:23–2:4) explain his handling of his travel plans and the journey never made.

With Candor and Clarity
2 Corinthians 1:12-14

> 1:12 **Indeed, this is our boast, the testimony of our conscience: we have behaved in the world with frankness and godly sincerity, not by earthly wisdom but by the grace of God—and all the more toward you.** [13] **For we write you nothing other than what you can read and also understand; I hope you will understand until the end—** [14] **as you have already understood us in part— that on the day of the Lord Jesus we are your boast even as you are our boast.**

This short paragraph points in two directions. Its immediate focus in the letter is to defend Paul's oscillating journey plans. He knows that his decisions have upset people in Corinth, but he is keen to assure them of his good intentions. He has tried to be honest and caring, and he wants the church to trust his goodwill when they reflect on the rather confusing course of events.

Yet these verses surely have a broader intention too. They set the tone for the letter as a whole by presenting Paul as a credible leader and pastor. In all the issues that he will discuss in the chapters ahead—ministry, money, mission—he wants the Corinthians to recognize his "frankness and godly sincerity" (1:12). He wants them to trust what he writes (1:13) and to rejoice in him as he rejoices in them (1:14).

The "day of the Lord Jesus" (1:14) means the Parousia, the second coming of Christ. For Paul this was a bright hope, and he looked forward to it keenly and confidently. When Christ gathered the faithful, all of Paul's labor and love as a missionary would be worthwhile. Pastor and people could be proud of one another, with a gladness that would never end. In his letters he often looks forward to meeting his friends in heaven, and rejoicing in all that God has done in them.

Sealed and Certain
2 Corinthians 1:15-22

> 1:15 **Since I was sure of this, I wanted to come to you first, so that you might have a double favor;** [16] **I wanted to visit you on my way to Macedonia, and to come back to you from Macedonia and have you send me on to Judea.** [17] **Was I vacillating when I wanted to do this? Do I make my plans according to ordinary human standards, ready to say "Yes, yes" and "No, no" at the same time?** [18] **As surely as God is faithful, our word to you has not been "Yes and No."** [19] **For the Son of God, Jesus Christ, whom we proclaimed among you, Silvanus and Timothy and I, was not "Yes and No"; but in him it is always "Yes."** [20] **For in him every one of God's promises is a "Yes." For this reason it is through him that we say the "Amen," to the glory of God.** [21] **But**

> it is God who establishes us with you in Christ and has anointed us, ²² by putting his seal on us and giving us his Spirit in our hearts as a first installment.

Paul was accused of being careless and inconsistent when he changed his travel plans. Now he replies to the charge. "Was I vacillating?" he asks. Was he being indecisive or fickle? Did he act in a selfish and ungodly way, promising two different things at the same time (1:17)? People in Corinth surely thought so. So here he justifies himself, first by looking to God and saying, in effect, "God is not inconsistent" (1:18–22). Only when he has made this point well will he be ready to review his own actions (from 1:23).

Paul always aimed, he says, to be faithful in his words and actions. He did so because God is faithful (1:18). So he centered his preaching on Jesus, who has shown God's faithfulness to the world. With Jesus there is no indecision or disappointment. All the hopes of Scripture are fulfilled in him (1:19–20), and this is the basis of Paul's contact and relationship with Corinth. God holds pastor and people together "in Christ" (1:21). Faithfulness, as lived out by Jesus, has given the church its identity. Paul has every reason and motive to deal honestly and truly.

More than this, God dwells in and with his people, in the person of the Holy Spirit, who both testifies to God's faithfulness and good purpose and directs and guides the life of the church. Paul uses three images to describe what the Spirit does.

- "Anointing" (1:21) means enabling Christians to share the life of the great Anointed One, Jesus Christ.
- A "seal" (1:22) is a mark of ownership; the Spirit labels us as God's people (as in Eph. 1:13).
- The Spirit is "a first installment" (1:22) of greater salvation ahead, a foretaste and guarantee of "the day of the Lord" (1:14).

So the very presence of God shapes our life as Christian people. These gifts assure us that God is trustworthy and true and commit us too to faithful speech and action, both with one another and in the wider life of the world.

"I DID NOT COME"
2 Corinthians 1:23–2:4

> 1:23 But I call on God as witness against me: it was to spare you that I did not come again to Corinth. ²⁴ I do not mean to imply that we lord it over

> your faith; rather, we are workers with you for your joy, because you stand firm in the faith. 2:1 So I made up my mind not to make you another painful visit. ² For if I cause you pain, who is there to make me glad but the one whom I have pained? ³ And I wrote as I did, so that when I came, I might not suffer pain from those who should have made me rejoice; for I am confident about all of you, that my joy would be the joy of all of you. ⁴ For I wrote you out of much distress and anguish of heart and with many tears, not to cause you pain, but to let you know the abundant love that I have for you.

Paul has made strong claims about his consistency and care in the verses above. Now he must show how these ideals have worked out in practice in his decisions and actions. It was out of compassion, he says, that he canceled his planned journey to Corinth (1:23). Deciding not to visit was meant as a constructive and helpful gesture.

Clearly Paul's earlier problem-solving visit to Corinth had not been easy. It may have been one step toward resolving the difficulty (as we see in a few verses' time), but it had also been "painful" (2:1). Indeed one of the church members was at the hub of the dispute, and both he and Paul had been left sore and hurt by the encounter (2:2, 5). A cooling-off period was needed. If Paul came back too quickly, the memories and misunderstandings would still be fresh. Others, such as Titus and indeed some of the Corinthians themselves, would have a more constructive role to play in the meantime.

So Paul had written, instead of coming to Corinth. Even though he would not visit for a while, he wanted the Corinthians to know that he loved them (2:4), steadily and surely amid all of his changing plans. He hoped too that his letter would help to correct and improve the situation in Corinth, so that when he eventually did visit, relationships would be warmer and easier (2:3). Yet even writing had brought him to tears (2:4), and it is quite likely that this sorrowful letter is entirely lost to us. The Corinthians did act on his advice (see comments on 2:5–9), but they might not have wished to keep the letter, once the immediate problem had passed.

I am moved by Paul's intensity over all of this. His concern for his churches stayed alive and active, even in spells of long separation. A pastor who talks of writing "with tears" and "abundant love" (2:4), of "pressure" and "anxiety" (11:28), and of constant and joyful prayer (Phil. 1:4) is investing a lot of himself in the lives and well-being of his friends. True pastoral care is constant and costly. Today, when we are rightly concerned for balance rather than burnout in pastoral ministry, let us recognize what we ask of those who lead our churches and honor and enable the giving of it.

MOVING ON
2 Corinthians 2:5–13

> 2:5 **But if anyone has caused pain, he has caused it not to me, but to some extent—not to exaggerate it—to all of you.** [6] **This punishment by the majority is enough for such a person;** [7] **so now instead you should forgive and console him, so that he may not be overwhelmed by excessive sorrow.** [8] **So I urge you to reaffirm your love for him.** [9] **I wrote for this reason: to test you and to know whether you are obedient in everything.** [10] **Anyone whom you forgive, I also forgive. What I have forgiven, if I have forgiven anything, has been for your sake in the presence of Christ.** [11] **And we do this so that we may not be outwitted by Satan; for we are not ignorant of his designs.**
>
> [12] **When I came to Troas to proclaim the good news of Christ, a door was opened for me in the Lord;** [13] **but my mind could not rest because I did not find my brother Titus there. So I said farewell to them and went on to Macedonia.**

In these verses we see more clearly what the problem in Corinth had been. An individual church member had behaved in a way that Paul thought very wrong. What exactly this man had done we do not know, and any attempt to match this trouble to issues in 1 Corinthians can only be guesswork. Yet this offense was surely the focus of Paul's difficult visit, and Paul had left Corinth with the problem still festering. He then sent the so-called "tearful letter" to the church as a whole, urging them to take this concern in hand and bring the offender into line (2:9).

Evidently the church did take some decisive steps (2:6), which seem to have met their aim. Now, says Paul, it is time to turn from discipline to forgiveness. Let the Corinthians "forgive and console" this man (2:7)—"consolation," of course, was the main theme of Paul's opening prayer (1:3–7)—and Paul will forgive him too. This will help the church, it will reflect the presence and love of Christ (2:10), and it will prevent evil and dispute from marring and miring the life of the fellowship (2:11).

"Move on" is then the message of these verses. Progress has been made. It is time to heal, to leave the problem in the past, and to grow in love. And Paul too is on the move (2:12–13). His journey from Ephesus brought him north to the town of Troas, but he could not linger there; he was impatient to hear from Titus. So he crossed into Macedonia and found his own "consolation" when Titus arrived with news of Corinth and of all that had been done to mend the situation there (7:6–7).

So for the moment the letter itself moves to a new theme. Paul pauses his account of travel and pastoral difficulty. Later, in chapter 7, he will return for a while to the difficult memories we have explored here in chapter 2—not to keep the wound open but to forge his own reconciliation with the Corinthians and to establish the firmest possible basis for another visit.

In the meantime, however, he starts to think more broadly about his ministry and about what it means to serve Jesus. Indeed Christian service itself is like being on the move, in the triumphal procession of Christ (2:14).

So now we approach a new section of the letter. Up to this point Paul has been telling a story, recalling his dealings with the Corinthians and explaining his own actions and plans (1:15–2:13). And this sequence will resume later (at 7:5). But from 2:14 onwards it breaks for a while. For in telling the story of his work, Paul has begun to reflect on his role as a minister of Christ's good news, on the values that he holds, and the standards for which he aims. So the next few chapters explore the nature of Christian ministry.

Yet this long detour will have a strategy and purpose. For even though the theme of the writing is quite general, Corinth never vanishes from view. "You," he says; "your slaves"; "for your sake" (3:2; 4:5, 15). And eventually Corinth will come more directly into focus, as Paul appeals to the church to recognize and welcome his leadership and love (5:12; 6:1–2, 11–13; 7:2–4). He wants the Corinthians to know they can trust him. His message, his conduct, his pastoral relationships, and his care are all of a piece. So they can rely on him and believe what he preaches. He represents Jesus, he will claim, not only in word but also by the way he lives.

10. Confidence and Integrity
2 Corinthians 2:14–5:10

"SUFFICIENT FOR THESE THINGS"
2 Corinthians 2:14–3:6

As Paul turns to reflect on his ministry, he starts by giving thanks to God (2:14). This is one of many thanksgiving prayers in his letters. But usually these appear at the very start (as in 1:3–7). It is less common for the note of thanks to resume, as it does here, part way through a letter. But whether at the start of a letter or in the midst of it, these prayers regularly offer a preview of themes that will come up in the chapters ahead. The ideas and issues that Paul has in his mind, the things he means to write about, become part of the praise that he offers. He shares with God the concerns that he carries for his friends and his work.

So as Paul turns here to thanksgiving, he mentions three concerns that will crop up often in the coming portion of the letter. Together they take us to the heart of his view of Christian ministry. Confidence in God is the first theme (2:14). It will appear several times in the chapters ahead—in 3:4; 4:14 and 5:6, for example. The second is Paul's profound sense of the paradox and power of the gospel (2:15–16). The good news always has a double edge—life and death, salvation and judgment, triumph and suffering, crucifixion and resurrection. This issue returns at 4:7–12 and 6:8–10. And the third concern is integrity (2:17)—the standard of uprightness, of honesty, and of clear speech that the gospel demands. We shall hear of this again at 4:2, 5:1, and 6:3. So as these three issues—confidence, paradox, and integrity—shape Paul's thanksgiving, he focuses them in three compact but rich illustrations.

Images of the Gospel
2 Corinthians 2:14–17

> 2:14 **But thanks be to God, who in Christ always leads us in triumphal procession, and through us spreads in every place the fragrance that comes**

> from knowing him. ¹⁵ **For we are the aroma of Christ to God among those who are being saved and among those who are perishing;** ¹⁶ **to the one a fragrance from death to death, to the other a fragrance from life to life. Who is sufficient for these things?** ¹⁷ **For we are not peddlers of God's word like so many; but in Christ we speak as persons of sincerity, as persons sent from God and standing in his presence.**

The first picture is a Roman triumph—a sort of ancient version of a ticker tape parade (2:14). When a general came home from winning a battle, he would ride into town with his armies, laden with the spoils of war. Crowds would roar with praise and delight. But in the procession would also be a sorry company of prisoners, captives of the fighting, a broken remnant of the enemy forces. For them there was no celebration. They were brought along under duress to be humiliated and put to death.

We may ask why Paul uses this image to describe his ministry. Some suggest that his line of thought is upbeat and assertive: he thinks of himself as a soldier beside his commander, an apostle of the victorious Lord, riding in power with Christ and sharing his glory. But perhaps this is too easy a reading of the text. It may be truer to Paul to explore a more complex sort of confidence and to think instead of the harsher and more painful aspects of a triumph. For in these Corinthian letters Paul speaks often of the prospect and presence of death (1 Cor. 4:9; 2 Cor. 1:9; 4:11; 6:9). His life as an apostle is filled with setbacks and threats. Often he feels like a dying man, a captive caught up in the cause of Christ.

Throughout these letters to Corinth, we find this strange counterpoint in Paul's ministry. His whole existence as a messenger of Christ is a constant paradox. Even when death is near, his journeys are a kind of victory parade. He travels from place to place, proclaiming the triumph of the resurrection. He shows the world that Jesus is Lord by the pains and pressures of his own suffering and service (1 Cor. 15:31; 2 Cor. 4:10–11). Like a Roman triumphal procession, the work of the gospel carries an odor both of death and of life (2:15–16).

So the second illustration in these verses is of fragrance. The image is used in other Jewish writing too, and some of these texts may shed light on Paul's use of the idea. For example, we read of faithful sacrifice rising to God with a pungent sweetness (Gen. 8:21). Does Paul, then, think of his own life and service as a kind of bittersweet sacrifice? Another text speaks of wisdom as a penetrating aroma—wholesome, pleasant, and holy (Sir. 24:20–21). So as Paul thought of the gospel as God's wisdom (1 Cor. 1:21)—attractive to some, folly to others—the idea of wisdom that divides may be in his mind again here, as an odor that brings both death and life. Indeed some Jewish rabbis talked of God's law as a powerful drug, bringing healing in lives that obey but potentially toxic to any who do not. So for Paul too the gospel carried different effects according to the response of those who heard it. The paradox of this good news, of strength and love embodied in the weakness and pain of the cross, would always polarize and divide. Many would be drawn into life; others would turn away in contempt and disgust. To preach such a gospel requires resolution. The preacher must be committed to the task and to the consistent integrity it demands.

So the third image is that of "peddling God's word" (2:17). The term implies dishonest trading, selling shoddy goods as quality material—a bartender who waters down the wine, a philosopher who teaches for gain and reputation rather than for the sake of truth. Paul's own ideal is very different: purity, honesty, and candor. He takes God seriously and has to be serious about his own standards too.

Finally, amid the images we overhear a hint of an Old Testament text and the start of a scriptural reflection that will run all through chapter 3. The question of "sufficiency" matches the thought and language of Exodus 4:10—particularly in the Greek Old Testament, which Paul knew. So Paul's question—"Who is sufficient for these things?" (2:16)—recalls the excuses and protests Moses offered when God called him to lead Israel (Exod. 3 and 4). It suggests that Paul sees Moses as a role model, and it points forward to his discussion of Moses' ministry as precedent and pattern for his own (3:7–18). As an overture to this longer reflection, Paul speaks next of his work as a kind of writing, yet very different from the written law that Moses brought.

Living Letters
2 Corinthians 3:1–3

> 3:1 **Are we beginning to commend ourselves again? Surely we do not need, as some do, letters of recommendation to you or from you, do we?** ² **You yourselves are our letter, written on our hearts, to be known and read by all;** ³ **and you show that you are a letter of Christ, prepared by us, written not with ink but with the Spirit of the living God, not on tablets of stone but on tablets of human hearts.**

After the claims of the last few verses, Paul pauses for a word of explanation. He has not been, he says, introducing himself as if he were a newcomer to Corinth. The Christians there know him well. Nor does he need anyone to write him a reference (3:1).

Letters of commendation were common in the ancient world. You might write to help a friend make contacts in a new place—in business, for example, or in connection with education or religion. Indeed Paul himself writes on occasion to commend fellow workers to distant churches (Rom. 16:1–2; 2 Cor. 8:16–24). But he does not need this at Corinth. The Christians there know his work. Their lives carry a message from Christ, for which Paul has been the scribe (3:2–3). It is not a message carved on stones, like the law Moses brought down Mount Sinai (Exod. 34:29) but is scripted and brought to life by the Holy Spirit within their hearts.

This contrast between letter and Spirit, and between old covenant and new, will shape the whole chapter ahead. Yet we should not think that Paul wanted to belittle the work of Moses. He valued highly what Moses achieved. He believed, however, that he was living in a different era. God's purposes had moved forward to a new stage. The Spirit had been released into the world, and God's presence could now be known more closely and intimately than before. It is this frame of understanding—of eschatology working itself out in time, of God's work moving from one phase to another, of an era of promise turning into one of fulfillment—which will help us to understand this third chapter of the letter.

Resources and Sufficiency
2 Corinthians 3:4–6

> **3:4 Such is the confidence that we have through Christ toward God. ⁵ Not that we are competent of ourselves to claim anything as coming from us; our competence is from God, ⁶ who has made us competent to be ministers of a new covenant, not of letter but of spirit; for the letter kills, but the Spirit gives life.**

Paul writes confidently. He is aware of the Spirit stirring around and through him. Many times in this chapter he describes the Spirit as the vital ingredient in Christian ministry, bringing a new kind of life (3:6) and a new weight of glory (3:8). For although he calls on Moses as a model for his work, he senses that he serves in an era of new opportunity and revelation, when a fuller experience of God's grace and goodness can be known. So these verses answer the question, "Who is sufficient for these things?" (2:16) with a firm and resonant "Our sufficiency is from God" (3:5). (Although the NRSV reads "competence" in 3:5, the same Greek word is used in both verses.)

Indeed this whole section of the letter rejoices in the resources God gives for the Christian to possess in Christ. Like a chorus line almost every paragraph begins with the words "We have:" "we have confidence" (3:4); "we have hope" (3:12); "we have this ministry" (4:1, literally translated); "we have treasure" (4:7); "we have faith" (4:13); "we have an eternal home" (5:1). With all these rich possessions Paul pursues his service for Christ. He is an agent and messenger of a "new covenant" (3:6), and he goes on now to write of the "glory" that he has discovered in it.

SPIRIT OF GLORY: THE FACE OF JESUS CHRIST
2 Corinthians 3:7–4:6

The background to the remainder of this third chapter is an episode in the book of Exodus (34:29–35). As Moses came down the mountain with the tablets of Israel's law, his face gleamed and shone with the glory of God. The people were afraid, and he had to veil his face as he went to and fro among them. But when he went in to meet with God, he would take the veil off. So there are three stages in the story, and Paul reflects on these in sequence: the shining (3:7–11), the veiling (3:12–15), and the removal of the veil (3:16–18).

Glory after Glory
2 Corinthians 3:7–11

> 3:7 **Now if the ministry of death, chiseled in letters on stone tablets, came in glory so that the people of Israel could not gaze at Moses' face because of the glory of his face, a glory now set aside, ⁸ how much more will the ministry of the Spirit come in glory? ⁹ For if there was glory in the ministry of condemnation, much more does the ministry of justification abound in glory! ¹⁰ Indeed, what once had glory has lost its glory because of the greater glory; ¹¹ for if what was set aside came through glory, much more has the permanent come in glory!**

The big idea in these verses is "glory." The word repeats eleven times in one short paragraph. Paul is drawing on the first stage of the Exodus episode, with its account of Moses' shining face. The main point he wants to make is that the gospel gives a larger and clearer vision of God than Moses had given. There was "glory" in the old (3:7); there is "greater glory" in the new (3:8–11). This connects quite well with the way that Paul has just turned to Moses as a model for his work (2:16; 3:5–6). So as he talks here about Moses, his point is not that Moses' ministry was wrong or bad but that this ministry has now been surpassed. The good news of Jesus is "Mosaic," because it carries and makes known God's glory. It fulfills the ancient tradition, but it does so in an even brighter way than Moses did.

Paul makes this point by exploring the theme of "new covenant" (3:6). This is an Old Testament idea that comes originally from the prophet Jeremiah (31:31–34). It speaks of a new relationship between God and the people, rooted firmly in Israel's covenant tradition but refreshing this for a new day and in a new way. Jesus took up the thought at his Last Supper (Luke 22:20), and the theme is also important in Hebrews, as well as in this chapter. Paul contrasts the old and the new in several respects. All of these contrasts reflect, in various ways, the idea of eschatology: a new era brings new possibilities. All of them are explored more fully in other letters than they are here.

So Paul speaks of the animating energy of the Holy Spirit, which the ancient legal code had not been able to make available (3:6; Gal. 3:13–14). He rejoices that through the Spirit, the law's promise of life has been realized, in ways that it never was before (3:6–7; Rom. 8:2–4). He talks of "justification"—a secure bond between humanity and God—in contrast to the severe voice of legal judgment (3:9; Rom. 3:20, 24). And, most significantly, he talks of permanence (3:11). The old covenant was never meant to last. Like Moses' face, it glowed in its own time, but when Christ came its work was done (Gal. 3:19). So it was "set aside" (3:7, 11), like an actor whose part is played, to usher in a fresh era in God's work.

For all these reasons, Paul could speak here of the new splendor that is in Christ. He did not despise the old, and he valued highly all that he knew of Moses. But he also believed that Moses' ministry was a signpost to something better. The "ministry of the Spirit" (3:8) had brought a "greater glory" (3:10) into view—brighter than even the light of Moses' face. In the paragraphs ahead, the thought of this "glory" will inform Paul's writing at several points (3:18; 4:4, 6, 15, 17). The next few verses explore the ways in which he believed this glory could be seen and known.

Veil and Vision
2 Corinthians 3:12–18

> 3:12 **Since, then, we have such a hope, we act with great boldness,** [13] **not like Moses, who put a veil over his face to keep the people of Israel from gazing at the end of the glory that was being set aside.** [14] **But their minds were hardened. Indeed, to this very day, when they hear the reading of the**

old covenant, that same veil is still there, since only in Christ is it set aside. [15] **Indeed, to this very day whenever Moses is read, a veil lies over their minds;** [16] **but when one turns to the Lord, the veil is removed.** [17] **Now the Lord is the Spirit, and where the Spirit of the Lord is, there is freedom.** [18] **And all of us, with unveiled faces, seeing the glory of the Lord as though reflected in a mirror, are being transformed into the same image from one degree of glory to another; for this comes from the Lord, the Spirit.**

This paragraph takes up the second and third movements in the Exodus episode—Moses' wearing of a veil (used in 3:12–15) and his removing it when he turned to face God (3:16–18). So Paul starts by speaking of "hope" (3:12)—a word that emphasizes the movement of God's purposes through time from promise to fulfillment. Which is exactly the way Paul looked on his own era, as a moment that fulfilled and made real the potential of the Old Testament.

So Paul was keen to speak "with boldness" (3:12)—to be frank, candid, open, and direct—about Jesus. And this theme will run on into the next chapter, where he talks about his methods in ministry (4:2–5). But first he contrasts boldness with veiling: the open message of the gospel is the opposite of using any sort of barrier or shield. Yet the "glory" of the old covenant had been hidden by "a veil," so that the Israelites could not see it directly (3:13). And in a strange and sad way, Paul suggests, a barrier still exists. There is a kind of obscurity over the Old Testament, which can only be dispelled when a person turns to Jesus Christ (3:14). So most of his fellow Jews, Paul believed, had read the message but had missed its meaning (3:15). They had encountered the promise but not the Messiah who fulfills it—as if a veil were over their minds.

So, says Paul, just as Moses took off his veil when he met with God, it is when a person "turns to the Lord" (3:16) that the veil of misunderstanding can fall aside. And "the Lord" now means the Holy Spirit (3:17). So when Paul writes of turning "to the Lord," he thinks of the Holy Spirit giving a person fresh clarity of vision. The Spirit makes it possible to recognize God's true glory. Now nothing gets in the way, and those who belong to the Spirit will be renewed by what they see. They will be transformed by God's presence, as Moses was, and changed "into the same image" (3:18)— the image of God that is in Jesus. God will do a work of new creation in them. They will become, in a gradual but genuine way, copies of Christ.

As we leave this chapter, it is clear that the Moses story has given Paul a strong and sustained basis for his argument. But we do not know why he chose to use it so heavily—much more fully than he does in any other letter. One suggestion is that his opponents, the newcomers in Corinth, looked to Moses as a role model; so Paul decided to meet them on their own territory, to draw attention to the power of the gospel. They may have cast themselves as visionaries and talked of their profound spiritual life. If so, Paul may be saying, in effect, that the gospel gives a clearer sight of God than any other sort of experience (3:17).

It is also possible that Moses' story, with its gleaming light and bright vision, reminded Paul of his meeting with Christ at Damascus and that this led him to reflect on the light that is in Jesus. Yet he is keen to stress that the experience of the Spirit is for "all of us" (3:18). If he is thinking of his Damascus encounter, he sees this as a taste and a symbol of a much wider work of God. The chance to know God more truly and be changed into the likeness of Jesus is not for a few visionary Christians alone. It is for everyone who believes. Paul saw the gospel as not only a word to believe but as a lively relationship with God, kindled by the Holy Spirit and leading the Christian steadily forward in renewal, growth, and "glory."

So as Paul speaks of "all of us . . . being transformed" (3:18), he is ready to write again about his own ministry and about God's creative power working in and through him.

Face of Christ
2 Corinthians 4:1–6

> 4:1 **Therefore, since it is by God's mercy that we are engaged in this ministry, we do not lose heart.** ² **We have renounced the shameful things that one hides; we refuse to practice cunning or to falsify God's word; but by the open statement of the truth we commend ourselves to the conscience of everyone in the sight of God.** ³ **And even if our gospel is veiled, it is veiled to those who are perishing.** ⁴ **In their case the god of this world has blinded the minds of the unbelievers, to keep them from seeing the light of the gospel of the glory of Christ, who is the image of God.** ⁵ **For we do not proclaim ourselves; we proclaim Jesus Christ as Lord and ourselves as your slaves for Jesus' sake.** ⁶ **For it is the God who said, "Let light shine out of darkness," who has shone in our hearts to give the light of the knowledge of the glory of God in the face of Jesus Christ.**

Paul describes his service for Christ and the church as "ministry" (4:1). The Greek word is *diakonia*, and at root it means "being an intermediary" or "helping one person to deal with another." So it came to have quite a broad range of association, and two of its aspects are worth exploring here.

Firstly, *diakonia* can refer to domestic duty, such as serving at table. Think of waiters at a dinner, acting as intermediaries, moving to and fro between kitchen and dining hall. In that setting *diakonia* suggests humble and patient service, and some passages in the New Testament reflect this aspect of the word. True *diakonia* cares neither for status nor reward but focuses on the needs and well-being of others. Church work is not meant to be a platform for ego or pride but is a lowly gift to God and God's people.

Yet *diakonia* can also describe roles of great responsibility—acting as a trusted envoy or passing on an important message. And Christian ministry is representative work of this kind. The preacher speaks for God. As messenger and agent of the gospel, Paul saw himself as a bridge between his Lord and his hearers. He was an intermediary: *diakonia* of this sort is a high and holy privilege.

So both aspects of this word contribute to Paul's view of his task. It is highly responsible work, requiring trust, integrity, and care. The preacher is "ambassador for Christ" (5:20), writing "a letter of Christ . . . on tablets of human hearts" (3:3). Such work is not to be done carelessly. Yet ministry is lowly duty too, offering little by way of social prominence or prestige. Paul calls himself a "slave" (4:5). He writes of carrying the cross (4:10). His work of *diakonia* was always double-edged—honorable and dignified, also humble and demeaning. Yet this is how God effects the "ministry of the new covenant" and "of the Spirit" (3:6, 8). This is the reason Paul "does not lose heart" (4:1). The task is tough, but the end product is lives renewed in Christ. The next verses discuss three aspects of practical Christian ministry: candor (4:2), opposition (4:3–4), and God (4:5–6).

First, as Paul has already said (2:17), ministry demands candor, clarity, and commitment to truth (4:2). The preacher ought to be open and direct in both manner and matter. The gospel deserves honesty. It would be shallow and shoddy practice to adjust the good news to the hearers' preference and pleasure.

Frankness, of course, can produce very mixed reactions, and opposition may well be among these. As with Jesus, so with his messengers: the seed is widely sown, but the soil is patchy (Matt. 13:3–9). Some people delight in the gospel; others despise it. And behind this Paul sees a spiritual battle, as "the god of this world" (4:3–4) puts a veil across human minds to prevent people seeing the light of Christ. He is thinking here of the figure Jesus called "ruler of this world" (John 12:31; 14:30; 16:11), also known as the devil or the evil one.

Yet Paul was aware of another and greater spiritual power at work, in and alongside the preaching of the gospel. For when the preacher tells of "Jesus Christ as Lord" (4:5), God gets involved. And as God works, the power that gave the world its first morning—"Let there be light" (Gen. 1:3)—shines again in the human heart to bring fresh hope and dawn into that person's life (4:6). "If anyone is in Christ, there is a new creation" (5:17). God is known, in "the face of Jesus Christ" (4:6). The preacher has not been working alone. The gospel enables people to encounter Jesus. And with Jesus there is no veiling of the face but a clear sight of God's glory.

For this reason above all—his confidence that God was working with him and through him—Paul would "not lose heart" (4:1). He had learned, however, that glory and suffering go together in Christian service. The "face of Christ" (4:6) carries the light of Easter but also the memories and marks of Good Friday. So the verses ahead will reflect graphically and deeply upon the costly task of living by that message and of representing Jesus in the world.

HOPE OF GLORY: SUFFERING AND RENEWAL
2 Corinthians 4:7–5:10

Treasure in Clay Jars
2 Corinthians 4:7–12

> 4:7 But we have this treasure in clay jars, so that it may be made clear that this extraordinary power belongs to God and does not come from us. [8] We are afflicted in every way, but not crushed; perplexed, but not driven to despair; [9] persecuted, but not forsaken; struck down, but not destroyed; [10] always carrying in the body the death of Jesus, so that the life of Jesus may also be made visible in our bodies. [11] For while we live, we are always being given up to death for Jesus' sake, so that the life of Jesus may be made visible in our mortal flesh. [12] So death is at work in us, but life in you.

This is one of Paul's best known pieces of writing, and it has resonated with many Christians across the ages. For we know ourselves to be vulnerable and mortal; we are made from the "dust of the ground" (Gen. 2:7); we get damaged; and we carry the wounds. Yet we often see in sisters and brothers around us the treasure that is Christ. Sometimes it is especially in hurting and humble people that the light of his presence seems to radiate most strongly, bringing life and hope to both friend and stranger. Those who carry Christ's cross also reveal his resurrection.

The paragraph starts, like so many in this part of the letter (3:4, 12; 4:13; 5:1), with the strong assurance, "we have." The treasure that is the "light of... the glory of God" (4:6) is one of the rich resources for Christian living. Yet God chooses to store this in the "clay jars" of fragile humanity. So any strength or splendor that others find in the good news, they will credit to God, not to the messenger (4:7). The power comes from God, and as people recognize this, their thanksgiving will rise back to God (4:15).

For carrying the treasure is not a comfortable calling. Paul's experience as an apostle is of pressure, persecution, problems, and pain. Yet these difficulties have not defeated him or laid him low. Four times in a couple of verses he says emphatically "but" (4:8–9). He suffers but he has not suffocated; he is bruised but not broken. His fellowship with the cross of Christ brings him knocks and hurts, but the resurrection sustains him in the midst of these. Both aspects—the weakness and the strength to handle it—are evidence of the presence of Jesus.

Amid the various passages in 2 Corinthians that speak of stress and strain (1:3–7; 6:4–10; 11:23–28), this is one of two places (the other is 12:7–10) where Paul reflects most deeply on the ways that these experiences have brought him near to Christ. Other ancient authors might write of peril and hardship to highlight the courage of the people involved or to tell a dramatic story of rescue and deliverance. But for Paul the aspects of suffering that mattered most were his dependence on Jesus and his strange but potent contact with the cross and empty tomb. Christians sometimes speak of "thin places," where the realities of heaven seem very near. And although this is not Paul's language, he does seem to think of his sufferings as a "thin place." In the troubles he bears, others will see Jesus (4:10–11). When he is pressed hard, life seeps out from him to refresh those he serves (4:12).

There is an echo here of the opening paragraphs of 1 Corinthians. There Paul spoke of the cross as the center of his gospel (2:2). Many around him would have thought the crucifixion a foolish and shameful message, a sign to shrink from and to shun. Yet he had found it a source of power and strength (1:22–25). And here in 2 Corinthians we get a fresh glimpse into Paul's inner life, into the man behind the message. We see how the cross was more than a doctrine for him, more than a distant event in history. It was a daily reality too, a matter of both faith and experience. He lived the crucifixion himself, and in doing so, he found he was living the resurrection. As he says elsewhere, "to me, living is Christ" (Phil. 1:21).

Faith and Hope
2 Corinthians 4:13–18

> 4:13 **But just as we have the same spirit of faith that is in accordance with scripture—"I believed, and so I spoke"—we also believe, and so we speak, ¹⁴ because we know that the one who raised the Lord Jesus will raise us also with Jesus, and will bring us with you into his presence. ¹⁵ Yes, everything is for your sake, so that grace, as it extends to more and more people, may increase thanksgiving, to the glory of God.**
>
> ¹⁶ **So we do not lose heart. Even though our outer nature is wasting away, our inner nature is being renewed day by day. ¹⁷ For this slight momentary affliction is preparing us for an eternal weight of glory beyond all measure, ¹⁸ because we look not at what can be seen but at what cannot be seen; for what can be seen is temporary, but what cannot be seen is eternal.**

Once again a paragraph begins "we have" (as in 3:4, 12; 4:7; 5:1). For faith too is one of the resources of the Christian life, as is the Spirit who kindles that faith (4:13). The Scripture quote—"I believed, and so I spoke"—is from Psalm 116:10, a hymn that looks back at a time of crisis, by a psalmist who has trusted God in trouble and gives praise when danger is past. And that is exactly Paul's outlook: he aims to see his pains from the perspective of faith and to look beyond them to the promise of resurrection (4:14).

So Paul speaks. He preaches the resurrection. He tells that Jesus is Lord. He watches God's grace ripple out across the world, much of this through his own work. He rejoices in the hope of meeting his friends in heaven. And he revels in the thought of voices in many lands rising in thanksgiving to God (4:14–15). As we have noticed before and shall see again (1:11; 9:12), Paul thinks of praise as a natural outflow of Christian life and service. For this we were made and to this we are called. Our "chief end," says the Westminster Confession, "is to glorify God, and to enjoy him forever." This letter too speaks of glory and joy, even when life is lived in the shadow of the cross.

For the servant of Christ need "not lose heart" (4:16, echoing 4:1). The Christian life is a life of renewal, refreshment, and resurrection. Indeed within a few verses Paul tells of three ways that he experiences the risen life of Christ. First, "the life of Jesus" flows out of him to others (4:11–12). Second, resurrection waits to meet him when "the earthly tent we live in is destroyed" (4:14; 5:1). And third, there is an inner resurrection going on right now (4:16). Even though our bodies decay with the years, our spirits may delight in the Lord. The "affliction" of life will pass, but the "glory" of Christ will endure (4:17). The invisible world is stable and sure, as this world of sight and hand can never be (4:18).

Paul's reference to "outer nature" and "inner nature" (4:16) is more than a distinction between body and soul. Certainly we are complex beings, and much of our live is lived on the inside, in the private personal space of mind and heart. But that is not the whole of Paul's meaning. He is concerned for what happens when that inner life is lived in fellowship with Jesus. For then we are transformed within, and this gives us new energy for outward service too. It also gives us hope: of life beyond death, of glory and gladness to come, of promise that will last, and of confidence to take away our fear. All of this is the theme of the next part of the letter.

Dwelling Place
2 Corinthians 5:1–10

> 5:1 **For we know that if the earthly tent we live in is destroyed, we have a building from God, a house not made with hands, eternal in the heavens.** ² **For in this tent we groan, longing to be clothed with our heavenly dwelling—** ³ **if indeed, when we have taken it off we will not be found naked.** ⁴ **For while we are still in this tent, we groan under our burden, because we wish not to be unclothed but to be further clothed, so that what is mortal may be swallowed up by life.** ⁵ **He who has prepared us for this very thing is God, who has given us the Spirit as a guarantee.**
>
> ⁶ **So we are always confident; even though we know that while we are at home in the body we are away from the Lord—** ⁷ **for we walk by faith, not by sight.** ⁸ **Yes, we do have confidence, and we would rather be away from the body and at home with the Lord.** ⁹ **So whether we are at home or away, we make it our aim to please him.** ¹⁰ **For all of us must appear before the judgment seat of Christ, so that each may receive recompense for what has been done in the body, whether good or evil.**

These verses look directly at the prospect of death and at what lies beyond. The two processes of decay and renewal (4:16) will one day run side-by-side to their final destination. Our human bodies wear out. And Christ beckons us forward to share his risen life. "We have," says Paul once again (5:1; as in 4:7, 13), but this time he is speaking of a future possession. We do not yet have our resurrection home; but we shall have it, and the hope of this sustains us even now.

Paul uses several images to speak about resurrection. These have some points of contact with Greek and Roman thought, but the content stands out as characteristically and particularly Christian. For the ancient world generally did not look at death with much optimism, and amid this general gloom the gospel struck a distinctive note of hope. (There is more on this in our comments on 1 Corinthians 15.) Here are the pictures Paul outlines:

- *Moving house.* Death and resurrection involve a change of address. When the "tent" that is our mortal body eventually collapses (5:1), there is a solid home to move into, of which God is the architect and owner. First Corinthians calls this the "spiritual body" (15:44), a dwelling place that is alive with the presence and energy of God's Holy Spirit.
- *Changing clothes.* Dying and rising is like putting on a new suit of clothing (5:2). Death will destroy our outer covering, the physical shell in which we move. But this will not reduce us to a hollow and disembodied "nakedness" (5:3)—as some in the ancient world believed. It will cover us with "glory" and "power" (1 Cor. 15:43).
- *Born over again.* Paul speaks of "groaning" (5:2, 4) beneath the load of this present life. And he reaches for this same word in Romans (8:22) to speak of creation as a birthing mother, longing and striving to bring forth new life. In 2 Corinthians too, he surely thinks of our mortal groaning as a yearning for life, an eager desire to start again in a new and wider world.
- *Gathered and grasped.* "What is mortal" is to be "swallowed up" (5:4)—taken in and absorbed—not by the shadowy realm of death but by a world of goodness and life. The idea is in Isaiah: "the LORD of hosts . . . will swallow up death forever" (25:6, 8), and Paul quotes from that text in 1 Corinthians (15:54). We may fear that our mortal selves will be devoured by death; the truth is, in Christ, the direct opposite.
- *Taste and testimony.* The Spirit dwelling in Christ's people is "guarantee" of all this (5:5). The Greek word (also used in 1:22) means the deposit on a business transaction—the first slice of a larger amount to come and a positive pledge that the buyer means to complete the deal. That is how Paul thought of the Spirit, as the first taste of God's eternal reality, the "first fruits" (Romans 8:23) of a fuller harvest, the Christian's first contact with the risen life of Christ.
- *Home and away.* Lastly the idea of moving house returns, with the words "home" and "away" (5:6, 8, 9). Dying and rising involve taking a journey, traveling a distance, settling down in a new home,

enjoying new company. As long as we are "at home in the body," we are "away from the Lord" (5:6)—not absolutely apart from God but living in trust rather than by direct sensory contact (5:7). Death will change that. It will bring us home to a new and better dwelling (5:8).

Around all these illustrations, these verses are deeply emotional. Talk of death will always touch our feelings as well as involving our mind. There is "groaning" (5:2, 4), the weary longing of a burdened soul for a fuller, better, and brighter world. And there is "good cheer" ("confidence" in the NRSV, in 5:6, 8)—a buoyancy of heart in the face of difficulty and a mood of courage, optimism, and resolve. Hope always gives the Christian a reason and purpose for living.

So Paul speaks also of a steady moral commitment, a constant desire to please the Lord (5:9). Although our mortal body will not endure forever, it is for the moment our place of Christian service. This is where we make choices between good and evil (5:10) and turn our choices into actions, habits, and lifestyles. So resurrection is an incentive to godly living. What we shall be, says Paul, should shape what we do now. We met this in 1 Corinthians (see comment on 6:13–14), and here he follows the same line of thought as he thinks of facing the judgment of Christ (5:10).

For even as Christians live in hope, we are to reckon with judgment. Only then will we know for sure what our service has been worth and how well it has lasted. So, although Paul reminds us that salvation is not earned by Christian service (1 Cor. 3:12–15), he did expect God to audit and appraise his work. He regarded himself as accountable to heaven. He realized that actions matter and that only eternity will show us how. He looked to Jesus to measure and monitor his living, and he knew that the final verdict was ahead. So as he lived with a cheerful confidence, he lived too in awe. Life is a serious task and a solemn trust. Distant as we are, heaven still gives Christ's people our aim and aspiration—"whether we are at home or away . . . to please him" (5:9).

With this thought, the theme of Paul's writing starts to change and develop. This aim, of pleasing the Lord, sums up and concludes his exposition of his ministry, which started in 2:14. He has laid out the way that he understands his task—as agent and herald of God's new covenant, as fellowship with the crucified and risen Jesus, and as a sharing of the Spirit's life in the world. Now the accent of the letter will shift a little as he starts to call more directly and deliberately for a response from his readers.

For Paul wants the Corinthians to take him seriously and to trust him. He wants to mend fully and finally the division and dispute that he mentioned in chapter 2 (this theme will come in chapter 7). He means to ask for their help in his collection for Jerusalem (8 and 9). And he will press them to distance themselves from the influence of the false teachers in Corinth (10 to 13). The foundation for all this is the gift of God in the cross of Christ. There is the source of reconciliation and new beginnings. There we now turn.

11. Repair and Reconciliation
2 Corinthians 5:11–7:16

GOD AND RECONCILIATION: THE CROSS OF CHRIST
2 Corinthians 5:11–21

These verses are the heart of the letter, and they take us to the heart of the gospel. For as Paul moves toward making a deliberate appeal to the Corinthians in the hope of mending damaged relationships, he comes first to the place where all true healing and wholeness are found: in the brokenness of the crucified Jesus. From the pain and weakness of the cross come power and possibility; we see this here in three particular ways. The love of Jesus as he gave himself is what motivates and stirs Paul and presses him forward in purposeful Christian service (5:11–14). The transforming death and life of Jesus enable Paul to think of new beginnings (5:14–17). And the reconciling work of Jesus allows Paul to speak of restored relationships in Corinth (5:18–21). These themes—motivation, transformation, and reconciliation—are thoroughly practical. They shape Paul's actions and his pastoral leadership. Yet they are also deeply theological. Their root and basis are in the cross of Christ.

Love That Motivates
2 Corinthians 5:11–14

> 5:11 **Therefore, knowing the fear of the Lord, we try to persuade others; but we ourselves are well known to God, and I hope that we are also well known to your consciences.** [12] **We are not commending ourselves to you again, but giving you an opportunity to boast about us, so that you may be able to answer those who boast in outward appearance and not in the heart.** [13] **For if we are beside ourselves, it is for God; if we are in our right mind, it is for you.** [14] **For the love of Christ urges us on, because we are convinced that one has died for all; therefore all have died.**

These verses begin not in love but in "the fear of the Lord" (5:11). This Old Testament phrase (Psalm 111:10, for example) need not mean an insecure fearfulness; rather it is a deliberate reverence for a God whose ways we know and whose might and majesty we respect. For Paul this arises directly from his belief in the coming judgment of Christ (5:10): with that in prospect it is right to live in reverent awe and to pursue a life of active goodness and service.

So Paul seeks to convince others (5:11) and to spread the news of Christ's resurrection across the world. Yet, as he has said before (2:17; 4:2), his persuasion is not founded on trickery and technique. He claims to speak with integrity, as God surely knows, and he hopes the Corinthians can recognize this too (5:11). He wants them to be proud of him and of their connection with him (5:12). Not that he needs their praise, but he believes his version of the gospel is truer and more wholesome than other ideas that are being preached in Corinth. So he wants to give the Corinthians some reason and confidence to stay loyal to his teaching and leadership.

The theme of "commendation" (5:12) has surfaced before (1:12–14; 3:1), and it will return in force at the end of the letter as an almost constant theme in chapters 10 to 12. There we shall see that Paul's opponents have plenty to say about themselves, and he feels the need to answer back. But it will be an uncomfortable sort of response from a man who would prefer to speak about Christ rather than about himself (4:5). So when he has to defend and justify himself, there can be a self-conscious awkwardness in his writing. And we see a hint of that in this chapter. Paul wonders if the Corinthians think him odd. Do they find him spiritually crazy? "Believe me," he says (to paraphrase 5:13), "All of my strangeness and all of my sanity are part of a life's commitment, to God and to you."

Which brings us to Paul's greatest and deepest motivation: "the love of Christ" (5:14). He is a man energized, driven forward and controlled by Jesus. He looks on the cross as God's loving gift to sinners (Rom. 5:8; Gal 2:20), and he finds this love overflowing into the lives of Christians around him. The cross stirs him and sends him, because Jesus gave himself in love, and because that same love reaches out into the world when Jesus is preached and known as Lord. What better motivation could there be for seeking to "persuade others" (5:11)? Truth changes people. Love makes them new. This is the theme of the verses ahead.

Life That Transforms
2 Corinthians 5:15–17

> 5:15 **For the love of Christ urges us on, because we are convinced that one has died for all; therefore all have died.** ¹⁵ **And he died for all, so that those who live might live no longer for themselves, but for him who died and was raised for them.**
> ¹⁶ **From now on, therefore, we regard no one from a human point of view; even though we once knew Christ from a human point of view, we know him no longer in that way.** ¹⁷ **So if anyone is in Christ, there is a new creation: everything old has passed away; see, everything has become new!**

The headline of Paul's gospel was "Christ died for our sins." This was a core element of his message—"of first importance," he says (1 Cor. 15:3). What Jesus suffered on the cross had become a word of good news, of pardon and of peace. One individual death had turned out to be the center of history. And two thousand years later, the cross still has a strange ability to summon and focus our attention and send us away changed and renewed. It seems that this is what Paul discovered too.

For even when Paul wrote to Corinth, the crucifixion was twenty years past and hundreds of miles away. Yet he saw in that event a power that was almost magnetic, to reach across the miles and the years, to draw other people into itself and to include them in the story of Jesus. So Jesus' death became their death, and his resurrection their door to new life. "One has died for all; therefore all have died" (5:14). When people turn to Jesus an old way of living comes to an end. No longer need life be centered on itself and on its own interests and preferences. A new center is given, and there is a new focus for attitude and action—to "live . . . for him who died and was raised" (5:15). To belong to Jesus is to be a new person.

So as Paul thought of his friends at Corinth, he knew that there is always more to a person than meets the eye. No one should be rated "from a human point of view" (5:16). "From now on"—because of the cross and resurrection—no human life can be truly measured by its outward and visible aspect. Paul had once reckoned with Jesus on that basis (5:16), as a crucified criminal, a failed prophet, a false messiah. And he had learned to think differently. He had met Jesus as risen Lord, and now that he had been given a new way of knowing Jesus, this changed the way he looked at other people. For when people turn to Christ, they are renewed inwardly. Nothing about them is quite the same again: "if anyone is in Christ, there is a new creation" (5:17).

This idea of the Christian life as a "new creation" is quite common in Paul's writing. We have met it before in this letter, with the thought of God's image being renewed (3:18) and God's creative light shining in the human heart (4:6). In Galatians (6:15) Paul uses the expression to describe the new life that the cross makes possible. And in Romans (5:12–21) he talks of Jesus as a counterpart to Adam, the prototype and pattern of a fresh and different way of being human.

Yet on this occasion, Paul may have two particular reasons for writing in this vein to Corinth. First, he is keen to move the Corinthians away from a scale of judgment based on "outward appearance" (5:12). He wants them to be less impressed when his opponents "boast according to human standards" (11:18). He wishes they could set aside the normal standards of their city, which so often accented style over substance, and think more seriously about the cross and resurrection as the true measure of a church leader. Second, Paul knew that the renewing love of Christ is the only power that can truly restore broken relationships in the church. As he writes this letter, he knows that there is some deep damage to repair. It will be important for all concerned to think and act in new ways. A proper reconciliation is needed, and this is the aspect of the crucifixion that the letter explores next.

God Who Reconciles
2 Corinthians 5:18–21

> 5:18 **All this is from God, who reconciled us to himself through Christ, and has given us the ministry of reconciliation;** [19] **that is, in Christ God was reconciling the world to himself, not counting their trespasses against them, and entrusting the message of reconciliation to us.** [20] **So we are ambassadors for Christ, since God is making his appeal through us; we entreat you on behalf of Christ, be reconciled to God.** [21] **For our sake he made him to be sin who knew no sin, so that in him we might become the righteousness of God.**

Paul's concern for a restored relationship with the Christians at Corinth will run right through the next two chapters, with many words of appeal and entreaty (6:1–3, 11–13; 7:2–4). He wants the church to value and honor his ministry, as a way of receiving surely and truly the gospel he proclaims. So he grounds this appeal for personal and pastoral healing in the much larger reconciliation that God has made possible by the cross. We will always seek peace more truly with one another when we have a secure peace with God.

The verb "reconcile" and the noun "reconciliation" come five times very close together (5:18–20). The words are as cumbersome in Greek as they are in English. A person reading the letter aloud would be bound to emphasize them. And Paul surely meant to be emphatic. For these verses track the whole path of reconciliation—from the purpose of God, through the work of Christ, by the mouth of the preacher, to the hearts of the Corinthians. Paul makes a series of dense and close-knit points.

- Reconciliation is God-given (5:18). The reconciliation of which the gospel speaks is not a human attempt to placate a distant and disaffected God. It starts with God, reaching out to the world in the person of Jesus, taking our flesh, entering into our conflicts and pains, and dying our death. "All this is from God" (5:18): the possibility of living a new life and entering a new creation starts with God's initiative and involvement. God comes into our place.
- Reconciliation includes forgiveness (5:19). When God reaches out to reconcile, no record is kept of sins or wrongdoings. We start again. The slate is clean. "Forgive us our trespasses," we pray. God does. Verse 21 will speak about how.
- Reconciliation is for sharing (5:20). Paul has talked of a "ministry" (5:18) and a "message" (5:19). He calls himself an "ambassador," speaking on God's behalf, as he urges and encourages people to respond to what God has done. And this is still part of the church's task, to tell of God's reconciling love and invite people to trust it for themselves.
- Reconciliation costs (5:21). This verse is one of the most intense and solemn texts in the New Testament: the sinless Christ "made to be sin." The words surely refer to the crucifixion and the way that Jesus was drawn into the ugly web of human shame and spite. Two Old Testament motifs help to uncover the meaning.

> First, we turn to the sacrificial worship of Israel, where an animal victim would carry and represent human sin and guilt (e.g., Lev. 4). So here the death of Jesus gathers into itself the meaning of that ancient system. Jesus was identified in his dying with the sins of others: he suffered for us, carried our guilt, and offered us forgiveness and freedom.
>
> The second motif to shed light on this text is the Servant figure of Isaiah 53, whose life was made "an offering for sin," so that he would "make many righteous . . . and bear their iniquities" (53:10–11). There is quite an echo of that text in this present verse. It seems that,

for Paul, this mysterious figure in Isaiah is a signpost to the meaning of the cross.

Yet all this is only the background to verse 21. In the foreground is the crucifixion, place of sin and shame, sign of healing and hope. For we know in our own living that forgiveness, the mending of damaged relationships, is neither easy nor cheap. Someone has to bridge the gap, handle the tension, and bear the pain if there is to be true reconciliation. God has done this for the world (5:19) at the cross of Jesus.

- Reconciliation is to be received (5:20). Notice how directly Paul asks his readers to respond: "we entreat you . . . be reconciled." The gospel invites people into new relationship with God. The messenger can appeal and persuade. It is for the hearer to accept the invitation.

There will be much more by way of appeal and persuasion in the next couple of chapters. But as we check out from this dense little section about God's reconciling love, the task remains of making that love known in God's world. The church is still called to herald this gospel, and surely one way we do so is by the way we handle conflict ourselves in our personal lives and our congregations. When we can show reconciliation, we may be better at helping others to know it. What this means in practice will not be simple; conflict rarely is. Yet we shall always bring something of Christ into these situations if we have allowed the reconciling love of the cross to shape and sustain our own relationship with God.

PAUL AND RECONCILIATION: "OPEN YOUR HEARTS"
2 Corinthians 6:1–7:4

This chapter takes the theme of reconciliation forward from the peace that God offers in the death of Jesus to the new relationship Paul seeks with the Christians at Corinth. The language is personal and emotional. Paul tries to be open, and he seeks openness in return. He declares his love for the church and asks for their loyalty. He wants them to trust him and his gospel and to let this gospel influence the choices and commitments that they make.

Acceptable Time
2 Corinthians 6:1–2

> **6:1 As we work together with him, we urge you also not to accept the grace of God in vain.** ² **For he says,**

> "At an acceptable time I have listened to you,
> and on a day of salvation I have helped you."
> See, now is the acceptable time; see, now is the day of salvation!

Paul speaks as an ambassador. He thinks of his life as a working relationship with his Lord (as in 1 Cor. 3:9), and he appeals in Christ's name. He does not want the Corinthians' faith to be "vain"—hollow and fruitless, without depth or reality. Elsewhere he uses this word to describe wasted effort—all struggle and no end product (Gal. 2:2; Phil. 2:16; 1 Thess. 3:5). Here, then, he asks for faith that has an end product, faith that can help the Corinthians to shape their living, select the company they keep, and sift the claims and influences that others set before them.

The line about "an acceptable time . . . and a day of salvation" (6:2) is from Isaiah 49:8, from another of the Servant Songs, on which Paul also drew in 5:21. It speaks of a moment of grace, a day of blessing and deliverance when promise will turn into fulfillment and hope into reality. Paul takes up this joyful text as an invitation: it is time for Corinth to grasp the moment, to realize that they live in a day of salvation, and to embrace God's gracious love as fully as they can.

Marks of Ministry
2 Corinthians 6:3–10

> 6:3 We are putting no obstacle in anyone's way, so that no fault may be found with our ministry, ⁴ but as servants of God we have commended ourselves in every way: through great endurance, in afflictions, hardships, calamities, ⁵ beatings, imprisonments, riots, labors, sleepless nights, hunger; ⁶ by purity, knowledge, patience, kindness, holiness of spirit, genuine love, ⁷ truthful speech, and the power of God; with the weapons of righteousness for the right hand and for the left; ⁸ in honor and dishonor, in ill repute and good repute. We are treated as impostors, and yet are true; ⁹ as unknown, and yet are well known; as dying, and see—we are alive; as punished, and yet not killed; ¹⁰ as sorrowful, yet always rejoicing; as poor, yet making many rich; as having nothing, and yet possessing everything.

These verses are an interlude in Paul's appeal, between two passages of direct address. They describe the way that Paul ministers to remind the Corinthians of how strongly his lifestyle supports his message. So the church need have no reason to reject what he stands for. Let there be "no obstacle" in their minds, no blame nor fault-finding, over his ministry (6:3). His deeds ought to "commend" him (6:4). And even though he is sometimes reluctant to commend himself (3:1; 5:12; 10:12, 18), he will list the deeds. A lengthy, paradoxical list we shall find it.

We split the list into three shorter sections. There are nine items in each. In the first (6:4–5) are difficulties that Paul and his friends have faced for Christ. "Great endurance" he says by way of opening summary (6:4), and then he sets out the sorts of things he has had to bear: "afflictions, hardships, calamities, beatings, imprisonments, riots, labors, sleepless nights, hungers." In Paul's Greek, all nine words are plural; these were not isolated events but a repeated pattern of service and suffering. Here is the downbeat of the Christian life, the rough aspect of walking with Jesus.

The second sequence (6:6–7) is much more upbeat. It is reminiscent of another Pauline list, of "the fruit of the Spirit" (Gal. 5:22–23). Here, in the main, are features of Christian character, qualities of life and of personality that come as gifts from God: "purity, knowledge, patience, kindness, holiness (or "the Holy Spirit"), love, truth, power, righteousness." These are virtues and resources for Christian living, graces and strengths for bearing the strain, sharing the word, and caring for the church.

Finally the third phase of the list (6:8–10) draws these two aspects of Christian experience—the vicissitudes and the virtues—together into nine pairs of words. Every pair is a paradox, a coupling of opposites, linking items that would not normally match or join: "honor and dishonor, ill repute and good repute, impostors and true, unknown and well known, dying and alive, punished yet not killed, sorrowful and rejoicing, poor yet making many rich, having nothing, and yet possessing everything." In musical terms, this is the chord, the fusing of different notes and tones, that is the life of faith. It is neither a simple upbeat nor a plain downbeat but is both at once. Credible Christian service echoes and embodies both the pain of the cross and the power of the resurrection. The resources God gives are often seen best against a background of hardship and stress.

This is one of four or five places in 2 Corinthians where Paul outlines his afflictions and troubles. Yet always there is more than difficulty; there are resources to bear it and to serve others through it. So Paul talks of reliance on God (1:9), of daily renewal (4:16), of power in weakness (12:9), and here of the utter paradox of sharing gladness amid hardship and wealth out of poverty. This is what it means to represent the good news and life of Jesus.

Open Mouth, Open Heart
2 Corinthians 6:11–13

> 6:11 **We have spoken frankly to you Corinthians; our heart is wide open to you.** [12] **There is no restriction in our affections, but only in yours.** [13] **In return—I speak as to children—open wide your hearts also.**

In the lines above Paul has spoken candidly, sincerely, and unreservedly. And his candor comes, he says, from the heart. Indeed all the pressures and qualities of which he has just been speaking are sign of his love. They are service and suffering for the church, his gift to them. So this short paragraph uses the metaphor of narrowness and breadth. It speaks of emotions in Corinth that seem to be ingrown and weak and of Paul's own love reaching out passionately and persistently, keen to give, yearning to care, and longing that others might gain and grow.

So the language of these verses is laden with feeling and emotion. Christians in the New Testament were often very ready to speak of their love for one another, and in some church traditions today we do not say this quite so easily. But perhaps the key point from these verses is not how we speak but how we care for our sisters and brothers in Christ, for those who lead us, and for those who depend on our leadership. If care comes from deep within us, if it is a matter of heart as well as hand, if it is grounded in the love of Christ, then it will always carry in it the gladness and generosity of the gospel.

A People Apart
2 Corinthians 6:14–7:1

> 6:14 **Do not be mismatched with unbelievers. For what partnership is there between righteousness and lawlessness? Or what fellowship is there between light and darkness?** [15] **What agreement does Christ have with Beliar? Or what does a believer share with an unbeliever?** [16] **What agreement has the temple of God with idols? For we are the temple of the living God; as God said,**
>
> **"I will live in them and walk among them,**
>   **and I will be their God,**
>   **and they shall be my people.**
> [17] **Therefore come out from them,**
>   **and be separate from them, says the Lord,**
>   **and touch nothing unclean;**

> then I will welcome you,
> ¹⁸ and I will be your father,
> and you shall be my sons and daughters,
> says the Lord Almighty."
> 7:1 **Since we have these promises, beloved, let us cleanse ourselves from every defilement of body and of spirit, making holiness perfect in the fear of God.**

This is, on any reckoning, a clutch of difficult verses. The tone of writing has shifted abruptly from warmth to warning, and there is a change in writing style too. In 6:11–13 Paul's talk was all affection and generosity. Then suddenly he speaks of demand, division, and detachment. Not only this: the tight sequences of rhetorical questions (6:14–16a) and of Old Testament quotations (6:16b–18) stand out from the writing immediately around. Rhetorical questions, to be sure, are plentiful in this letter; and there is another series at 12:17–19. But this little nest of Scripture citations is unique in 2 Corinthians; there is much more of this sort of thing in Romans. So why have Paul's words become so fierce and stark? Why has his style changed? And why has all this happened without anything obvious by way of lead-in or anticipation?

One quite common theory (mentioned in the introduction to 2 Corinthians) is that these verses do not really belong here. They have landed at this point by some quirk of editing or transmission and broken up an otherwise smooth and intelligible passage of writing. If that were so, it would now be very difficult to know what to make of them: we would have almost no idea who wrote them, what situation they originally addressed, and what point they were making about it. So we shall ask a simpler and more accessible question instead. What sense can be found in them in the place where they now appear, and how might they connect with the material on either side? First we look more closely at their content.

The five rhetorical questions are all about the "yoking together" (6:14; "mismatched" says the NRSV) of good and evil. The image is of two animals pulling a plough, side by side. So, says Paul, light and darkness cannot walk in easy partnership. Righteousness cannot work with anarchy. Belief and unbelief will not be happy yokefellows. Beliar—a great evil angel, often mentioned in Jewish writing of that era, although rarely in the Bible itself—can have nothing to say to Christ. Nor can idol worship find any home in God's temple.

It is no accident that the sequence ends with God's temple. For the very center of this clutch of verses, the link between the rhetorical questions and the Old Testament quotes, is in v.16: "we are the temple of the living

God." As in his earlier letter (1 Cor. 3:16–17; 6:19) Paul has used the idea of temple as a symbol of the Christian life. His point is that God's temple is a holy place, and the church too is a holy people.

So the Scripture quotations that follow all concern, in one way or another, the theme of holiness. They tell of God calling a people apart, to be faithful, separate, and distinct. The church too, suggests Paul, is also a people apart, a sacred company and a fellowship where God dwells. And you do not profane God's sacred territory. The people of the church should guard their commitment to Christ, with the reverence and care that befit holy ground. So we hear of "cleans[ing] . . . from every defilement . . . making holiness perfect" (7:1); this is the language of Jewish worship applied to the pastoral life of the church in Corinth.

So what might Paul have been getting at through all of this? Two suggestions are worth taking seriously.

One is that he may be returning to the theme of idol worship, which he discussed at such length in 1 Corinthians, to remind the church that they cannot enjoy deep fellowship with Christ if they share at the same time in a very different religious life. They should set firmly behind them any involvement in events and ceremonies that honor the deities of Greece and Rome. Reading the verses in this way would make sense of the strongly religious language, and that may be a point in its favor. But it would also introduce the theme of idol worship into 2 Corinthians without any explanation or forewarning.

So a second possibility may be worth considering: that these very stark verses were meant to reinforce a concern that Paul carries through much of this letter. He wants the Corinthians to be wary of the claims and company of his opponents. He refers to these men as "deceivers and false apostles" (11:13); he says they bring "a different spirit and a different gospel" (11:4). So it may be that he casts them here as sirens of Satan, threats to the church's relationship with its Lord, tempters who are leading the Corinthians away from the heart of their faith. Paul urges his friends not to be duped.

From our vantage point, two thousand years later, it is difficult to know which of these interpretations—if indeed either of them—is correct. Yet these verses clearly suggest that Paul's personal warmth toward the Christians at Corinth was matched by a strong desire for them to make some decisive choices. They would not easily keep their footing in the faith he taught them unless they distanced themselves from certain other influences that were bearing on their lives. Honest pastoral care must sometimes involve not only warmth but warning too.

One further point, by way of postscript. The opening line of 6:14 has often been used to warn Christians against marrying non-Christians. And that issue does need careful thought; marriage and faith do affect one another. But it may not have been the point Paul was making here. Nothing else in this letter suggests this issue as a major concern. Paul says much more about marriage relationships in 1 Corinthians 7.

Comfort and Joy
2 Corinthians 7:2–4

> 7:2 **Make room in your hearts for us; we have wronged no one, we have corrupted no one, we have taken advantage of no one.** [3] **I do not say this to condemn you, for I said before that you are in our hearts, to die together and to live together.** [4] **I often boast about you; I have great pride in you; I am filled with consolation; I am overjoyed in all our affliction.**

The previous section ends with positive and inviting words—"let us cleanse ourselves . . . and make holiness perfect" (7:1)—which lead well into the warm and loving words of this short paragraph. Several themes from earlier recur here as Paul gathers his thoughts and goodwill in preparation for moving onto more delicate ground later in the chapter.

"Make room," he says—as he did in 6:13. There has been nothing in his ministry to invite resentment (7:2)—a point he made in 6:3 and elaborated in the verses that followed. He holds the Corinthians warmly in his heart (7:3; as in 6:11). Indeed if he had to die in their service he would be confident of meeting them in resurrection (as he says in 4:14). He boasts in them (7:4; as in 1:14). And in the midst of affliction, every thought of his friends brings him consolation and delight; this echoes the opening of the letter, with its frequent repetition of the word "console" (1:3–7). So although there will be difficult issues to discuss later, there is no doubt of the warmth and care that Paul brings to these. Even sensitive and painful truths may be heard more easily if they are spoken in love.

CORINTH AND RECONCILIATION: GRIEF AND COMFORT
2 Corinthians 7:5–16

> 7:5 **For even when we came into Macedonia, our bodies had no rest, but we were afflicted in every way—disputes without and fears within.** [6] **But God, who consoles the downcast, consoled us by the arrival of Titus,** [7] **and not**

only by his coming, but also by the consolation with which he was consoled about you, as he told us of your longing, your mourning, your zeal for me, so that I rejoiced still more. [8] For even if I made you sorry with my letter, I do not regret it (though I did regret it, for I see that I grieved you with that letter, though only briefly). [9] Now I rejoice, not because you were grieved, but because your grief led to repentance; for you felt a godly grief, so that you were not harmed in any way by us. [10] For godly grief produces a repentance that leads to salvation and brings no regret, but worldly grief produces death. [11] For see what earnestness this godly grief has produced in you, what eagerness to clear yourselves, what indignation, what alarm, what longing, what zeal, what punishment! At every point you have proved yourselves guiltless in the matter. [12] So although I wrote to you, it was not on account of the one who did the wrong, nor on account of the one who was wronged, but in order that your zeal for us might be made known to you before God. [13] In this we find comfort.

In addition to our own consolation, we rejoiced still more at the joy of Titus, because his mind has been set at rest by all of you. [14] For if I have been somewhat boastful about you to him, I was not disgraced; but just as everything we said to you was true, so our boasting to Titus has proved true as well. [15] And his heart goes out all the more to you, as he remembers the obedience of all of you, and how you welcomed him with fear and trembling. [16] I rejoice, because I have complete confidence in you.

Here the letter picks up the travelogue that we left in 2:13. Paul had moved on from Ephesus as far as Troas. But he would not wait there, because he was restless to meet Titus and hear about his visit to Corinth. So he pushed on northwest into Macedonia in the hope of running into Titus coming in the other direction. And when in due time they met (7:6), Titus brought good and heartening news.

The situation seems to have developed along these lines. Titus had been in Corinth, probably delivering Paul's so-called "tearful letter" (2:4; 7:8) and using his own pastoral gifts to help the church to respond. In due course the matter of misconduct (which we met in 2:5–13) was well and truly settled. The Corinthians had been willing to take the matter seriously, to challenge the errant brother, and to guard the purity of their life as a church. The problem, whatever it had been, was now fading into the past, and the church was moving on, wiser, stronger, and more mature. All this is the main theme of 7:7–12.

There was an outstanding difficulty, however, around the church's relationship with Paul. His last visit to Corinth had been difficult in the extreme (2:1). Since then he had canceled a promised visit (1:23) and sent a sharp letter of reproof (2:4; 7:8). It would not be altogether easy for him to appear in the city again. There would be a welcome for sure, but some awkwardness too, a few strained friendships to repair, and certain no-go areas in conversation and reminiscence.

This explains all the argument of the last four or five chapters. Paul has been outlining his pattern of ministry (chapters 3 and 4), speaking of the reconciling cross of Jesus (5), and appealing to Corinth (6), because he knows that he needs to regain their trust. All along he has said "we," but most of the time he has been thinking primarily of his own role and relationships. It really matters to him to recover his pastoral bond with the Corinthian church.

His reasons for wanting this are, of course, personal—friendships have been damaged, and it is time to mend them—but much more than personal. There is a collection to gather for Jerusalem, and Corinth could be a good contributor (chapters 8 and 9). The newcomers have brought a different version of the gospel to town and made an inroad into the life of the church (10 and 11). Paul fears that when he visits, he will be drawn into tense and troubling exchanges (12 and 13). For all these reasons, he wants to reestablish himself with the Corinthians as a respected and beloved church leader.

So perhaps the warm and assuring language of this chapter has a double meaning and purpose. Firstly and most obviously, it affirms all that has been done for good. It revisits the writing and receiving of a difficult letter (7:8–9, 12), the church's willingness to deal with an offender in its ranks (7:9–11), the assurance this had given Titus (7:7, 13, 15), and the pleasure his news had brought to Paul. The words "consolation" and "rejoicing" ring like a chorus across the whole chapter. The middle verses (7:8–11) are thick with "grief"—the effect of Paul's letter—but the outflow has been assurance, uplift, and thanksgiving to God.

A second aspect of these verses, however, is surely concerned with the future more than with the past. Paul writes about past healing, because he knows there is more healing yet to do (7:2). He writes of repentance, because it may be needed again (12:21). He writes of challenge and grief, because he is aware of possible conflict ahead (10:2; 13:10). He uses language of trust and bonding to prompt generosity and avert new misunderstandings (8:8, 20).

So as this first long movement of the letter comes to an end, the repeated "consolations" of the opening thanksgiving (1:3–7) sound again to draw Paul and Corinth back into mutual trust (7:4, 6, 7, 13). The "confidence" that Paul claims (7:16) will be the basis of his appeal for funds. And his right to challenge the church and to ask them to respect this rather than resent it may very well be invoked when he visits again.

Along the way, Paul the pastor names a couple of moods that most of us know well: "godly grief" and "worldly grief" (7:9–11). These two kinds of sorrow regularly compete for our attention when we come to terms with particular faults, sins, or mistakes. "Worldly grief" is sorrow in being found out, sorrow for the dent in our personal pride, sorrow for the trouble we have caused ourselves. It "produces death" (7:10); it is a sterile and destructive reaction. "Godly grief" is more likely to involve genuine repentance and shame, and sorrow for any damage done to other people. It is harder to live with in the short term than the worldly kind of sorrow but more wholesome in the long run. It "leads to salvation" (7:10), to truer relationships, and to deeper integrity.

Part 5: Collecting for the Saints
2 Corinthians 8–9

12. A Call to Contribute
2 Corinthians 8–9

These two chapters are all about money. Paul is collecting for poor Christians in Jerusalem. He asked the Corinthians to start saving when he wrote before (see 1 Cor. 16:1–4 and the comments there). Now he is trying to bring the project to fruition and to gather the money that has been saved. As ever when the church talks about money, two issues need to be discussed—management and motivation. How will the money be gathered; when should it be given, and to whom; how will it then be used, and for whose benefit? These are management issues, and they need to be secure if people are to give with confidence and purpose. But motivation must also be rooted in deeper issues of faith and fellowship, which set the invitation to give within the wider context of the church's whole life in Christ.

When we read these chapters, we find little in the opening verses about the purpose of the collection. Paul has explained this to the Corinthians long ago, and he seems to assume that they know it. So he starts with a narrative, of what others have given (8:1–15). Then he moves on to tell of messengers who will come to Corinth to gather the church's gifts (8:16–9:5). Only toward the end does he write more fully about what the gifts will achieve (9:6–15). All the way through are snippets of motivational advice, a host of good practical and spiritual reasons for Corinth to be generous.

OPPORTUNITY FOR GIVING: AS OTHERS HAVE GIVEN
2 Corinthians 8:1–15

Friends in the North
2 Corinthians 8:1–6

> 8:1 We want you to know, brothers and sisters, about the grace of God that has been granted to the churches of Macedonia; ² for during a severe ordeal

of affliction, their abundant joy and their extreme poverty have overflowed in a wealth of generosity on their part. ³ For, as I can testify, they voluntarily gave according to their means, and even beyond their means, ⁴ begging us earnestly for the privilege of sharing in this ministry to the saints— ⁵ and this, not merely as we expected; they gave themselves first to the Lord and, by the will of God, to us, ⁶ so that we might urge Titus that, as he had already made a beginning, so he should also complete this generous undertaking among you.

Paul is writing this letter from Macedonia (2:13; 7:5), an area in northern Greece around Philippi and Thessalonica, two hundred miles from Corinth. Christians in Philippi had been generous at other times; they sent several gifts to support Paul and help his work (Phil. 4:10–18). And clearly the Macedonian churches were keen to contribute to this current cause. So Paul uses their generosity as an incentive to prompt the Corinthians to give too.

The language of these verses is warm and appreciative. We hear of grace, of abundance and joy, and of willing and eager giving (8:1–4). Although they were not wealthy, the Macedonians had reached deep into the resources they had to offer far more than one might have expected (8:2–3). For their giving was grounded in a fresh commitment, first to Christ and so to Paul and his work (8:5).

Paul was greatly heartened by this enthusiasm for the collection, and he wanted to make sure that the Corinthians played their part too. So he was sending Titus back to Corinth to gather together gifts that had long ago been pledged and promised (8:6).

In Paul's eyes this collection was much more than a practical project. He calls it a "ministry" (8:4). The word is *diakonia* (see comment on 4:1)—a service to Christ and to the well-being of other believers. He also speaks of "sharing" (8:4); this word *koinonia* means involvement and participation with others. So just as he pointed out earlier that light has no *koinonia* with darkness (6:14), here now is a proper opportunity for *koinonia*, a network of relationship and care to which the Corinthians may be glad to belong.

Completers in Christ
2 Corinthians 8:7–15

> 8:7 Now as you excel in everything—in faith, in speech, in knowledge, in utmost eagerness, and in our love for you—so we want you to excel also in this generous undertaking.

⁸ I do not say this as a command, but I am testing the genuineness of your love against the earnestness of others. ⁹ For you know the generous act of our Lord Jesus Christ, that though he was rich, yet for your sakes he became poor, so that by his poverty you might become rich. ¹⁰ And in this matter I am giving my advice: it is appropriate for you who began last year not only to do something but even to desire to do something— ¹¹ now finish doing it, so that your eagerness may be matched by completing it according to your means. ¹² For if the eagerness is there, the gift is acceptable according to what one has—not according to what one does not have. ¹³ I do not mean that there should be relief for others and pressure on you, but it is a question of a fair balance between ¹⁴ your present abundance and their need, so that their abundance may be for your need, in order that there may be a fair balance. ¹⁵ As it is written,

"The one who had much did not have too much,
and the one who had little did not have too little."

Some people have the sort of personality that makes them completer-finishers. They may not be the most creative contributors at the start of a task, but they have the stamina and vigilance to bring it to a proper conclusion. Paul here speaks to the Corinthians about completing and completeness from two different angles.

First he asks them to complete, to balance, the strengths of their Christian lives. God has been gracious to them: they are full in faith and rich in many fine Christian qualities (8:7; as in 1 Cor. 1:5–7). Will they then be equally abundant in their giving? Often in this letter, Paul has used images of plenty to describe Christian experience—abundant comfort (1:5; 7:4), overflowing love (2:4), radiant glory (3:9), expansive thanksgiving (4:15), fullness of joy and of heart (7:13, 15). When life is lived in fellowship with God, then the current of grace flows swift and broad; life is generously resourced; what right kind of giving could there be other than abundant, free, and glad?

He also asks them to bring their own plans forward to completion (8:10–11). It is a year since they started to give, since they set their hearts and hands to this project. Now is the time to turn desire into delivery. Their own consistency of action and purpose is at stake. He wants them to show that their Christian love is genuine and solid (8:8).

Around these words of encouragement, Paul offers two thoughts in motivation. First, he points out that no one is expected to give above and beyond their means. Macedonia may be doing this, but he does not ask it of Corinth (8:11–12). Yet in terms of wealth and resources, there is shortage in Jerusalem, and Corinth does have the means to help (8:13).

So Corinth ought to give. Israel's experience with manna on the Exodus journey sets an example (8:15, quoting Exodus 16). People gathered different amounts of the bread, but everyone eventually found they had just enough. This is what Paul is aiming for—"a fair balance" (8:14), and enough for all.

The other piece of motivation is "the generous act of our Lord Jesus Christ" (8:9). Here Paul seems to summarize very compactly thoughts that he sets out more fully in Philippians 2. The richness of Jesus, mentioned so briefly here, is his existence "in the form of God" and his "equality with God" (Phil. 2:6) And the "generous act" of Jesus is his humble journey into incarnation and on to crucifixion, his embodiment of the life of God in human form and in death on a cross (Phil. 2:7–8). In Philippians Paul used this teaching to shape and sustain the church's pastoral life and to remind his readers to be humble in attitude and action (2:1–5). With the Corinthians he uses it to press for financial generosity. He wants them to give in gratitude for what Jesus has given them. And he is confident that their giving in Jesus' name will surely enrich the lives of others.

The very brevity of Paul's reference to this story of Jesus must mean that he expected the Corinthians to know what he had in mind. It suggests that he had already taught them about Jesus' "preexistence"—his life within the godhead before his human birth. Indeed First Corinthians seems to bear this out when it refers to "Jesus Christ, through whom are all things and through whom we exist" (1 Cor. 8:6). And of course Paul surely spoke often of the cross of Christ (1 Cor. 2:2; 15:3). So by taking up these thoughts so succinctly and allusively, Paul does here what he does often in his letters. He uses weighty gospel beliefs in pastoral teaching. Then as now, Christian practice will be true and sure when it is informed and inspired by what God has done for us.

OCCASION FOR GIVING: TITUS'S VISIT AND PAUL'S
2 Corinthians 8:16–9:5

Titus and the Team
2 Corinthians 8:16–24

> 8:16 **But thanks be to God who put in the heart of Titus the same eagerness for you that I myself have.** [17] **For he not only accepted our appeal, but since he is more eager than ever, he is going to you of his own accord.** [18] **With him we are sending the brother who is famous among all the churches for his proclaiming the good news;** [19] **and not only that, but he has also been**

appointed by the churches to travel with us while we are administering this generous undertaking for the glory of the Lord himself and to show our goodwill. [20] We intend that no one should blame us about this generous gift that we are administering, [21] for we intend to do what is right not only in the Lord's sight but also in the sight of others. [22] And with them we are sending our brother whom we have often tested and found eager in many matters, but who is now more eager than ever because of his great confidence in you. [23] As for Titus, he is my partner and co-worker in your service; as for our brothers, they are messengers of the churches, the glory of Christ. [24] Therefore openly before the churches, show them the proof of your love and of our reason for boasting about you.

Paul now moves on to explain the arrangements for the collection. Titus is coming (8:17), as he came once before and found much to support and encourage in the church (7:7). If we ask what Paul was doing while Titus traveled south, there may be an answer in Acts 20:2—he was busy in Macedonia, building up the churches. Only later did he come "to Greece" (20:3), and surely to Corinth, for three months.

When money is being handled, it will not do to send one envoy alone. Issues of personal safety and security must be considered; one man traveling alone could be an easy victim. Paul was keen too to avoid any accusations of carelessness or dishonesty (8:20–21), and a larger team would be altogether more credible. So two other men are being sent, "brothers" in Christ and in Christian service. Paul does not mention their names; nevertheless many have tried to work out who they might have been.

The first "brother" whose "praise is in the gospel" ("famous for proclaiming the good news" says the NRSV; 8:18) was once quite commonly thought to be Luke. This theory rests partly on Acts, where the writing slips into first-person plural for a while from 20:5; so Luke, it is said, was with Paul at about the time of this letter. But that theory has faded in recent decades, now that Luke's Gospel is generally dated about 80 CE, much later than Paul wrote to Corinth. And no other theory is really convincing; we just do not know who this man was. Most clearly, however, he was "appointed by the churches" (8:19), perhaps by Christians in Macedonia, to escort their money and to represent their love and care for the Christians in Jerusalem. So he embodies a basic principle of church management: those who handle money should be people the donors can trust.

The second "brother" was evidently a long-time associate of Paul's, and he apparently knew Corinth; otherwise why would Paul speak of "his great confidence in you" (8:22)? Is he then Timothy, mentioned at the start of this letter as "our brother" (1:1) who came to Corinth during

Paul's first spell there (Acts 18:5) and may have visited subsequently (1 Cor. 16:10)? But if so, why does Paul not name him here, as he does so readily in other letters? So again, we cannot know for sure who this man was. Yet if Titus and his colleagues had brought this letter to Corinth, the Corinthians would know, long before they read through to these words of commendation in chapter 8.

A People Prepared
2 Corinthians 9:1–5

> 9:1 **Now it is not necessary for me to write you about the ministry to the saints,** [2] **for I know your eagerness, which is the subject of my boasting about you to the people of Macedonia, saying that Achaia has been ready since last year; and your zeal has stirred up most of them.** [3] **But I am sending the brothers in order that our boasting about you may not prove to have been empty in this case, so that you may be ready, as I said you would be;** [4] **otherwise, if some Macedonians come with me and find that you are not ready, we would be humiliated—to say nothing of you—in this undertaking.** [5] **So I thought it necessary to urge the brothers to go on ahead to you, and arrange in advance for this bountiful gift that you have promised, so that it may be ready as a voluntary gift and not as an extortion.**

This little section explains what Titus and his colleagues are coming to do. They have been sent as an advance party to remind the Corinthians of their financial commitment before Paul himself comes to town. This is a practical measure. He wants the money to be ready when he gets there. So if some in Corinth had saved for a while and then let their intentions lapse, now is the time to start again. If any have thought only vaguely about giving, this is the moment to consider more deliberately and urgently how they might contribute. If any have lost interest in the project, because of their difficulties with Paul, here is a reminder that others too depend on their involvement.

To press the point, Paul talks about shame: "we would be humiliated," he says, "to say nothing of you" (9:4). He had spoken of Corinth as an example to stir up support for the collection in Macedonia. "Achaia has been ready since last year," he told the Christians there (9:2), and this proved a strong incentive. The Macedonian churches got involved and gave well. How embarrassing it would now be if he brought Macedonian friends with him to Corinth and all his fine words turned out to be hollow. Paul would look foolish for having bragged about the Corinthians. And they would be even more ashamed; their lack of resolve and consistency would have been found out.

The ancient Mediterranean world is often described as an "honor-shame" culture where people were deeply influenced by convention and by pressure to conform to the roles and duties that others expected. Of course all cultures show this to some extent, but many of the ancients were more affected by this sort of concern than we are used to in the West today. So for Paul to speak of shame was to reach for quite a powerful and deep-seated cultural instinct.

He tells the Corinthians on the one hand that he is so confident of their generosity that he does not even need to mention the collection (9:1–2). In theory that is true. On the other hand, he reminds them quite forcibly to be ready (9:3–5). It matters that they show the Macedonians a good example. Paul wants the money to be on hand when he gets to Corinth so that it can be contributed gladly rather than in haste or duress.

Yet despite Paul's use of shame as a motive here, most of the language in these two chapters about money is upbeat and uplifting. Indeed even in these verses Paul calls the collection a "bountiful gift" and "voluntary gift" (9:5); the Greek word in both places is literally "blessing." And often he talks of "grace"—a multifaceted word, expressing almost any kind of favor or goodwill. So "grace" might refer to the "privilege" of participation (8:4), the "generous undertaking" of the collection itself (8:6, 7, 19), God's many sided goodness to his people (8:1; 9:8, 14), or the thanks the church offers in return (8:16; 9:15). Talking so ceaselessly of "grace" might seem in some settings merely an astute tactic, the appropriate mood music for a financial appeal. Yet I suspect it reveals something deeper here. Paul thinks of the church's whole life as a matter of grace, tended by a constant stream of loving goodness, with its source in the heart of God. He will explore this theme much more fully in the verses ahead.

OBJECTS OF GIVING: SHARING AND PRAISE
2 Corinthians 9:6–15

These last few verses about the collection speak of giving as a spiritual experience (9:6–9) and of giving as an investment in the faith of other people (9:10–15). Paul believes passionately that God is involved in Christian giving, both in the place where money is offered and at the point where it is received. God is neither absent nor inert nor bound by human habits and expectations. God is present, active, and surprisingly generous.

Sowing and Reaping
2 Corinthians 9:6–9

> **9:6** **The point is this: the one who sows sparingly will also reap sparingly, and the one who sows bountifully will also reap bountifully.** ⁷ **Each of you must give as you have made up your mind, not reluctantly or under compulsion, for God loves a cheerful giver.** ⁸ **And God is able to provide you with every blessing in abundance, so that by always having enough of everything, you may share abundantly in every good work.** ⁹ **As it is written,**
> "He scatters abroad, he gives to the poor;
> his righteousness endures forever."

These verses draw on some Old Testament texts and use them as maxims or principles for Christian giving. The first comes from the world of farming: giving should be generous. You must sow plenty of seed if you want to reap a good harvest (9:6). Paul may be thinking here of Proverbs 11:24: "Some give freely, yet grow all the richer; others withhold what is due, and only suffer want." But whether or not he is thinking of this particular text, his meaning is plain. Lavish giving will do much good; modest and measured giving should always expect a thinner return.

The second principle is that giving should be voluntary. "The Lord blesses a glad and generous man," says the Greek version of Proverbs 22:8, and Paul quotes this text and adapts it a little. He wants the Corinthians to be committed and cheerful in their offering; for then they will grow and rejoice through the experience. If they grudge what they give, it will feel an arid sort of action.

The third principle is that giving can be confident. God is generous. God can provide both the means to give and the means to live (9:8). The word translated "enough" is *autarkeia*, an idea often found in Greek thought. Stoic philosophers taught it as "self-sufficiency"—the ability to live in ways that do not depend on other people and to manage and sustain life out of one's own resources. Understood this way, *autarkeia* is a detached, contained sort of notion. Yet Paul thinks differently, of sufficiency richly supplied by the love of God, reaching out freely in care for others. Such a life is neither detached nor contained but is full with abundance and gratitude—"every blessing . . . always . . . every good work" (9:8). The text in 9:9 comes from Psalm 112:9. This psalm describes the life of a righteous person, living in the "fear of the Lord" (112:1) and rejoicing to share wealth and well-being. That is the pattern of life to which Paul invites the Corinthians.

Harvest of Praise
2 Corinthians 9:10–15

> 9:10 **He who supplies seed to the sower and bread for food will supply and multiply your seed for sowing and increase the harvest of your righteousness.** [11] **You will be enriched in every way for your great generosity, which will produce thanksgiving to God through us;** [12] **for the rendering of this ministry not only supplies the needs of the saints but also overflows with many thanksgivings to God.** [13] **Through the testing of this ministry you glorify God by your obedience to the confession of the gospel of Christ and by the generosity of your sharing with them and with all others,** [14] **while they long for you and pray for you because of the surpassing grace of God that he has given you.** [15] **Thanks be to God for his indescribable gift!**

The metaphor of harvest continues, drawing again on themes from the verses above. A generous God supplies the seed—the means to give—then people sow it, and God turns it into harvest (9:10). Paul's phrasing echoes texts from the prophets Isaiah (55:10) and Hosea (10:12), but he does not explore these Scriptures in any depth. He moves on to pursue the thought of harvest, which will surely come through what the Corinthians are giving.

The result of the collection, says Paul, will be above all a harvest of "thanksgiving to God" (9:11). As gifts from Corinth assist needy Christians in Jerusalem, many voices will rise in praise (9:12). There will be a new solidarity of prayer and gratitude between Jewish believers in Jesus and the Gentile churches (9:14). This sharing of money will testify to God's grace and to the Christian church's unity, which spans the miles and reaches across divisions of heritage, culture, and race.

In 9:13 Paul uses words that speak of the church's common faith and fellowship. "Ministry" and "sharing" he says—service to one another and involvement with one another (see comment on 8:4). And "confession of the gospel of Christ" is the belief that all Christians share, in Jesus crucified and risen. Paul had "handed on" this faith in Corinth (1 Cor. 15:3); surely he had first "received" it from Christians whose roots were in the Holy Land. Yet, "Whether then it was I or they," he says—whether Paul the apostle to the Gentiles or the Jerusalem believers—"so we proclaim, and so you have come to believe" (1 Cor. 15:11). This was the common faith of the church. So now the Gentile Christians' gifts and the shared trust in the gospel to which these gifts bear witness will strengthen the bond between Corinth and Jerusalem.

Finally the chapter sounds an extravagant note of praise, recalling God's "surpassing grace" (9:14) and "indescribable gift" (9:15). Words cannot measure God's goodness to the world in Jesus. The church returns "thanks" (literally "grace") to the one true source of all favor, love, and bounty.

Part 6: Challenge to Corinth
2 Corinthians 10–13

13. A Call to Discern and Decide
2 Corinthians 10–13

TENSION IN THE AIR

As I turned to write this, in a quiet library, a mighty clap of thunder rolled across the sky. The stillness of the day was rent by crash and storm. And that is exactly what some interpreters of 2 Corinthians have found in chapter 10. Suddenly there is electricity in the air, a mood of clash and challenge, the harsh sound of conflict and controversy. The language of generosity, grace, and gift (9:13–15) passes abruptly into talk of opposition, warfare, destruction, and punishment (10:2–6).

There is not a totally new agenda at this point in the letter. But there is definitely a change of tone. Here is a head-on challenge, of a kind that has not been obvious before. Paul feels threatened and indignant, and he responds with passion and force. The problem, in his eyes, is that new preachers have come to Corinth, and they are undermining his good work in the church there.

We shall refer to these people in commentary as "the opponents." You will find more information about them in the introduction to 2 Corinthians (in the section headed "A Different Gospel"). But we do not know everything about their ministry and message. All that we really know comes from "mirror-reading" these chapters and gleaning from Paul's reaction what the opponents had said and done. Yet this method cannot be precise, and it surely highlights their differences and disagreements with Paul. So we may still see only a fraction of the opponents' story. Such insight as we do have into their work in Corinth is as follows.

These people were proud of their Jewish ancestry (11:22). They thought Paul a poor speaker (10:10), so perhaps rhetorical skill was a talent they rated highly. Their leadership style was assertive and even confrontational (11:20). They may have been glad to accept long-term hospitality from the Corinthians, which Paul had not done (11:7–9). Perhaps they spoke of visions and signs and were glad to be regarded as spiritual people who knew God in more intense and intimate ways than other people (12:11–12). They had plenty to say about themselves and their gifts and merits; Paul responds by talking of "commending" (10:12, 18) and "boasting" (10:8, 13; and often in chapters 11 and 12).

Putting all this together has suggested to many that the opponents had roots in dispersion Judaism. They were Jewish but seem not to be concerned with issues around the Jewish law or with ties to Jerusalem in the way that these matters appear in Galatians. So they may not have come from the tight Jewish communities of the Holy Land. But even this point is uncertain, and beyond that we know little about them—for example, where they first heard about Jesus, what might have caused them to head out on mission, or where they had been before Corinth.

However, in the course of commending their own ministry, these men seem to have criticized Paul. He was a man who ministered in a merely human way rather than being a truly spiritual character (10:2). He was a poor public speaker. Indeed he was an unimpressive figure altogether: he could only impress on paper; in person he had little to offer. "Weak," they thought him, and "contemptible" (10:10).

Some of these criticisms would have found a ready hearing among the Corinthian Christians. The city had an eye for style, cleverness, and power. In public life of any kind, people with rhetorical talent, networking skills, a competitive attitude and a high opinion of themselves would tend to rise to the top. And some in the Corinthian church were keen on "wisdom," on "spiritual gifts," and on associating themselves with strong leaders. For them the claims of the opponents would have carried influence and conviction.

So as Paul writes, he tries to convince the Corinthians to take a different point of view. He wants them to value the merits and methods of his ministry and to set aside their affection for the opponents. He regards the opponents' influence as sinister and unhealthy, as a false version of the faith, and as a threat to the well-being of the church. So he appeals to his friends, not only because he wants to remain on good terms with them but also because he believes his version of the gospel has an integrity that he fears the opponents lack.

It would be a mistake, however, to think that these concerns have dawned suddenly, at the start of chapter 10. Much earlier in this letter Paul defends his own integrity (1:12; 4:2). He refers to speakers who strive for popularity and water down God's word (2:17). He handles rather self-consciously the matter of commendation: even though he is reluctant to brag, he feels he needs to make himself credible (3:1; 5:12; 6:4). He dislikes boasting about superficial matters (5:12) and will not rate people by human talents alone

(5:16). Most significantly, he has spoken several times of the theme of suffering (1:3–7; 4:7–12; 6:3–10). There he finds his identity, as suffering brings him near to the cross of Christ (4:10). This is a line of thought that the opponents would have reckoned very strange.

So although there is heavy tension in the air in these chapters, it has not arisen abruptly or without anticipation. Paul's argument and explanation in the earlier parts of the letter have given him a basis to defend himself in this later section. And as we shall see, out of this uneasy controversy have come words about Christian experience that have stood the test of the years and spoken with gentle power in many weary lives.

So we turn now to read through these chapters. First Paul confronts the criticisms that have been made against him (10:1–18). Then he speaks of his own experience, as testimony to Christ's power working in him (11:1–12:13). Finally he looks forward with some uncertainty to visiting Corinth and to what will happen when he arrives (12:14–13:13).

FACING THE CRITICS
2 Corinthians 10:1–18

Weapons of Gentleness
2 Corinthians 10:1–6

> 10:1 **I myself, Paul, appeal to you by the meekness and gentleness of Christ—I who am humble when face to face with you, but bold toward you when I am away!—** [2] **I ask that when I am present I need not show boldness by daring to oppose those who think we are acting according to human standards.** [3] **Indeed, we live as human beings, but we do not wage war according to human standards;** [4] **for the weapons of our warfare are not merely human, but they have divine power to destroy strongholds. We destroy arguments** [5] **and every proud obstacle raised up against the knowledge of God, and we take every thought captive to obey Christ.** [6] **We are ready to punish every disobedience when your obedience is complete.**

These verses tackle two accusations made against Paul, by his opponents and perhaps also by some Christians in Corinth. The first charge is inconsistency. His letters sounded weighty and authoritative, but in person he was a mild and unassuming character—not at all an impressive leader, said some (10:10). And it seems that Paul accepts the analysis. He bases his appeal on "the meekness and gentleness of Christ" (10:1). So if he has acted humbly and unassertively in Corinth, that very behavior is a sign of Christ's gentle presence in him. Indeed there may also have been pastoral reasons for a calmer style. It is easier to "build people up" (as in 10:8) by that sort of approach.

But Paul will also act strongly if he has to, and will not shirk a challenge, should the need and occasion arise (10:2). Which brings him to the second criticism—that people have called him unspiritual. He lacks, they were saying, the religious polish and power that a Christian leader ought to show. He operates, say some, at a merely human level.

In response to this, Paul reaches for the metaphor of spiritual warfare (10:3–6), using ideas that echo later in the "armor of God" passage in Ephesians (6:10–17). So, says Paul, the gospel that he preaches is a weapon of war: it has the strength and force to change minds, hearts, and lives. He lives in a fleshly body, but he is fighting spiritual battles (10:3). He spreads "the knowledge of God" into places where people defy and resist it (10:5). And once he has won the Corinthians 'round, he will not hesitate to deal boldly and decisively with any opposition that remains (10:6).

Building Up and Tearing Down
2 Corinthians 10:7–11

> 10:7 **Look at what is before your eyes. If you are confident that you belong to Christ, remind yourself of this, that just as you belong to Christ, so also do we.** [8] **Now, even if I boast a little too much of our authority, which the Lord gave for building you up and not for tearing you down, I will not be ashamed of it.** [9] **I do not want to seem as though I am trying to frighten you with my letters.** [10] **For they say, "His letters are weighty and strong, but his bodily presence is weak, and his speech contemptible."** [11] **Let such people understand that what we say by letter when absent, we will also do when present.**

In the verses above we have seen a strange counterpoint in Paul's attitude. He talks of gentleness and will speak at length in the chapters ahead about his personal weakness. In some important ways he seeks to be a humble, restrained character, and he dislikes any sort of showmanship or aggression in a pastoral leader. On the other hand he is ready, if need be, for battle, and he will clash strongly and directly with any who damage or disturb the church. He can be abrasive if he must. This next paragraph is abrasive indeed and dense with challenge.

Someone—probably an opponent—has claimed to belong to Christ more truly than Paul does (10:7). Perhaps this man reckoned to be a better sort of apostle—a claim that Paul rebuts later on (11:5; 12:11). Or this may be a way of stating the criticism mentioned above, that Paul was an unspiritual character (10:2).

Paul's counter is that he has a God-given authority, "for building you up" (10:8), and he will not hesitate to use it in person. There is an echo here of Jeremiah's prophetic call, "to tear down and to build up" (Jer. 1:10), and indeed Paul will quote Jeremiah again in a few verses' time (10:17). But at this point he reflects on the two different aspects of Jeremiah's text. His own primary call is to "build up" the church (10:8; 12:19; 13:10), and if he has to "tear down" (10:4) obstacles and opposition along the way, he will always look on this as a secondary and less savory aspect of his task.

Paul much prefers, then, to be gentle than to be contentious. He looks on this as a truer expression of God's calling to him and perhaps too a better way of expressing the life of Christ (10:1). So this may be the reason that he writes so candidly, and even severely. His words of challenge and warning are intended to goad the Corinthians, to get them to take proper responsibility for the spiritual well-being of their church. If problems can be sorted out before he arrives, his visit will not be soured by clashes and quarrels (13:10), and he will be able to act more gently. There has been one difficult visit already; Paul has no wish to make another (2:1–3).

New Territories
2 Corinthians 10:12–18

> 10:12 **We do not dare to classify or compare ourselves with some of those who commend themselves. But when they measure themselves by one another, and compare themselves with one another, they do not show good sense.** [13] **We, however, will not boast beyond limits, but will keep within the field that God has assigned to us, to reach out even as far as you.** [14] **For we were not overstepping our limits when we reached you; we were the first to come all the way to you with the good news of Christ.** [15] **We do not boast beyond limits, that is, in the labors of others; but our hope is that, as your faith increases, our sphere of action among you may be greatly enlarged,** [16] **so that we may proclaim the good news in lands beyond you, without boasting of work already done in someone else's sphere of action.** [17] **"Let the one who boasts, boast in the Lord."** [18] **For it is not those who commend themselves that are approved, but those whom the Lord commends.**

This short portion is all about "boasting" (10:13, 15, 16, 17). Reading through it invites us to think about our own speech and our self-image.

When is it right to speak proudly and about what—ourselves, our talents, our achievements, our God? The opponents, says Paul, "commend... measure... and compare themselves" (10:12). They have a high opinion of what they are worth and are quick to let others know this. But Paul is skeptical. Their boasting, he says, is secondhand and parasitic. They have moved in on work that someone else started and are trying to take credit for it (10:13, 15).

He, by contrast, was the first Christian preacher in Corinth (10:14). He was breaking new ground when he brought the gospel to the city. And now he would like the Corinthians' help to send him on to fresh openings and opportunities (10:16). This pattern of work is, he believes, more authentic and honest than the opponents' ways.

It is difficult to know precisely what was behind the opponents' coming to Corinth. Did they think Paul had a deficient message, so that they had to supplement what he had taught? That seems to be the problem in Galatians; but Galatians is a very different letter. Or were they perhaps influenced by the agreement mentioned in Galatians 2:9, that Jerusalem should send missions to Jewish people and Paul would go to the Gentiles? Had the opponents then come to evangelize Jews in Corinth? Yet Paul does not mention or discuss this agreement. He simply seems to argue that it is more genuinely apostolic to tell the gospel in places where Christ's name is not known than to linger with an existing congregation. His own missionary career had begun that way (Acts 13:1–3), when it would surely have been more comfortable for him to stay in Antioch. That was the way he meant to continue.

As another quite basic concern, Paul is wary of people who are keen to commend themselves. He quotes from Scripture (Jer. 9:24), as if to say, "We should boast about God, and must leave God to boast about us" (10:17–18). Effective Christian service depends on God's assigning us a task (10:13) and God's approval as we do it (10:18). If our service in the church ever makes us think we are better than other people—as seems to be the case with the opponents—then we may well be in the wrong place, and we are certainly living with a wrong attitude.

"A LITTLE FOOLISHNESS"
2 Corinthians 11:1–12:13

Rough Résumé

After confronting the complaints against him, Paul turns to reflect on his own career and experience. He does not care to "commend himself"

(10:18), but he does want to tackle the criticism that he does not "belong to Christ" as genuinely as some of his opponents (10:7). So he follows a backhanded and quite subtle line of argument that stretches through more than a chapter: he lists his weaknesses. All the things that have hurt him, assailed him, distressed him, strained him, and made him look foolish—these he stacks up as an upside-down sort of personal résumé. All this, he will say, has actually brought him nearer to Christ (12:10).

Eventually, then, Paul manages to make this list of difficult experiences into a way of boasting "in the Lord" (10:17). He boasts "in weakness" (11:30; 12:9), because his sufferings have led him into closer contact with Christ. He can accept the charge of being weak, because it has helped him to be more deeply Christian. This is weakness with credibility in it, and strength and spirituality too.

Yet along the way, Paul seems to be speaking "as a fool" (11:1, 16, 17, 21; 12:11). What does he mean by this? Perhaps there are three layers of meaning. First, it was odd and countercultural to brag about failures. Corinth was an arrogant and competitive place. Its citizens were assertive and boastful; they liked others to know about their gifts and talents. People in Corinth did not boast of their weaknesses. They would think it mad. But Paul is doing it.

A second layer of meaning appears when we notice that Paul is uneasy about what he is doing. By writing in this vein, he is going some way toward self-commendation. So although he resents it when opponents commend themselves, he finds himself talking in a way that is not wholly dissimilar (11:16–18). This feels foolish. He has reached for a method he disapproves of and started to respond in kind to people whose talk he dislikes.

So a third thought lurking in this language of "folly" may be that the opponents who regularly talk in this way are themselves foolish. "You gladly put up with fools," says Paul to Corinth (11:19). Boasting about yourself is a great foolishness. The wise person should boast only in the Lord (10:17). So perhaps Paul is giving a hint to the Corinthians that they should start to be more critical of the opponents. "I speak as a fool," he says. Yet he is evidently speaking with some astuteness and wisdom.

Fearful for Friends
2 Corinthians 11:1–21

> 11:1 **I wish you would bear with me in a little foolishness. Do bear with me!** ² **I feel a divine jealousy for you, for I promised you in marriage to one husband, to present you as a chaste virgin to Christ.** ³ **But I am afraid**

that as the serpent deceived Eve by its cunning, your thoughts will be led astray from a sincere and pure devotion to Christ. ⁴ For if someone comes and proclaims another Jesus than the one we proclaimed, or if you receive a different spirit from the one you received, or a different gospel from the one you accepted, you submit to it readily enough. ⁵ I think that I am not in the least inferior to these super-apostles. ⁶ I may be untrained in speech, but not in knowledge; certainly in every way and in all things we have made this evident to you.

⁷ Did I commit a sin by humbling myself so that you might be exalted, because I proclaimed God's good news to you free of charge? ⁸ I robbed other churches by accepting support from them in order to serve you. ⁹ And when I was with you and was in need, I did not burden anyone, for my needs were supplied by the friends who came from Macedonia. So I refrained and will continue to refrain from burdening you in any way. ¹⁰ As the truth of Christ is in me, this boast of mine will not be silenced in the regions of Achaia. ¹¹ And why? Because I do not love you? God knows I do!

¹² And what I do I will also continue to do, in order to deny an opportunity to those who want an opportunity to be recognized as our equals in what they boast about. ¹³ For such boasters are false apostles, deceitful workers, disguising themselves as apostles of Christ. ¹⁴ And no wonder! Even Satan disguises himself as an angel of light. ¹⁵ So it is not strange if his ministers also disguise themselves as ministers of righteousness. Their end will match their deeds.

¹⁶ I repeat, let no one think that I am a fool; but if you do, then accept me as a fool, so that I too may boast a little. ¹⁷ What I am saying in regard to this boastful confidence, I am saying not with the Lord's authority, but as a fool; ¹⁸ since many boast according to human standards, I will also boast. ¹⁹ For you gladly put up with fools, being wise yourselves! ²⁰ For you put up with it when someone makes slaves of you, or preys upon you, or takes advantage of you, or puts on airs, or gives you a slap in the face. ²¹ To my shame, I must say, we were too weak for that!

But whatever anyone dares to boast of—I am speaking as a fool—I also dare to boast of that.

Everything in these verses is anticipation and scene setting for what is ahead. The "fool's speech" only really begins at 11:21, but Paul announces it much sooner than that. He says he is about to launch into "a little foolishness" (11:1) and then turns aside for a while to outline his reasons for doing so. Only later does he actually start "speaking as a fool" (11:21), after reminding his readers of the role into which he is stepping (11:16–18). All else is background, the concerns that have led him to speak like this, and the points about which he hopes to convince the Corinthians.

Paul is fearful. He dreads the thought that the Corinthians will be "led astray" (11:3). He thinks of the opponents as a bunch of smooth-tongued religious con men. They are talented but seriously off track. They offer, he reckons, "another Jesus . . . a different spirit . . . a different gospel" (11:4). But exactly what they had been saying we do not know. The best guess—although we are far from sure about this—is that they thought of Jesus in terms of power and saw themselves as representatives of that power. Signs, visions, and eloquence were their stock-in-trade, and they had little to say about the cross. Paul would have seen this as a faith without any real salvation. But it might have been readily accepted in Corinth.

So Paul makes the matter personal. He refers to the opponents ironically as spiritual superstars: "super-apostles" he calls them and says he is "not in the least inferior" to them (11:5). So now he must set out to show why he is "not inferior." That is the point and purpose of the "fool's speech," and Paul will draw together at the end the case he has made (12:11). But before this long speech begins, there are three preliminary issues to tackle: preaching ability (11:6), financial dependence (11:7–12), and leadership style (11:19–20).

On preaching ability, Paul admits that he lacks formal rhetorical polish (10:10). But he defends the content of what he says. He knows God and enables others to know God too (2:14; 4:6; 10:5). This knowledge is deeper and truer than any ordinary human knowing (5:16), and he has shared it generously with the Corinthians (11:6). There is no cause for criticism here.

The matter of financial support came up in 1 Corinthians too. Paul was independent. He would not take money from the church. When he made the gospel available without charge, everyone would know it was a free gift of God (1 Cor. 9:12, 18; 2 Cor. 11:7). Even if some in Corinth would gladly have been his patrons and enjoyed a measure of kudos and influence from hosting him, this was not an opportunity he offered. Instead he worked in a leather shop (Acts 18:3) and accepted gifts from other churches, particularly from Macedonia (11:9). But when the opponents arrived in town, it seems that they did accept hospitality and made themselves materially dependent on Christians in Corinth. This would explain why Paul gives so much attention to this issue and sees it as an important difference (11:12) between him and them. If they take money from the church, he is not impressed. He serves the church freely because he loves the people (11:11; 12:15) and he will stay committed to this policy (11:9, 12). He thinks of himself as a spiritual father (1 Cor. 4:14–15) and offers his ministry in a spirit of fatherly love and provision (12:14). On this issue he feels he is some way ahead of his opponents (11:12): they gain from the church; he gives himself to it.

The third preliminary point concerns the opponents' manner of leadership. Paul is indignant. "Put up with me," he has said, "when I speak as a fool" (to paraphrase 11:1). "For you put up with them when they act as fools and treat you badly" (11:19–20). The opponents were taking advantage, he feels, of the Corinthians' resources, their goodwill, and even their dignity. Ironically he says, "We were too weak for that" (11:21). Weakness may be no bad thing, he implies, if that is the sort of conduct to which strength has led.

In the midst of these three preliminary points come Paul's sharpest words about the opponents (11:13–15). He reckons that their influence in Corinth is seriously at odds with the cause of the gospel. He may not mean that they have knowingly adopted a disguise, but he does think they should know better. They are, in his view, bad and unworthy ministers, and he fears they will do much damage.

If the strength of Paul's language here shocks us, we might reflect on a couple of points. One is that forms of speech vary from one culture to another. Controversy in New Testament times in both the Jewish and the Greco-Roman worlds was generally sharper and more hostile than is typical in my country today. Language tends to reflect its cultural setting as well as its subject matter. Second, although his words are harsh, Paul is actually arguing here toward a gentle and quite fragile pattern of ministry. He knows he cannot always be tough and uptight. The church cannot live on a diet of contention and controversy. Disagreement, even when it is earnest and serious, should try to point the way back to constructive and secure pastoral relationships. Even when opinions differ, we are generally better to aim at "building up" than at "tearing down" (10:8).

Catalog of Weakness
2 Corinthians 11:22–33

> 11:22 **Are they Hebrews? So am I. Are they Israelites? So am I. Are they descendants of Abraham? So am I.** [23] **Are they ministers of Christ? I am talking like a madman—I am a better one: with far greater labors, far more imprisonments, with countless floggings, and often near death.** [24] **Five times I have received from the Jews the forty lashes minus one.** [25] **Three times I was beaten with rods. Once I received a stoning. Three times I was shipwrecked; for a night and a day I was adrift at sea;** [26] **on frequent journeys, in danger from rivers, danger from bandits, danger from my own people,**

danger from Gentiles, danger in the city, danger in the wilderness, danger at sea, danger from false brothers and sisters; ²⁷ in toil and hardship, through many a sleepless night, hungry and thirsty, often without food, cold and naked. ²⁸ And, besides other things, I am under daily pressure because of my anxiety for all the churches. ²⁹ Who is weak, and I am not weak? Who is made to stumble, and I am not indignant?

³⁰ If I must boast, I will boast of the things that show my weakness. ³¹ The God and Father of the Lord Jesus (blessed be he forever!) knows that I do not lie. ³² In Damascus, the governor under King Aretas guarded the city of Damascus in order to seize me, ³³ but I was let down in a basket through a window in the wall, and escaped from his hands.

Now we have come to "the fool's speech" proper. Paul is "boasting" in the way that others have done (11:21), but he is boasting "as a fool." This will be a topsy-turvy sort of boast, naming and apparently celebrating all that has been harsh and hurtful in his life. He lists the insults and hardships as a kind of badge of honor, as marks of the cross and signs of the presence of Christ.

He starts with a simple factual point. If the opponents revel in their Jewishness, in their ethnic, genetic, and linguistic credentials, he can match that. He can speak Hebrew (Acts 22:2), and his roots and genes are Jewish. "So am I," he says, three times over (11:22).

The next little question and answer open up a line of thought that will run right through the speech. "Are they servants of Christ? I am a better one." This is the word *diakonos*, which Paul has used already to speak of his own ministry: he is a servant of the new covenant, of reconciliation and of God (3:6; 5:18; 6:4). And, foolish though it may be to say so, he is a better servant of Christ than the opponents (11:23). He can proclaim the crucified and risen Christ better than they can, because he has suffered more. That is why he is "not inferior" (11:5). He has endured "greater labors ... more imprisonments ... countless floggings" (11:23). The list is long (11:24–28), and it is meant to give the reader pause for thought.

Many of the episodes recounted here are not mentioned anywhere else, either in Acts or in Paul's other letters. But that should not surprise us. Acts squeezes a decade or so of his work into eight chapters (13–20), and most of the letters carry only a few snippets of current personal news. There must have been a lot of his life that never appears on screen.

There were five floggings, for example (11:24); when Paul spoke of Jesus in synagogue services, the reaction could be swift and sharp. Being "beaten with rods" was a Roman penalty (11:25), handed down by civil authorities; one of these three incidents was at Philippi (Acts 16:22). The stoning happened at Lystra (Acts 14:19). The three shipwrecks do not figure in Acts at all; the calamitous voyage of Acts 27–28 was some years after 2 Corinthians. But sea travel was always hazardous in those days; Paul knew the risks, evidently at firsthand on occasion. Land journeys were arduous too: towns could be rowdy, the countryside lonely and lawless, distances long, and weather bad (11:26). Then if Paul settled for a while, the physical stresses of leatherwork brought another sort of "toil and hardship' (11:27). And with it all went care and concern for a scattered network of churches with all their problems and people (11:28). When his friends struggled, Paul struggled too. As pastor, he carried the weaknesses of others alongside the weakness and stress of his own living (11:29).

This mention of weakness now leads Paul on, to recall one of the most dangerous and undignified episodes of his career—being let down a city wall in a basket (11:30–33). Acts records the event too (9:23–25), and Paul may be mocking himself by offering a deliberate parody of a Roman military honor—the *corona muralis*, awarded during a siege to the first soldier to scale the city wall. Paul inverts the image. His honor is not in going up but in coming down.

So "the fool's speech" moves toward its climax. Paul knows he is weak (11:29), as others have said about him too (10:10). Yet he is ready to "boast of . . . my weakness" (11:30). He has taken the criticism and is turning it into his calling card as apostle of Jesus. The one remaining move he has now to make is to tell of "a thorn in the flesh."

Vision and Thorn
2 Corinthians 12:1–10

> 12:1 **It is necessary to boast; nothing is to be gained by it, but I will go on to visions and revelations of the Lord.** ² I know a person in Christ who fourteen years ago was caught up to the third heaven—whether in the body or out of the body I do not know; God knows. ³ And I know that such a person— whether in the body or out of the body I do not know; God knows— ⁴ was caught up into Paradise and heard things that are not to be told, that no mortal is permitted to repeat. ⁵ On behalf of such a one I will boast, but on my own behalf I will not boast, except of my weaknesses. ⁶ But if I wish to boast, I will not be a fool, for I will be speaking the truth. But I refrain from it, so that no one may think better of me than what is seen in me or heard from me, ⁷ even considering the exceptional character of the revelations. Therefore, to keep me from being too elated, a thorn was given me in

> the flesh, a messenger of Satan to torment me, to keep me from being too elated. [8] Three times I appealed to the Lord about this, that it would leave me, [9] but he said to me, "My grace is sufficient for you, for power is made perfect in weakness." So, I will boast all the more gladly of my weaknesses, so that the power of Christ may dwell in me. [10] Therefore I am content with weaknesses, insults, hardships, persecutions, and calamities for the sake of Christ; for whenever I am weak, then I am strong.

These verses talk of two remarkable experiences but describe neither in detail. So we do not know exactly what Paul is referring to. In the first case he does not want to give detail, and perhaps he cannot. In the second he probably could be specific, but he has not been. Yet despite the lack of information, we can learn from the way that he links these two events and reflects on what they have taught him.

He starts by saying that he will boast about "visions and revelations" but admits that "nothing is to be gained" by this (12:1). So he may well be trying to match the opponents by showing that he too has had intense spiritual experiences. Yet he wants also to move away from talking of such things and bring the focus of his writing back to weakness. For visionary moments may be a gracious gift of God, but they can never be the constant heartbeat of Christian living. Weakness is the setting where the strength of Christ is most fully known. So when Paul says that the heavenly encounter involved "a person in Christ" (12:2), he surely means himself. This oblique wording captures the awkwardness that he feels in boasting: he thinks it wrong, yet he has to do it. He wants to tell of the experience but does not want any credit or kudos for doing so.

The event itself had happened fourteen years earlier (12:2). However, that does not tell us much. For according to Acts, Paul had numerous mystical experiences (9:3; 16:9; 18:9–10; 22:17–21; 23:11; 27:23), but none of those is likely to be the incident he mentions here. Generally the chronology is wrong: the Damascus Road episode is too early; most of the others are too late. So we have no other information about this event, apart from what Paul says here.

Yet much in this account defies any precise analysis (12:2–4). Almost every word suggests mystery or remoteness. The mention of a "third heaven" reflects a Jewish notion of layered heavenly spaces; it suggests an exalted place where God's reality is clear and near. "Paradise" too suggests the presence of the Lord and of the righteous dead (Luke 23:43); but it is a rare word in the Bible. As for Paul's own involvement, he cannot decide whether the encounter was a bodily experience or not. Nor will he tell what he heard or saw. Although he speaks often of "glory" in this letter, he does not do so here. Perhaps, then, he discovered what many Christians have learned since: that God's holiness is far beyond the grasp of human words. The truest response to direct revelation is a reverent silence.

So Paul will not boast of the experience. He has been ready to name it but not to describe it. He attributes it cryptically to "a person in Christ" but claims no personal credit, lest people start to judge him on the basis of his visions rather than his service (12:5–6). It is a hidden part of his story—not part of his public profile as a minister of the gospel. Indeed, even in the privacy of his inner life, he had to learn not to be fascinated by experiences of this kind. "A thorn was given," to prevent this (12:7).

We have no idea at all what the thorn was. Guesses are legion and varied. Most of them are medical—gallstones, epilepsy, malaria, gout, depression, leprosy—and this would make some sense of the reference to "flesh" (12:7). Alternatively it might be temptation, opposition, remorse— we simply cannot be sure. Yet the very fact that we do not know may be a gift from God. For this somehow opens the text to us all to find our own story in it and to use it as a conversation with God about the particular "thorn" that besets our living. Your troubles and mine—the worst, ugliest, and most intractable of them—find a home in these verses, and we find a way to live with them and with God through Paul's words and through his relationship with Christ.

Whatever the "thorn" was, it hurt. The word originally meant something more than a "splinter"; more a "stake" or "spike." It poked unpleasantly and painfully into Paul's peace and well-being. He sees it as evil in origin, "a messenger of Satan" (12:7). But God can use even evil for good purposes, and this is what God chose to do here. Three times Paul asked for release (12:8)—just as Jesus prayed three times in the garden to be spared the cross (Matt. 26:36–46). And the Lord spoke to him—how we are not told but Paul was in no doubt about the message. Instead of release he would know the presence of Christ and would be given strength to bear the hurt (12:9). Grace would carry him, and Christ's power in him would be fuller and surer because he was weak.

So Paul wanted to "boast in weakness" (11:30; 12:5, 9). He would live with the knocks and strains of ministry and of the years, and when he was at his weakest, he would know he was nearest to Christ. And through this he has left the church a pattern for living through hard times: "whenever I am weak, then I am strong" (12:10). Across the centuries many Christians have found an anchor here. For this sort of spirituality is sane and sure. Trust of this kind does not extract Christians from our ordinary living but sustains us in it. It offers to you and me a faith that will not be easy but will be enough. It reminds us that God's power will most likely come to us through life's hardships and hurts. I am grateful for the people I have known whose lives have made that plain.

Back into Role
2 Corinthians 12:11–13

> 12:11 **I have been a fool! You forced me to it. Indeed you should have been the ones commending me, for I am not at all inferior to these super-apostles, even though I am nothing.** [12] **The signs of a true apostle were performed among you with utmost patience, signs and wonders and mighty works.** [13] **How have you been worse off than the other churches, except that I myself did not burden you? Forgive me this wrong!**

This short section rounds off "the fool's speech." It allows Paul to acknowledge the odd way that he has spoken. It enables him to reengage with his normal role and responsibilities as founding pastor of the church in Corinth. Yet as he does this, he can set his relationship with the church on a surer basis, because of all that he has said in the guise of a fool. There are three short movements in the three verses.

First Paul steps out of the role of fool (12:11). If the Corinthians had been loyal to him, he says, he would not have needed to speak like this. But now he has done so, he has shown them that he is "not at all inferior to these super-apostles"—just as he said in 11:5. His very weakness enables him to serve Christ better than they do.

More than this, God did great things through Paul in Corinth (12:12). There were deeds of power and grace when he worked there. So if the opponents claim power, they have no advantage over Paul. Miracles were part of his ministry (Rom. 15:19; Gal. 3:5; and often in Acts), and although these were not the heart of his relationship with Jesus, they should help the church to value and trust him.

Paul's apostolic portfolio is, then, complete. He served Corinth quite as well as he did other churches. The only possible failing in his ministry was, he says ironically, that he did not ask for their money (12:13). It is time now for them to respect him and to look forward to the visit that he will shortly make. This will be the theme of the last portion of the letter.

As we move on from the fool's speech, it leaves us with a model and pattern for serving God and perhaps for church leadership too. For Paul does not expect Christians to be people without any sort of vulnerability.

Like most of us, he lived with problems and pains and he found that the key to effective Christian service lies in sharing those with Christ. Only then can we become properly strong in ourselves and learn how to offer Christ's strength to others.

COMING TO CORINTH
2 Corinthians 12:14–13:13

After confronting the opposition and criticisms that were put against him (10:1–18) and offering a long justification of the character of his ministry (11:1–12:13), Paul is ready to speak directly about his next visit to Corinth. The writing in these paragraphs blends care and challenge. Paul loves the Corinthians, but if he finds them going astray, he will not hesitate to be frank and forthright. So this last part of the letter is a warning, an attempt to get them to put their Christian lives into order before he arrives. He wants to be warm and encouraging when he comes. An earnest letter of this kind should help to make such a visit possible.

Pastoral Care
2 Corinthians 12:14–21

> 12:14 **Here I am, ready to come to you this third time. And I will not be a burden, because I do not want what is yours but you; for children ought not to lay up for their parents, but parents for their children.** [15] **I will most gladly spend and be spent for you. If I love you more, am I to be loved less?** [16] **Let it be assumed that I did not burden you. Nevertheless (you say) since I was crafty, I took you in by deceit.** [17] **Did I take advantage of you through any of those whom I sent to you?** [18] **I urged Titus to go, and sent the brother with him. Titus did not take advantage of you, did he? Did we not conduct ourselves with the same spirit? Did we not take the same steps?**
>
> [19] **Have you been thinking all along that we have been defending ourselves before you? We are speaking in Christ before God. Everything we do, beloved, is for the sake of building you up.** [20] **For I fear that when I come, I may find you not as I wish, and that you may find me not as you wish; I fear that there may perhaps be quarreling, jealousy, anger, selfishness, slander, gossip, conceit, and disorder.** [21] **I fear that when I come again, my God may humble me before you, and that I may have to mourn over many who previously sinned and have not repented of the impurity, sexual immorality, and licentiousness that they have practiced.**

These verses set the tone for sterner words ahead. Their theme is love. Because Paul loves the Corinthians, he will not take their money or material help. He has never exploited them nor have any of his team. Rather he looks on them as a father looks on his family. He wants to provide for them, to give himself for their welfare, and to show his love in practice when he is with them (12:14–18).

All he has wanted, as he has spoken about himself in this letter, is to build them up (12:19). All his concern is to reestablish trust, to show them the true contours of Christlike ministry, and to renew his relationship with them so that he can help them again. Yet as he looks forward to visiting, he is anxious. It would hurt him deeply to find them ignoring the ways he taught. A quarrelsome, chaotic, and wayward church would reduce him to tears. Such a state of affairs ought to humble the Corinthians; yet Paul speaks of it humbling him (12:20–21). As their pastor, evangelist, and apostle, he feels responsible. When they are weak, so is he (11:29). They are the script, the living record, of his ministry (3:2–3). He serves them, loves them, and reaches out to them (6:11–13). He cares very much that they love him in return. But above all, he wants them to love Jesus and walk in Jesus' ways. He would rejoice to find them doing this; but as he looks forward to visiting, he is aware of other possible scenarios too.

The Challenge of Christ
2 Corinthians 13:1–4

> 13:1 **This is the third time I am coming to you. "Any charge must be sustained by the evidence of two or three witnesses."** [2] **I warned those who sinned previously and all the others, and I warn them now while absent, as I did when present on my second visit, that if I come again, I will not be lenient—** [3] **since you desire proof that Christ is speaking in me. He is not weak in dealing with you, but is powerful in you.** [4] **For he was crucified in weakness, but lives by the power of God. For we are weak in him, but in dealing with you we will live with him by the power of God.**

Paul's next visit to Corinth will be his third after his first long stay in the city (Acts 18) and a subsequent "painful" visit (2:1). He quotes from Deuteronomy (19:15) to make the point that the evidence of two or three visits would give him a solid basis to challenge members of the church about their conduct. If he finds there are faults to correct and sins to name and shame, then he will be on firm ground in so doing, and he will not hesitate to be severe (13:1–2).

If this should seem very different to the portrait of weakness Paul drew a little earlier in the letter, the reason is Christ. Christ will speak through Paul, and although Paul is weak, Christ is risen and mighty. So Paul will bring to Corinth the power of the resurrection and of God. That would indeed be power to reckon with in any pastoral exchange. Let the Corinthians be warned (13:3–4).

So a circle has been closed in the testimony of these last four chapters. Others had spoken of him as weak in person and only strong on paper (10:1, 10). So in the course of these chapters, Paul has accepted the label and spoken of the strength of Christ that is present in his weakness, which means that when he is present he can speak and act with strength, just as he said he would (10:2–6, 11). There is authority in his ministry, which works through his weakness. This is the paradox of the gospel and of living with a crucified and risen Lord.

Building Up
2 Corinthians 13:5–10

> 13:5 **Examine yourselves to see whether you are living in the faith. Test yourselves. Do you not realize that Jesus Christ is in you?—unless, indeed, you fail to meet the test!** [6] **I hope you will find out that we have not failed.** [7] **But we pray to God that you may not do anything wrong—not that we may appear to have met the test, but that you may do what is right, though we may seem to have failed.** [8] **For we cannot do anything against the truth, but only for the truth.** [9] **For we rejoice when we are weak and you are strong. This is what we pray for, that you may become perfect.** [10] **So I write these things while I am away from you, so that when I come, I may not have to be severe in using the authority that the Lord has given me for building up and not for tearing down.**

The Corinthians too live in fellowship with Jesus (13:5). So they can reach for his strength and goodness as they audit and review their living. Paul speaks of quality control—of checking, testing, proving, and perfecting (13:5–7, 9). He wants his friends to attend to their Christian practice, to look hard at what they do, and to straighten out anything that is wayward in their lives. This would be far more important to him than his own reputation (13:7). If they still think him "weak," that scarcely matters, as long as they are "strong" in their faith and Christian behavior (13:9).

For his chief aim is to "build them up" (13:10; as in 10:8; 12:19). His God-given authority as a pastor is first and foremost for this purpose, and he does not want to use it in clash and criticism, if he can properly avoid doing so. "Tearing down" may be the flip side of his vocation, but it is not a tune he is eager to play. He writes "boldly" from afar, so that he need not act severely when he comes in person. As we move toward the final greetings and blessing, Paul's last word has echoed the opening of these four chapters (13:10; and 10:8). Along the way, love has moved him to write with candor and challenge. And in that same love he longs to meet the Corinthians face-to-face and to rejoice in the strength and sureness of their faith in Christ.

The Grace of the Lord
2 Corinthians 13:11–13

> 13:11 **Finally, brothers and sisters, farewell. Put things in order, listen to my appeal, agree with one another, live in peace; and the God of love and peace will be with you.** [12] **Greet one another with a holy kiss. All the saints greet you.**
> [13] **The grace of the Lord Jesus Christ, the love of God, and the communion of the Holy Spirit be with all of you.**

All of Paul's letters end with warmth and blessing. All of them end with "grace." So here Paul sets the life of the church and the challenges ahead within the care of God. The Corinthians, erratic as they are, are a people "graced" by the love and peace of heaven. Let them then strive for truth, sustain one another, and rejoice in the support of God's wider church (13:11–12).

For around and within is the goodness and care of the Holy Trinity (13:13). Grace provides, love enfolds, and "the communion of the Holy Spirit" draws Christians into the life of God and of the Lord Jesus Christ.

For Further Reading

Any writer on Scripture learns much in libraries and from other authors. I have certainly done so. Here are some suggestions for further reading for anyone who would like to delve more deeply into these two letters than this short commentary allows. Below that is a list of a few works that especially deserve to be credited because they helped me to understand Paul more clearly.

On Both Epistles

Adams, Edward, and David G. Horrell, eds. *Christianity at Corinth*. Louisville, KY: Westminster John Knox Press, 2004.

Keener, Craig S. *1–2 Corinthians*. New Cambridge Bible Commentary. Cambridge: Cambridge University Press, 2005.

Witherington, Ben. *Conflict and Community in Corinth*. Grand Rapids: Eerdmans, 1995.

On the First Epistle

Blomberg, Craig L. *The NIV Application Commentary: 1 Corinthians*. Grand Rapids: Zondervan, 1994.

Furnish, Victor Paul. *The Theology of the First Letter to the Corinthians*. Cambridge: Cambridge University Press, 1999.

Garland, David E. *1 Corinthians*. Baker Exegetical Commentary on the New Testament. Grand Rapids: Baker, 2003.

Hays, Richard B. *First Corinthians*. Interpretation: A Bible Commentary for Teaching and Preaching. Louisville, KY: John Knox Press, 1997.

On the Second Epistle

Furnish, Victor Paul. *II Corinthians*. The Anchor Bible, vol. 32A. New York: Doubleday, 1984.
Harris, Murray J. *The Second Epistle to the Corinthians*. The New International Greek Testament Commentary. Grand Rapids: Eerdmans, 2005.
Matera, Frank J. *II Corinthians: A Commentary*. The New Testament Library. Louisville, KY: Westminster John Knox Press, 2003.
Minor, Mitzi L. *2 Corinthians*. Smith and Helwys Bible Commentary. Macon, GA: Smith and Helwys, 2009.

Other Works That Helped Me

Deming, Will. *Paul on Marriage and Celibacy: The Hellenistic Background of 1 Corinthians 7*. 2nd ed. Grand Rapids: Eerdmans, 2004.
Finney, Mark. "Honour, Head-Coverings and Headship: 1 Corinthians 11.2–16 in Its Social Context." *Journal for the Study of the New Testament* 33, no. 1 (2010): 31–58.
Friesen, Steven J., Daniel N. Schowalter, and James C. Walters, eds. *Corinth in Context: Comparative Studies on Religion and Society*. Studien zum Neuen Testament 134. Leiden: Brill, 2010.
Lakey, Michael. *Image and Glory of God: 1 Corinthians 11:2–16 as a Case Study in Bible, Gender and Hermeneutics*. The Library of New Testament Studies. New York: T. & T. Clark, 2010.
Newton, Derek. *Deity and Diet: The Dilemma of Sacrificial Food at Corinth*. Journal for the Study of the New Testament Supplement. Sheffield: Sheffield Academic, 1998.
Schowalter, Daniel, and Steven J. Friesen, eds. *Urban Religion in Roman Corinth: Interdisciplinary Approaches*. Harvard Theological Studies. Cambridge, MA: Harvard, 2005.
Watson, Deborah Elaine. "Paul's Collection in Light of Motivations and Mechanisms for Aid to the Poor in the First-Century World." PhD diss., University of Durham, 2006.
Winter, Bruce W. *After Paul Left Corinth: The Influence of Secular Ethics and Social Change*. Grand Rapids: Eerdmans, 2001.
Wire, Antoinette Clark. *The Corinthian Women Prophets: A Reconstruction through Paul's Rhetoric*. Minneapolis: Fortress, 1990.
Wright, N. T. *The Resurrection of the Son of God*. London: Society for the Promotion of Christian Knowledge, 2003.

www.ingramcontent.com/pod-product-compliance
Lightning Source LLC
Chambersburg PA
CBHW011613290426
44110CB00020BA/2576